Bad Blood and Economics

Lois,

Thanks!

Mike

Monks!

Bad Blood and Economics

Michael Resman

North Star Press of St. Cloud, Inc.
Saint Cloud, Minnesota

Copyright © 2011 Michael A. Resman

On the cover: A young picket in Mahtomedi during the 1981 strike., *St. Paul Pioneer Press* December 11, 1981, p. 1.
Photographer Buzzz Magnuson, Minnesota Historical Society Collection,
Courtesty: Minnesota Historical Society

ISBN: 0-87839-563-6
ISBN-13: 978-0-87839-563-7

All rights reserved.

First Edition, September 2011

Printed in the United States of America

Published by
North Star Press of St. Cloud, Inc.
P.O. Box 451
St. Cloud, Minnesota 56302

www.northstarpress.com

Table of Contents

Author's Notes   vii
Introduction   xi
List of Strikes   xv

Part One - Politics and Economics of Teachers' Strikes

Chapter One—Strikes and the Law   3
Chapter Two—Unions and Teachers' Strikes   9
Chapter Three—Incidents During Strikes   14
Chapter Four—Substitutes During Strikes   20
Chapter Five—Effects of Strikes   29
Chapter Six—Wants Versus Needs   34
Chapter Seven—Economics   43
Chapter Eight—Bad Blood   52
Chapter Nine—Preventing Teachers' Strikes   58
Chapter Ten—Right to Strike   69

Part Two - Chronology of Teachers' Strikes in Minnesota

Chapter Eleven—The Early Strikes   77
Chapter Twelve—Legal Strikes Begin   96
Chapter Thriteen—Faribault—The strike that nearly failed   111
Chapter Fourteen—The Late 1970s   122
Chapter Fifteen—Factors Contributing to the Strikes of 1981   134
Chapter Sixteen—1981 Strikes Begin   140
Chapter Seventeen—Strikes the Week Before MEA   153
Chapter Eightten—MEA Week   169
Chapter Nineteen—After MEA   190
Chapter Twenty—1984 Strikes   211
Chapter Twenty One—1988-1992   234
Chapter Twenty Two—Recent Strikes   251

Conclusion   272

Index   275

Author's Notes

Few people are neutral about the subject of teachers' strikes. Many are adamantly opposed, believing that teachers shouldn't have the right to strike. Others feel that even if they have the right, striking betrays the teacher's role in society. Most teachers, on the other hand, are convinced that the possibility of a strike is the only tool they have to prevent school boards and superintendents from stepping all over them.

I worked in a public school in Minnesota for twenty-five years as an occupational therapist and was a member of the Rochester Education Association, a union local affiliated with the Minnesota Education Association and later Education Minnesota. For five years late in my career, I served on the local's Executive Board and one term on the Negotiations Committee.

Many will say this puts me exclusively on the side of the union. I will agree that I can certainly understand the viewpoint of teachers. The intent of this book is not to advance the cause of unions or teachers. Instead, my hope is to prevent future strikes by documenting what has happened during Minnesota teachers' strikes.

I have a message—a bias if you will—that I am happy to make up front. During contract negotiations over school contracts, both sides must compromise. That's it. Simple. Straightforward. And, some of you are thinking, self-evident.

Time and time again—seventy-one times at least—that understanding has broken down. In some cases, school boards were adamant that they would not pay raises that would necessitate providing fewer services to students. In others, teachers absolutely wouldn't accept losing rights or benefits they'd had and felt a right to. A strike seemed the only solution.

However, in the end both the school board and the union face the same two choices: compromise during negotiations and accept an unpleasant outcome, or go through a strike—angering most of the residents and poisoning the atmosphere in the district for years—and then compromise, accepting an unpleasant outcome. If neither side is happy with a new contract, but feels it's the best they could do, that's a successful negotiation.

Similarly, if I have done an appropriate job on this book, people on both sides will be unhappy. There are some very difficult realities at work in contract negotiations. Teachers often don't want to believe (or don't realize) the direct connection between their raises and service provision. School boards can get so caught up in what appear to be beneficial or necessary changes that they overlook how teachers will react. Strong-willed board members and superintendents sometimes fuel disagreements without regard for the consequences. It's likely that none of them will appreciate an effort to expose their foibles.

This book had its origins in December of 1991 when I stood on a snow bank for hours in a wind chill that was fifty-four degrees below zero, wondering what in the heck I was doing. Not an active member of the union, I'd attended informational meetings and read the union newsletter that said we had struck over the issue of subcontracting. I didn't understand why a settlement hadn't been reached or why I was out freezing.

I knew our superintendent was unpopular with most teachers, and the union leaders were very unhappy about the way they'd been treated. Union bulletins and the news reports about negotiations were full of talk about subcontracting, but things didn't add up to me. It seemed there was another, unspoken agenda playing out. Teachers were furious with the superintendent and it seemed to me those feelings had spilled over into contract negotiations.

That was never talked about by the parties involved. I could see that the community was angry about the strike and was looking for someone to blame. The brutal cold built sympathy for teachers walking picket lines, and many came to blame the superintendent. He became the target of vituperation and vicious rumors. The strike was settled after only 4 days, but things in the district weren't the same. The superintendent became much more conciliatory and left the district a year and a half later. Teachers involved in the strike remained militant and angry for years.

What was it all about? How was it possible that the whole community was in an uproar over issues that were never brought out in the open? Why did the school board—some of whom I knew well—have such a different viewpoint of what was going on than the teachers? What had led up to the strike, and how could another one be avoided? I mulled these questions over for fifteen years before setting out to find some answers. That seeking and the age-old maxim that those who don't know history are destined to repeat it, led to this book.

Introduction

Minnesota has traditionally placed a high value on public education. With its public image of "Minnesota nice" it comes as something of a surprise to find that teachers have gone out on strike seventy-one times. But perhaps it shouldn't be a surprise, considering the number of changes that have occurred in economic conditions, the laws governing school district functioning and the interplay of personalities in hundreds of school districts in the state.

The subject of teachers' strikes generates strong emotions. Parents'—and the public's—concerns about the well-being of children come to the fore. Public schools are the focus of identity and pride for many communities, functioning as one of the major employers. They are the recipient of a significant portion of tax dollars, and the only unit of local government in Minnesota which has to turn to local voters to seek additional tax revenue.

School boards have a number of incentives to keep the public informed, and local citizens keep an eye on student performance and district finances. In outstate communities, high school sporting events are a major source of entertainment, generating lengthy discussions in local coffee shops.

Given the variety of religious, economic and political viewpoints present in any group of people, local citizens respond differently to school issues. Most will be averse to disruptions or perceived threats to their schools. School strikes are often viewed locally as calamities, ranked with major fires, accidents and plant closings.

Stories abound about communities in Minnesota ripped apart by a teacher's strike. Churches, clubs, sporting teams, friendships and family members became estranged from one another. Community leaders typically call for healing after the strike is settled, but the emotional impact persists. The effects of the 1981 strikes are still evident in some communities—thirty years later.

The Minnesota Bureau of Mediation Services has compiled a list of teacher's strikes, beginning in 1974.[1] It provides a definitive record of where strikes occurred from that point on. Records of strikes before 1974 were not kept by the Minnesota Department of Education, Minnesota School Board Association or Education Minnesota. It is thus very likely that the list of strikes provided in this first edition doesn't include some early strikes. Hopefully, communities and individuals will provide additional information.

One of the first questions to resolve is a definition of what constitutes a teacher's strike. A dictionary definition states: to stop work in order to obtain a change in conditions of employment.[2] Seemingly straightforward, several examples complicate the issue.

A one day walkout occurred in the Duluth school district in the mid-1960s. Because it was in the summer, no contract was in effect. Later termed a "walkout" the local paper didn't consider it a strike.[3] In December of 1989, a strike appeared inevitable in St. Paul. The school board had issued what it said was its final offer, which the union leadership rejected. The superintendent called Mayor George Latimer for help the day before the strike was to begin. The mayor was a former labor lawyer and agreed to intervene.

Meeting first with the general membership and then with the union negotiating team, he got the union to commit to an agreement splitting the salary difference. He then went to the school board and finalized an agreement.[4] Because the settlement had occurred so late in the day, the next day was declared a snow day to allow for teachers to vote on the contract. While it could be argued that students missed a day of school because teachers stopped working, this one day event is not considered a strike by the Minnesota Bureau of Mediation Services. For this book, all other work stoppages by teachers that involve lost school days are considered strikes.

The length of strikes is another area of possible inconsistency. Strikes began after school on a Friday, on holidays or weekends and continued during holidays. In some cases this included winter break, involving a week or more. Strikes ended during the week and weekend near midnight. Newspapers sometimes provided running totals of the number of strike days and included each weekend. The Bureau of Mediation Services appears focused on the number of work days lost. My focus is on students, so I calculated the number of school days lost during strikes.

The number of days made up by teachers couldn't be calculated based only on student days. In a number of instances, strike days were made up by teacher work days on Saturdays or what would have been holidays. Whether students were in school on those days wasn't always clear. The full number of makeup days is included here to help calculate the economics of each strike.

A clear example of the importance of strikes' legal status occurred in Hortonville, Wisconsin, in 1974. This is a book about Minnesota teachers' strikes, but we need to turn to Wisconsin for an extreme example.

Teachers' strikes were illegal in Wisconsin, but occurred nonetheless. School districts often sought injunctions once strikes began, and most were quickly settled.[5] Hortonville was a small town with an economy based on farming and pulp wood. Conservative politically, there was a strong anti-union sentiment.

Negotiations had been ongoing during the 1974 school year. The two sides were very close—the board offering $7,900, union asking $8,100.[6] The teachers went out on strike March 19th, saying the board was unwilling to compromise. On April 2nd the school board fired all the teachers, withdrew its latest contract offer and hired new teachers.

During spring break, 500 Wisconsin teachers from across the state staged a mass march, and were confronted with police from five counties in riot gear. The dispute moved to the courts, where a decision limited the number of pickets. The right of the Board to fire the teachers was contested up to the U.S. Supreme Court, which ruled in favor of the district.

During the strike dozens of teachers and counter protestors were arrested, windows of the strike headquarters were smashed, school board members and teachers' homes were spray painted. The Hortonville Vigilante Association harassed pickets and escorted strikebreakers through the picket lines.

Some of the fired teachers left the profession while others scattered to new teaching jobs across the state. The strike increased support for a bargaining law legalizing strikes and providing an arbitration system.

The legal status of strikers was an issue in the early Minnesota teacher's strikes. If employees have in effect resigned, there was no one to negotiate with. The possibility of mass firings may have inhibited Minnesota teachers from striking. Only the two largest districts—Minneapolis and St. Paul—had so many staff that replacing all of them wasn't possible.

---

1. MN Bureau of Mediation Services, K-12 Teacher Strikes FY 1974—Present, undated. Concludes with fiscal years 2003-2005 and includes Crosby-Ironton Strike in 2005.
2. *Marriam-Webster Dictionary*, Springfield Massachusetts 2004.
3. *Duluth News Tribune & Herald,* December 2, 1983, p. 2A.
4. *St. Paul Pioneer Press Dispatch,* December 7, 1989, p. 1A, 6A.
5. *WEAC: A History, Wisconsin Education Association Council*, Chapter 5.
6. "Education: The Hortonville 84," *Time*, May 27, 1974.

Minnesota Teacher Strikes

1946
St. Paul November 25–December 27

1948
Minneapolis February 24–March 22

1951
Minneapolis January 23–February 14

1970
Minneapolis April 9–April 28

1973
Hermantown September 24–October 5

1975
Winona December 9–16, Roseau December 11–16, Howard Lake–Waverly December 9–11, Luverne December 12–December 18, Faribault December 18–February 1

1976
Sauk Centre January 5–17, Minnetonka January 22–23

1977
Lake Benton November 16–December 5, Lakefield November 30–December 1,

1978
Buhl April 3–April 21, District 916 May 2–May 18, Burnsville September 19–Oct 6

1979
Albany November 12–December 3

1980
Audubon April 2–12

1981

Anoka, Bemidji, Cambridge-Isanti, Cass Lake, Crookston, Deer River, Eden Prairie, Eveleth, Forest Lake, Fridley, Glenwood, Grand Meadow, Granite Falls, Hibbing, Hill City, Houston, Howard Lake-Waverly October 6, Isle, Jordan, Lake City, Lester Prairie, Mahtomedi, New Prague, Paynesville, Pine River, Prior Lake, Proctor, Randolph, Rockford, St Cloud, Sauk Centre, Thief River Falls, Tracy, Wabasha-Kellogg, Walnut Grove

1983

Duluth December 1–19

1984

Greenway-Coleraine January 3–30, Sauk Rapids January 5–February 27, Appleton January 16–25, Park Rapids January 17–January 23, Rural St. Louis County January 18–February 6, Moorehead January 26–February 10, Chaska February 27–March 26,

1988

Proctor January 6–January 10 , Elk River February 23–March 2

1990

Messabi East January 10–26

1991

Rochester December 4–December 9, Spring Lake Park December 16–January 6

1992

International Falls February 14–March 10

2002

International Falls September 20–October 13

2002

Red Wing October 22–November 13

2005

Crosby-Ironton February 9–April 6

A frustrated principal, speaking of both negotiating teams during the 1992 teachers' strike in International Falls:

"If I had a gun, I'd get them in a room with a Porta-potty in the corner and send in pizza. I wouldn't let them out until they settled."[1]

---

1. *The Daily Journal*, February 21, 1992, pp. 1, 8.

Part One

Politics and Economics of Teachers' Strikes

Chapter One
Strikes and the Law

Private industry deals with its employees under federal and state laws, and faces fewer restrictions when developing contracts. Local units of government are subject to state control. This control increased over the years resulting in school districts being told when to negotiate, and the length of contracts.

Well before the first teacher's strike, a 1933 Minnesota labor law prohibited courts from issuing restraining orders preventing participation in strikes.[1] While this early law supported labor's ability to strike, it didn't speak to the issue of public versus private employee's rights.

In 1939, the legislature passed the Minnesota Labor Relations Act, creating the Division of Conciliation and establishing a Governor's Commission to hear labor disputes and issue reports.[2] The Commission's findings weren't binding on either party in a labor dispute and could only apply the force of public scrutiny.

Teachers called on the state conciliator for assistance early in the 1946 St. Paul strike, but he refused to get involved. He said state law didn't permit him to enter a case between a political subdivision and its employees. Public employees were thus left on their own for the next twenty-five years.

The dearth of labor laws resulted in several other issues during that strike. It was not clear on either side who the negotiators would be. The city council—who ran the schools at the time—formed a subcommittee to meet with teachers in an attempt to avert the strike. Teachers refused to meet with the committee because they lacked authority to negotiate.[3]

On the second day of the strike, the administration refused to formally recognize the Teachers' Council, but agreed that they would negotiate with them. For their part, teachers said that formal recognition of the Joint Teachers' Council as their bargaining agent would have to be part of a settlement.[4] Recognition of the importance of formalizing bargaining agents in all school districts wouldn't occur for years.

Questions about the legality of public employee strikes lingered until the 1950s. In response to a scheduled janitor's strike in January of 1951, the Minneapolis school board obtained a temporary injunction while a permanent injunction was considered.[5] Two weeks later, the district Court judge ruled that there was no clear language in Minnesota law prohibiting strikes by public employees. The city attorney had argued that strikes by public employees were unconstitutional because they limited the scope of government.

The judge said that to contend that citizens of a state could not meet and negotiate with the government or any of its departments and officials would be "a reversion to old monarchial right of sovereignty and the divine right of kings which is repugnant to the ideas of a free citizenry."[6]

In preparing for a state Supreme Court hearing, union lawyers cited the 1933 law, claiming, "That public policy is that courts shall not interfere with normal labor relations nor grant any injunction to restrain peaceful concerted action by employees."[7]

Teachers' strikes have influenced the development of state laws. The legislature was in session during the 1951 Minneapolis strike. A number of Minneapolis school board members were invited to testify. The legislature then passed a draconian anti-strike law aimed at all public employees. It included the following statement: ". . . strikes by public employees are a real danger to the safety and welfare of the general public and are a dangerous threat to government on all levels, and constitute a strike against the public itself."

Included in the law were harsh penalties. Any public employee violating the law was considered to have terminated his employment. If they were re-employed, the following provisions applied:

- Compensation couldn't exceed what was being paid prior to the strike.
- Their pay could not be increased for a year after being re-employed.
- They were placed on probationary status for two years.

The law included a hearing process for individuals to establish that they hadn't been on strike.[8] Since that was the only way to avoid the harsh penalties, maneuvering around that provision would be a key part in the next Minneapolis strike.

Commenting on the anti-strike law, a member of the Minneapolis School Board in 1971 said, "That law came out of a previous strike in 1951, and the legislature at that time was vindictive, mean, brittle and unbending and passed a very stupid law."[9]

The 1951 strike spotlighted another gap in labor law. School boards were not obliged to negotiate with staff. Testifying before the education committee of the House of Representatives, the secretary of the Minneapolis School Board stated, "In my personal opinion, the main issue is control of the public schools—whether it will be by the school board or the Men Teachers' Federation. The issue is political and nothing else." Asked whether the School Board was meeting with the union committees, he replied that the board was "at all times ready to listen to the superintendent, but does not, unless you propose to change the laws, intend to sit down and bargain with unions over wages."[10]

Labor made some progress in the 1960s. A 1961 law established that labor organizations representing a majority of employees had the right to meet and confer with their employer.[11] While not the same as negotiations, employee groups gained some legal status. In 1967 teachers were given the right to form unions. Five member teacher counsels were specified for each school district, with membership proportional to the ratio of teachers belonging to each teachers' union.[12]

The 1970 Minneapolis strike was the only teachers' strike to take place under the no-strike law. The district attempted to keep schools open during the first two days of the strike. Legally, any teacher who didn't report for work was considered terminated.

Despite this, the superintendent and school board met with striking teachers to attempt to work out an agreement. Teachers contacted the governor's office the fifth day of the strike to request mediation. An assistant state conciliator said the Minnesota law specifically excluded teachers from services by the state bureau of mediation. Governor

Levander said teachers had no status to request assistance until they had been rehired.

The issues of whether teachers could still be considered employees and whether they could participate in negotiations were discussed in District Court as well. While these questions went on outside the district, school board members urgently sought a way around the no-strike penalties.[13]

The governor refused to call a special session of the legislature to change the law, and a taxpayer group sought to ensure that the penalties were enforced. The smaller teachers' union in Minneapolis filed suit to be allowed to participate in negotiations, and sought to protect its members who hadn't reported for work the first two days of the strike.

During all this, the board and teachers also had to make progress in the give and take of difficult negotiations during a strike. Even after an agreement was reached about contract language and salary, the strike lasted an additional week until the board developed a satisfactory solution that got around the harsh no-strike penalties. Teachers were given a written assurance of amnesty, and the board agreed to a lump sum payment one year after the strike ended.

One odd result of the Minneapolis settlement was payment to teachers for the seven days they were on strike. The law didn't speak to pay during strikes, and the board included it to sweeten the settlement.

The painful and public difficulties experienced in Minneapolis resulted a year later in the establishment of the Public Employment Labor Relations Act. It regularized many aspects of teacher negotiations, but wasn't a giveaway to labor.

Strikes by public employees remained illegal. Those who struck "may have his appointment or employment terminated." (Note the "may.") If re-employed, they were put on a probationary status for two years. It specified that employees could not be paid for days they were engaged in a strike.

It required that contracts be written. Grievance procedures including possible binding arbitration had to be part of teachers' contracts. Teachers' contracts would be two years in length, starting in July of even numbered years. Negotiation sessions had to be held in public, unless directed by the

Bureau of Mediation Services.[14] Teachers finally had legal access to mediation services.

The law was liberalized in 1973 to permit strikes only in cases when an employer refused binding arbitration.[15] Several strikes occurred under those circumstances. Seven years later, the 1980 law permitted strikes when contracts had expired and mediation services had been utilized. The language in the new law was convoluted. A complex series of dates had to pass before teachers could strike.

"The exclusive representative and the employer have participated in mediation over a period of at least 60 days, 30 days of which have occurred after the expiration date of the collective bargaining agreement provided that the mediation period established by section 31 shall govern negotiations pursuant to that section. For the purposes of this sub-clause the mediation period commences on the day following receipt by the director of a request for mediation; and

Written notification of intent to strike was served on the employer and the director by the exclusive representative on or after the expiration date of the collective bargaining agreement, or if there is no agreement, on or after the date impasse under section 31 has occurred and at least ten days prior to the commencement of the strike, provided that if more than 30 days have expired after service of a notification of intent to strike, no strike may commence until ten days after services of a new written notification;"[16]

Small wonder that in 1981 when hundreds of school administrators, boards and unions had to be trained in the new law that misunderstandings occurred. The most common was that some union locals (and a number of boards) appeared to believe that if an agreement hadn't been reached by July 1st, the strike timelines began. After that first and painful Autumn, it was clear that the strike timelines spelled out the earliest a strike could be held. Mediation and notification periods could take place any time later in the contract period.

The 1980 law remains largely in place. The 2009 version states that teachers (but not principals or assistant principals) may strike after a collective bargaining agreement has expired and thirty days have been spent in mediation. The union must provide written notification ten days prior, and a strike can occur for the next fifteen days. The strike period can be extended, if both parties agree, for an additional five days. Teachers are limited to one notice of intent to strike for each contract period. It can be renewed for an additional ten days, five of which are a notice period if an agreement had been reached during the first strike notice period but was rejected be either party.[17] Thus, unions now have to be ready to strike if they provide notice, for they will have only one opportunity in each contract period.

---

1. *Minnesota Revisor of Statutes, Session Laws of Minnesota for 1933* Chapter 416.
2. *Minnesota Revisor of Statutes, Session Laws of Minnesota for 1939* Chapter 440.
3. *St. Paul Pioneer Press*, November 17, 1946, p. 1, 2.
4. *St. Paul Pioneer Press*, November 26, 1946, p. 1.
5. *Minneapolis Star*, January 6, 1951, p. 1.
6. *Minneapolis Star*, January 22, 1951, p. 1, 7.
7. *Minneapolis Star*, January 25, 1951, p. 1, 6.
8. *Minnesota Revisor of Statutes, Session Laws of Minnesota for 1951*, Chapter 146.
9. *Minneapolis Tribune*, April 28, 1971 p. 4.
10. *Minneapolis Star*, January 25, 1951, p. 1, 6.
11. *Minnesota Revisor of Statutes, Session Laws of Minnesota for 1965*, Chapter 839.
12. *Minnesota Revisor of Statutes, Session Laws of Minnesota for 1967*, Chapter 633.
13. *Minneapolis Tribune*, April 16, 1970, p. 1.
14. *Minnesota Revisor of Statutes, Laws 1971—Extra Session* Chapter 33.
15. *Minnesota Revisor of Statutes, Laws of Minnesota for 1973* Chapter 635.
16. *Minnesota Revisor of Statutes, Laws of Minnesota for 1980* Chapter 617.
17. *Minnesota Revisor of Statutes, 2009 Minnesota laws*, Chapter 179.18.

of teachers' unions in Minnesota thus needs to be viewed at both the local and state level.

The National Education Association was founded in 1857.[2] An umbrella organization to promote public education, it included superintendents and principals. It developed significant political clout because it came to be seen as an advocate for improving the education system. It wasn't primarily an advocate for teachers and believed that an emphasis on teachers' welfare was unprofessional and beneath the dignity of the Association.

The American Federation of Teachers broke away from the NEA in 1916 and affiliated with the American Federation of Labor.[3] The tactics and tone of the AFT state and local affiliates were more closely aligned with the traditional militant labor movement.

In the 1940s and 1950s, working conditions and teachers' unions were much different than today. Men's and women's teacher unions often were separate entities within a school district. Pay was based in part on perceived need, with men receiving $300 more if they were married. A widow would receive $100 extra if she had dependent children. Some districts refused to employ a woman if she married, others if the woman had children under eighteen. Teachers had to leave after their fourth month of pregnancy and weren't guaranteed a job when they returned. If they were reemployed, it would be at the bottom of the scale.[4]

The independence of the men's and women's unions within a district were clear during the lead up to the 1951 Minneapolis strike. Men voted to strike, but the women's union initially voted not to. Men were asking for $1,000 more than women. Despite that inequity, the women's union changed their position and voted to support the strike.[5]

The AFT developed support in large metropolitan areas, in in conjunction with the growth of unionism. In Minnesota, the AFT represented the majority of teachers in Minneapolis, St. Paul, and Duluth. Like other unions, these locals developed their own pension systems.

The MEA grew in outstate districts. It was much less militant, with many members seeing it as an advocate for education. When a draconian anti-strike bill was being considered in 1948 by the Minnesota Senate,

Geneveve Johnaton, the legislative chairman of the Minneapolis division of the MEA spoke in support of preventing teachers from striking. The MEA was described in the paper as a non-union group of teachers.[6] Beginning in 1952, the MEA met annually with leaders from the Minnesota School Board Association.[7]

The MEA's early non-confrontational approach was apparent during the Minneapolis teachers' strikes. In 1948, they didn't join striking AFT teachers. Instead, they sent letters to the superintendent indicating that they were willing to work.[8] During the strike, they found themselves in an ambiguous position. Because they weren't on strike, they were left out of the negotiations process. At one point when an extended school year was discussed, they made it clear they wanted a chance to comment.[9] Since any settlement would determine wages for all teachers, non-striking teachers had a stake in the outcome, but no voice.

In the last day of the 1951 strike, the district attempted to open the schools. All the MEA teachers crossed picket lines staffed by their AFT colleagues. The janitors honored the lines and the cold temperatures in classrooms caused teachers to send students home.[10] While crossing the picket lines didn't affect the 1951 strike outcome, it was a dramatic example of one Minnesota teachers' union not supporting another.

The two unions vied for membership, the AFT working to expand its membership beyond the central cities. The AFT recruited with some success in suburban districts, leading the MEA to respond by adopting more militant tactics during the 1960s.[11] A former MEA president recalled that, "One of my major goals was to make the MEA look not only like we were dominant but the most militant and aggressive organization, able to get more things for teachers than the Federation."[12]

The change in MEA's stance toward becoming an advocate for teachers led the Minnesota Association of School Administrators to sever its ties with the MEA in 1968. By 1973 the last administrators—elementary principals—left the MEA.[13]

Their intense rivalry led the two unions to sabotage each other's legislative efforts. In 1965 the MFT persuaded the governor to propose a collective bargaining bill providing for exclusive representation in bargaining. It provided that the union representing the majority of teachers would be the only one at the table. The MEA supported an alternate bill allowing for multiple representation that would have allowed districts to negotiate separately with each union, with disputes settled by the state Commissioner of Education.[14]

When the PELRA law passed in 1971 calling for exclusive representation, the MEA won in 390 school districts, the MFT in 50.[15] Don Hill was elected MEA president in 1975 and called for locals to improve conditions for teachers. With the passage of the right to strike, he led the MEA strike efforts that culminated in thirty-five strikes. The AFT avoided strikes at that time, stating that it felt members were better served through negotiations.

Recognizing that they would be better off working together rather than against each other, the MFT and MEA began merger talks in 1991, resulting in the formation of Education Minnesota in 1998.

---

1. *St. Cloud Daily Times,* October 2, 1981, p. 1.
2. *NEA Today,* January 2006.
3. Winkels Henry, *Who We Are What We Stand For 1966 Minnesota Federation of Teachers,* p. 3.
4. *MEA 137 Years Proud,* MEA 1999.
5. *Minneapolis Star,* January 6, 1951 p. 1, January 11, 1951 p. 1, 5.
6. *Minneapolis Star,* February 16, 1951, p. 1.
7. Gestie Bernice, *Centennial Issue,* MN J of Education, September 16, 1960 p. 92.
8. *Minneapolis Star,* February 25, 1948, p. 1.
9. *Minneapolis Star,* March 13, 1948, p. 1.
10. *Minneapolis Star,* February 13, 1951, p. 1, 6.
11. *MEA 137 Years Proud,* MEA 1999, p. 29.
12. *MEA 137 Years Proud,* MEA 1999, p. 30.
13. *MEA 137 Years Proud,* MEA 1999, p. 32.
14. Winkels Henry, *The MFT Legacy to the Teaching Profession 1986,* p. 20.
15. *MEA 137 Years Proud,* MEA 1999, p. 37.

Chapter Three
Incidents During Strikes

For teachers, administrators, and school boards, heading into a strike means moving into the unknown. One assumption they may each bring to the strike is that they can control what happens. The record of what's happened during teacher's strikes in Minnesota says otherwise. Incidents ranging from minor to irritating to potentially life-threatening popped up. Court cases escalated. No matter how hard each side tried, getting their story out to the public didn't always help.

Anonymous petty incidents occurred like the manure smeared on teachers' strike headquarters one night during the Thief River Falls strike. Others were very public, such as the fire truck that sprayed picketing teachers on a cold morning in Audubon.

Picket lines are an uncommon sight and could engender strong feelings. One parent felt so concerned about being near a strike that he drove to school with a handgun on the dashboard of his car. He hoped that the empty gun would scare those union workers enough so that nothing would happen to his daughter. As he prepared to drive through the picket line after dropping off his child at dance lessons in an elementary school, he put the gun in his lap. He hoped the picketers wouldn't notice that the gun was empty.

A teacher reported the incident to police, who charged the driver with careless handling of a handgun. In a letter to the editor, the parent called the teachers' union a menace to society and the picketers a mob. He claimed he was charged because he had been "a little too American."[1]

You might think that he was somewhat unusual and confused, but that's the point—unusual and confusing things happen during teacher's strikes. The parent in the gun incident was fearful. A driver in Granite Falls was angry.

A local publisher drove through the picket line without stopping while delivering some printed materials to the vocational school. When he got out of the car, a picketing teacher asked him to honor the picket line. The publisher responded in a profane manner and said that if teachers were in the way, he'd run over them on his way out.

When he got back in the car, he accelerated toward the picket line hard enough to squeal the tires and leave twenty feet of rubber on the asphalt. As he approached the picketing teachers, he slammed on the brakes hard enough to leave a five-foot skid, but was unable to stop. He struck a teacher, knocking him onto the hood of the car. The teacher rolled off and called for the car to stop. Instead, the driver squealed away, shaking his fist at the teacher.

The driver was charged with reckless driving, failure to stop at a picket line and hit and run. All were considered misdemeanors because the teacher's bruises and chipped cartilage weren't considered serious enough for felony charges.[2]

Picket lines are rare enough that some drivers don't know that they are required to stop. During the District 916 strike in 1978, teachers were hit by vans in two separate incidents. In one case, the district's personnel director was the driver.[3]

On the other side of the coin, at least one positive incident occurred when a mother stopped her car in front of a picket line because her child was choking. Two teachers performed the Heimlich Maneuver and the child expelled a piece of candy.[4]

School Board members were sometimes distressed to find that the strike was carried so personally to them. In Faribault, one of the earliest strikes, teachers "bannered" a savings and loan where the board president worked.[5]

Teachers picketed for several days at a business owned by a school board member during the 1992 strike in International Falls. The board member said that the pickets cost him some business because it was a union town and customers weren't willing to cross a picket line. Another board member complained that the picketing was unfair and said that board members should be left alone in their private lives. He questioned whether those teachers were fit to be with students and characterized them as terrorists.[6]

Feelings run even higher when a district has hired subs to reopen schools during a strike. In Howard Lake-Waverly, the district sought a court injunction barring teachers from continuing to picket not only board member's jobs, but their homes as well.[7] Although they might not have fully realized the implications, students in Moorehead carried out what is generally considered a reprehensible act when they hung a substitute teacher in effigy.[8]

Schools and unions may feel that they will have to deal only with each other during a strike. Over the years, many others have gotten involved. Two strikes on the Iron Range in 1984 saw the involvement of powerful mining union locals. When the districts of Greenway-Coleraine and rural St. Louis County said they would open with subs, the miners announced that they would stage mass picketing. Both districts quickly settled.[9]

Local ministers spoke out about strikes. In three communities during the 1981 strikes, religious leaders got together to call for a settlement. Their intervention didn't appear to affect the duration of the strikes. In Walnut Grove, all the pastors in town preached sermons on forgiveness before the strike began, to no avail.[10] In Mahtomedi four church leaders preached the same message one Sunday and organized a march that occurred in the middle of the strike.[11] The Cambridge Ministerial Association published a letter in the local paper saying the strike was divisive, was damaging the ability of teacher and board members to work together and called for more mediation sessions. That strike ended shortly afterwards.[12] In spite of the minister's efforts, all three strikes appeared to engender very negative feelings throughout the communities.

Minneapolis and St. Paul early strikes necessarily involved city councils and mayors. Due to nebulous negotiating rules, others were called in to help resolve those first strikes, including the state Attorney General and Governor, who played a key role in resolving the Minneapolis strike of 1951. A state senator's involvement caused the Faribault school board to settle.

The involvement of state politicians wasn't limited to early strikes. The Eveleth teaching staff in 1981 included the wife of a state legislator. At a teacher's rally attended by another state representative and two state senators, he claimed that the Minnesota School Board Association had targeted the Eveleth district for a strike. That led the school board to charge that he was abusing his legislative office as a member of the house education committee.[13]

A state senator was a striking teacher in the St. Louis County District. Late in the strike, he attempted to bring together a meeting of school board members and teachers. It wasn't held because teachers wouldn't meet without a mediator.[14] The state Attorney General was involved in Crosby-Ironton, the most recent strike.[15]

The Attorney General's inclusion in a strike involving the use of substitutes was emblematic of the challenges associated with subs. Of the fourteen strikes that utilized subs, eight of them went to court during the strikes. The most common issue was the utilization of unlicensed substitutes. Any district planning to use subs during a strike should assume they will end up in court. Not only does this entail legal expenses, it hands control of some of what happens during the strike to a judge.

It might seem logical to both teachers' unions and school boards that if they could just articulate to the public how reasonable their positions were, the local populace would overwhelmingly agree and force the other side to capitulate. An examination of the print media shows little correlation between news coverage and strike settlements.

The Faribault paper published long explanations provided by the board and union.[16] The Eveleth school board published a lengthy letter in the local paper that it had also sent to parents.[17] Howard Lake—Waverly teachers placed five ads in the local weekly paper during their long strike.[18] The MEA placed an ad by its president in the local Howard Lake paper as well.[19]

Toward the end of the Howard Lake—Waverly strike, parents placed a full page ad listing teachers' past and proposed salaries by name and the signatures of hundreds of residents who supported the school board's position.[20] The League of Woman Voters held a radio debate between a union spokesman and the board president.[21]

International Falls teachers placed ads during their 1992 strike.[22] The school board in Aurora-Hoyt Lakes—Biwabik published letters explaining their positions.[23] None of these efforts by unions and school boards appeared to bring a quick end to strikes.

News coverage provided far more information than any full page ad. Here again, there appears to be little correlation between how thoroughly a strike was covered by local newspapers and the length of the strike.

Some of the 1981 strikes occurred in tiny towns without a local paper. The twenty-four teachers in Hill City resolved their strike after two days with virtually no news coverage while the strike by nineteen teachers in Walnut Grove lasted nineteen days under more print.

The strikes in Spring Lake Park and Rochester took place within days of each other. Perhaps because it's a small suburb, Spring Lake Park received very little coverage in print. Rochester on the other hand had a local daily paper that provided extensive coverage during both the negotiations and the strike. The Rochester strike lasted four days, Spring Lake Park, five. A few years later, when Red Wing went on strike there was again a local daily that provided a great deal of coverage. That strike lasted seventeen days. The strike in Crosby-Ironton received extensive TV and superb print coverage, yet went on and on to become the second longest teachers' strike in Minnesota history.

This is not to say that media coverage didn't affect strikes. In Red Wing, teachers struck the day before a sectional football game. The game had to be moved to Austin where the Red Wing team coached itself, losing by two points.[24] There was widespread TV coverage of the unusual occurrence of a team playing without its coaches. Many residents of Red Wing felt that teachers had timed the strike to coincide with the game to garner media coverage. Residents weren't happy about their team losing. Many in town had been feeling sympathetic toward teachers during the run up to the strike, but didn't support them after the game.[25]

It didn't appear to be the media coverage that influenced strikes. Rather, public perception was altered by events. Letters to the editor often showed that opinions held either for or against the strike strengthened as time went on. Support was gained by whichever side appeared to be willing to meet and compromise. Teachers lost support when incidents of vandalism in Prior Lake were attributed to them, and through yelling at substitutes in Crosby-Ironton. Teachers gained sympathy in Rochester when the weather turned brutally cold.

Parents and most citizens just wanted the strikes ended. Public opinion swung toward whomever appeared most willing to develop a settlement.

---

1. *Park Rapids Enterprise*, January 21, 1984, p. 1, 2.
2. *Granite Falls Tribune*, October 29, 1981, p. 1, 18.
3. *White Bear Press*, May 11, 1978, p. 1.
4. *Paynesville Press*, October 14, 1981, p. 1
5. *Faribault Daily News*, January 17, 1976, p. 1.
6. *The Daily Journal*, February 19, 1992, p. 1, 7.
7. *Wright County Journal-Press*, December 10, 1981, p. 1.
8. *The Forum*, February 4, 1984, p. A1.
9. *Duluth Tribune & Herald*, January 30, 1984, p. 1; February 4, 1984, p. 1.
10. *Daily Journal*, October 22, 1981, p. 6.
11. *White Bear Press*, December 3, 1981, p. 1.
12. *Cambridge Star*, November 11, 1981, p. 4.
13. *Mesabi Daily News*, October 25, 1981, p. 2, October 28, 1981 p. 1, 2.
14. *Mesabi Daily News*, February 5, 1984, p. 1.
15. *Brainerd Dispatch*, March 29, 2005.
16. *Faribault Daily News*, February 13, 1975, p. 4.
17. *Mesabi Daily News*, October 19, 1981, p. 3.
18. *Howard Lake Herald*, October 8, 1981, p. 8; November 12, 1981, p. 8; November 19, 1981; December 3, 1981, p. 6; December 10, 1981, p. 7.
19. *Howard Lake Herald*, November 19, 1981.
20. *Howard Lake Herald*, December 17, 1981, p. 8.
21. *St. Cloud Daily Times*, October 8, 1981, p. A1.
22. *The Daily Journal*, March 2, 1992, p. 12.
23. *Aurora Hoyt-Lakes Range Facts*, January 18. 1990, p. 5.
24. *The Daily Journal*, October 23, 2002, p. 1.
25. Interview with parent, February 2002.

Chapter Four
Substitutes During Strikes

One of the decisions districts have to make when planning for a possible strike is whether to attempt to reopen the schools using substitutes. Fourteen districts did so during Minnesota strikes. It has been the stance of the Minnesota School Board Association to encourage districts to use subs because it shortens strikes. The record doesn't substantiate that belief.

The following table records the length of strikes separated by districts that did and didn't use subs. The averages at the bottom shows that in Minnesota, strikes in districts who didn't use subs averaged 10.6 days, while those in districts that did averaged 26.

Effect of Using Subs

Saying that using subs prolongs strikes doesn't tell the whole story. In ten districts—indicated by italics—the administration announced that subs were being interviewed and/or schools would reopen within the following week. In every case, the strikes were settled within a week and a half. It thus appears that the threat of using subs can shorten a strike.

In looking at the entire picture of what happens to the students, staff and community, a stark metaphor comes to mind. Using substitutes is like announcing during an argument that you have a hand grenade. If the threat is credible, it certainly will get the other side's attention, and may well persuade them that it's in their best interest to settle. If the grenade is used however, great damage occurs.

Some of that damage occurs to students, first of all because the strike is likely to be prolonged. The rationale for using subs is typically an attempt to resume the education process. During the Faribault strike in 1975—the first to use subs—the day the first school reopened, the superintendent

Substitutes During Strikes

Districts advertising and planning to hire subs in italics.

Year	District	Strike Length w/o Subs	Strike Days w/Subs
1946	St. Paul Nov 25 – Dec 27	18	
1948	Minneapolis Feb 24 – March 22	19	
1951	Minneapolis Jan 23 – Feb 14	17	
1970	Minneapolis April 9 – April 28	14	
1973	Hermantown Sept 24 – Oct 5	10	
1975	Winona Dec 9 – 16	7	
	Roseau Dec 11 – 16	3	
	Howard Lake – Waverly Dec 9 – 11	2	
	Luverne Dec 12 – 18	6	
	Faribault Dec 18 – Feb 1		29
1976	Sauk Centre Jan 5 – 17		7
	Minnetonka Jan 22 – 23	2	
1977	Lake Benton Nov 16 – Dec 5		12
	Lakefield Nov 30 – Dec 1	2	
1978	Buhl April 3 – 21	15	
	916 May 2 – 18	13	
	Burnsville Sept 19 – Oct 6	14	
1979	Albany Nov 12 – Dec 3	13	
1980	Audibon April 2 – 12		5
	Anoka, Oct 6 – 18	7	
	Bemidji, Nov 4 – Nov 15	8	
	Cambridge–Isanti, Oct 12 –Nov 15?	22	
	Cass Lake, Dec 3 – Jan 4	12	
	Crookston, Oct 13 – Nov15	12	
	Deer River, Oct 1 – 20	11	
	Eden Prairie, Oct 9 – Nov 29		34
	Eveleth, Oct 21 – Nov 12	18	

Bad Blood and Economics

Year	District	Strike Length w/o Subs	Strike Days w/Subs
1980	Forest Lake, Oct 27 – Nov 14	14	
	Fridley, Oct 13 – Nov 4	10	
	Glenwood, Oct 12 – 18	3	
	Grand Meadow, Oct 20 – Nov 14	19	
	Granite Falls, Oct 14 – Nov 23		26
	Hibbing, Nov 2 – 8	5	
	Hill City, Oct 13 – 15	2	
	Houston, Nov 10 – Nov 17	4	
	Howard Lake–Waverly Oct 6 – Jan 10		58
	Isle, Oct 13 – 28	7	
	Jordan, Nov 2 – Nov 19	10	
	Lake City, Oct 6 – 11	4	
	Lester Prairie, Oct 14 – Nov 1?	10	
	Mahtomedi, Oct 30 – Dec 21		33
	New Prague, Oct 15 – 20	2	
	Paynesville, Sept 25 – Oct 18	14	
	Pine River, Nov 13 – 18	3	
	Prior Lake, Oct 1 – Nov 15		30
	Proctor, Oct 12 – 14	3	
	Randolph, Nov 18 – Dec 10	9	
	Rockford, Oct 6 – Nov 13	27	
	St Cloud, Oct 1 – 28	18	
	Sauk Centre, Oct 30 – Dec 4	22	
	Thief River Falls, Oct 13 – Nov 14	22	
	Tracy, sept 30 – Oct 6	5	
	Wabasha–Kellogg, Oct 6 – 13	7	
	Walnut Grove, Oct 9 – Nov 12		19
	Duluth Dec 1 – 19	12	
1984	*Greenway – Coleraine Jan 3 – 30*	19	
	Sauk Rapids Jan 5 – Feb 27	38	

22

Year	District	Strike Length w/o Subs	Strike Days w/Subs
1984	Appleton Jan 16 – 25	8	
	Park Rapids Jan 17 – Jan 23	5	
	Rural St. Louis County Jan 18 – Feb 6	13	
	Moorehead Jan 26 – Feb 10		12
	Chaska Feb 27 – march 26		22
1988	Proctor Jan 6 – Jan 10	3	
	Elk River Feb 23 – Mar 2	7	
1990	Messabi East Jan 10 – 26	13	
1991	Rochester Dec 4 – Dec 9	4	
1991	Spring Lake Park Dec 16 – Jan 6	5	
1992	International Falls Feb 14 – March 10	17	
2002	International Falls Sept 20 – Oct 13	16	
2002	Red Wing October 22 – Nov 13	17	
2005	Crosby–Ironton Feb 9 – April 6		39
	Average	10.6	26

said, "We are interested in getting the children back in school. We will open any school we can get staffing for. It is not my intention to break the strike. That is not my objective and I'm not thinking about that, I am just trying to get the children back in school and I am starting wherever I can."[1]

The school board chair during the 2005 Crosby-Ironton strike said, "Our primary goal is to bring the kids back to school with replacement teachers."[2] While these seem to be logical and laudable goals for the administration and school board, they have proven to be very difficult to implement.

Of the fourteen districts who attempted to reopen utilizing subs, only five were able to open all grades. Those districts were Lake Benton in 1977, Howard Lake-Waverly in 1981, Walnut Grove in 1981, Moorehead in 1984 and Chaska in 1984. The other nine districts—despite their best efforts—

were unable to find enough licensed substitutes to fill all their classrooms. Typically, the middle school grades were the last filled.

Some districts may feel that if five districts were able to open fully, they could as well. Several of the districts who were able to open were quite small. Lake Benton had only twenty-four teachers, Walnut Grove, nineteen. The 1981 strikes saw the creation of 'professional strike breakers' who substituted in as many as five different striking districts, including Howard Lake-Waverly.[3]

Moorehead was a fairly large district with 337 teachers. A number of teachers in town had been recently laid off and as a border city; it was able to draw subs from both Dakotas.[4] Chaska was a moderate sized district with 188 teachers, located close enough to draw subs from the Twin Cities. There's little cause for optimism in these five examples.

Athletic events were disrupted in every district. Coaching requires a specific and uncommon certification. Districts were rarely able to find qualified coaches who were not teachers or sympathetic to the teachers' strike.

These examples obviate the laudable goal of continuing student's educations during a strike through the use of substitutes. It's highly unlikely that enough qualified substitutes will be found to open all grades and extracurricular activities. The more likely outcome will be that some students will experience a longer disruption to their school year.

Along with the limited positives, using substitutes produces a number of negatives. Picket lines go from being relatively benign when schools are closed, to angry and confrontational when substitute teachers are crossing the lines. The heightened feelings have long-term consequences in the community and within districts.

Teachers are typically seen as well-mannered professionals. Many residents of Prior Lake were angered when teachers flattened substitutes' tires in a nearby Target parking lot and boxed in vans driving them to school, forcing them to drive slowly.[5] A parent in the Crosby-Ironton School District who witnessed striking teachers yelling at substitutes at the bus garage said, " I was stunned. They were yelling the most awful things you could imagine to these people. I thought, these are our teachers? They teach our kids?"[6]

In addition to losing the respect of community members and parents, friendships are damaged. A parent who accompanied her child to school during the strike in Moorehead was quoted, "I saw one of my friends out there and she told me she would never speak to me again. And all I did was bring my child to school."[7]

Students sometimes felt alienated by their substitutes. In Moorehead, high school students left the building to picket with teachers and hung a substitute in effigy.[8] They told school board members the substitutes teachers were little better than baby sitters and a growing rift had developed between students who did and didn't support the strike.[9] An editorial in the Howard Lake-Waverly school paper described the student body as split into bitter enemies because of the strike.[10]

Substitute teachers worked for a variety of reasons. Some of them were strongly opposed to strikes. A sub interviewed during the Moorehead strike said she was going to donate her wages to the school. She felt that students had a right to go to school, and that strikes—whether in private industry or public jobs—were wrong.[11]

Money was an incentive as well, with some districts paying what they calculated as their teachers' average wage or in one case a higher amount because they said it was the average salary they had offered in a rejected contract. In addition, some districts paid to house subs in motels and paid mileage for them to drive home once a week.

Teachers who crossed the lines of their own districts altered their relationships with colleagues. In Howard Lake-Waverly the two groups were described twenty-nine years later as being life-long enemies.[12] Even in cases where subs weren't used, teachers who don't support strikes encounter hostility from those who do. In Cambridge teachers wouldn't even look at a teacher for the rest of her career because she had crossed the line.[13] I witnessed the shunning of a teacher in Rochester whose only transgression was refusing to picket.

Moorehead provides the most optimistic example of the outcomes of a strike that used subs. They were able to hire hundreds of subs early in the strike, enabling them to open many classes by the third day and filled all classrooms shortly after that. Perhaps because the union was uncomfortable, the strike was settled in only twelve days. The settlement provided teachers with only two make up days and settled for significantly less than half the difference between the two salary positions at the start of the strike.

Was this a success for the district, providing support for the use of subs? The superintendent didn't seem to think so. He was teary-eyed when announcing the end of the strike.[14]

Substitutes during strikes cost a district nearly as much as their normal payroll. The average teacher's wage in a district was often used to set subs' salaries. Since this was much higher than normal day sub wages, it served as a source of irritation for unions, who sometimes viewed it as proof that the district was out to break the strike. Because some subs came from well outside the area, some districts also paid for them to stay in motels, and provided mileage money to travel home once a week. Security personnel were often hired to get subs through the picket lines.

During the Chaska strike, the board chair stated that payroll expenses for substitutes and guards ran $27,380 per day, higher than the normal per day teacher cost of $23,000.[15] By the end of the strike, the district had paid $625,000 in strike related expenses, compared to the $506,000 teacher pay would have cost for the same period.[16]

Given the expenses of operating schools with substitutes, it's no surprise that districts were reluctant to make up strike days. In their view, they'd already paid for those school days. Making up days was sometimes the last issue to hold up a settlement and contributed to prolonging some strikes.

Reopened schools must operate during a strike under the wide variety of state and federal mandates they usually face. Among them are the rules governing special education. During some strikes, special education classes were among the last to reopen. The Red Wing school district interpreted the federal law to read that they couldn't open regular education classrooms without also providing special education services. When special education subs couldn't be found, they didn't open any classes.[17]

The use of substitutes during strikes has triggered court actions. In Crosby-Ironton, the most recent strike, the union sought an injunction against the district for hiring unlicensed teachers. They also claimed unfair labor practices and violations of the Data Privacy Act.[18] The district agreed in court to release subs' names and that all subs would have proper licenses. The union dropped its request for an injunction, but the unfair labor practice lawsuit went forward and wasn't resolved until the strike settlement rendered the question moot.

The Minnesota attorney general weighed in, issuing a ruling that the board of teaching couldn't issue temporary teachers' licenses to replacement teachers on the basis of the district's hardship. Since a strike is not an event beyond a school board's control, the 2000 amendment to the rule on temporary licenses was not applied correctly. He said that four substitutes had been issued such licenses.[19] While the Crosby-Ironton school district didn't contest the attorney general's ruling, that strike illustrates the scope of possible actions that can occur when substitutes are hired.

So, the question remains. Should districts utilize subs during a strike? Unless it's clear that a full complement of teachers—including special education—can be quickly hired, it's likely that some students will lose more education if subs are utilized. There will be little if any money saved if the district will be paying average teacher's wages plus security services. The quality of instruction will be decreased, since substitutes don't know student's needs or the district's curriculum. The community will come to respect teachers less. Teachers will feel a deep resentment against the administration and/or school board and will be alienated for decades from colleagues who didn't support the strike.

On the other hand, teachers will probably be made to suffer a larger financial loss because the strike will last longer and fewer days will be made up. School boards and administrators will appear to some in the community to be stout defenders of children's right to an education. Replacing teachers, even temporarily, provides a strong statement of management's power.

Teachers find any strike unnerving. Not only are their routines completely disrupted, they face a number of unknowns. How long will it last? They might gain in the long run, but how much will it cost them? At least they have the reassurance in Minnesota that they can't be replaced permanently by subs hired during a strike. Unlike private industry where workers were replaced during the Hormel strike of 1985, teachers don't have to fear losing their jobs. Sooner or later, the district will have to forge an agreement with them, allowing them to return to work. If that law changes, the dynamics of teachers' strikes would change as well.

In the end, it comes down to the question asked other times in this book. What kind of school district does the community want? Is education to be the focus, or conflict? Using subs is guaranteed to inflame passions for years to come.

---

1. *Faribault Daily News,* January 19,1975, p. 1.
2. 65 *Brainerd Dispatch,* March 1, 2005.
3. *White Bear Press,* December 17, 1981, p. 1.
4. *The Forum,* February 8, 1984, p. A1, A4.
5. *St. Paul Pioneer Press,* November 4, 1981.
6. *Brainerd Dispatch,* February 26, 2005.
7. *The Forum,* January 31, 1984, p. A1, A5.
8. *The Forum,* February 4, 1984, p. A1.
9. *The Forum,* February 3, 1981, p. 1.
10. *Howard Lake Herald*—Open Channels—December 16, 1981, p. 2.
11. *The Forum,* January 31, 1984, p. A1.
12. Interview with local resident, Spring 2010.
13. Interview, MN Bureau of Mediation, Spring 2010.
14. *The Forum,* February 11, 1984, p. A1, A2, A3.
15. *Carver County Herald,* March 7, 1984, p. 1.
16. *Carver County Herald,* May 2, 1984, p. 1.
17. *Republican Eagle,* October 25, 2002, p. 1.
18. *Brainerd Dispatch,* March 22, 2005.
19. *Brainerd Dispatch,* March 30, 2005.

Chapter Five
Effects of Strikes

Many people in a community are affected by a teachers' strike, beginning with the students. The vast majority of strikes resulted in lost days of education. In several long strikes where enough substitutes were found to open part of the district, other students lost a significant amount of their school year. In most strikes, students lost only a few days. This may seem unimportant, but two groups of students can be adversely affected by any disruption in the school year—athletes and those applying for post-high school programs.

There were many cases of teams forfeiting not just individual games, but participation in sectionals. A high school senior commented about the return of his regular coach, "There will always be some resentment towards the teachers."[1] Win/loss records might alter an athlete's chances of a college scholarship. College scouts planning to observe may not be able to reschedule.

Parents of high school juniors and seniors are well aware of the crucial role counselors play in post-high school plans. Most colleges, and virtually every scholarship program, receive far more applications than they can accept. An easy way to process applications is by strictly enforcing submission deadlines. High school counselors complete some paperwork, and guide students and families through what can be a grueling process.

In small districts where an administrator acts as the counselor, a teacher's strike would be less disruptive to the application process. Most programs require letters of recommendation from teachers, however, so students may still miss deadlines from even a short strike.

Schools serve many roles these days. School nurses may be dispensing most of the medications a child receives during the week. A letter to the editor during the 2002 International Falls strike pointed out that kids getting free and reduced lunches might be going hungry because their parents hadn't budgeted for those meals.[2]

The student body was affected when hostility developed between students who supported and opposed the strike.[3] This was pronounced when schools were reopened with substitutes. The editor of the student newspaper in Howard Lake-Waverly described the student body as divided into bitter enemies.[4]

Strikes can take a heavy toll on superintendents. In outstate communities, the superintendent is one of the best paid and most respected members of the community. With the advent of a teachers' strike, the superintendent—particularly if he or she is the district spokesperson—will be the object of anger from parents and teachers' supporters. Inside the district, the superintendent will be transformed by a strike from someone to be respected and listened to, into the enemy.

Looking back over his many years as superintendent in a number of districts, the former superintendent of the Anoka schools said of the seven-day strike in 1981, "That was probably the low point in my career in Anoka-Hennepin."[5] The Red Wing superintendent said the strike was the worst experience of his career, and decided not to renew his contract.[6] The superintendent in Rochester adopted a more conciliatory tone after the strike and agreed with criticisms from the school board about his leadership style.[7] He resigned and left the state a few years later. In Crosby-Ironton the superintendent endured a vote of no-confidence by the teachers months after the strike. Her contract was renewed, but she announced that she was leaving the profession.

The divisions caused by teachers' strikes run deep within communities. In the metropolitan area, schools are a minor part of a complex landscape. The strikes in Minneapolis and St Paul were so big that they garnered attention. Some of those in the suburbs attracted very little. In outstate Minnesota, schools are a central aspect of the community. When consolidation is discussed, many towns fight hard to keep their school, saying they would lose their communities' identity. High school sports are a major draw not just for parents, but the whole town.

A disruption in the school system is, thus, a threat to the whole community. In the suburbs, families without children in school may shrug and turn to another story. In small towns, nearly everyone's concerned. In Walnut Grove, they'd never had a strike of any kind and thought it couldn't happen. The walkout by teachers in 1981 left a lot of people feeling numb. Others were angry. A man in the coffee shop said, "You can't put in print what the people are saying here."[8]

The state senator representing the Crosby-Ironton area said three weeks into the strike that, "The community is being ripped apart. It's time to end this before the community is so divided that it will take generations to heal the wounds."[9] He was right. Almost a year after the strike, it was reported that some friendships and even family relationships weren't what they were, and might never be the same.[10]

In addition to turning on each other, some community members turned against the schools after a strike. In Howard Lake-Waverly, after the strike many residents stopped attending school games. Support for the school district dropped, contributing to a delay of over twenty years before a new high school was built because enough new people had moved into the district to overcome the resentment felt by those who had been there in 1981.[11] The strike in Duluth continues to reverberate and polarize the school board almost thirty years later.[12]

Can all this residual pain be worth it? Most communities learned their lesson the first time. Very few chose to repeat a strike. Proctor's first strike in 1981 was over in three days. The local paper said that it was as if it hadn't happened, saying there was no polarization or animosity.[13] Perhaps because it had been relatively painless, Proctor teachers went out again six years later. The second time, there was said to be little support for teachers in the community. Picketing wasn't pleasant either, with wind chills at forty-three degrees below zero.[14] They haven't struck since.

The first International Falls strike lasted eighteen days, with only half made up. There was a fair amount of community support for teachers, in part because the superintendent wasn't popular. Ten years later teachers went out again, this time for sixteen days. There was much less support for teachers, and other unions were slower to express support.[15] Despite being in a strongly union community, nine years have passed without a threepeat.

Minneapolis is the only district to have experienced three teachers' strikes—in 1948, 1951 and 1970. One advantage they had was that their sheer size made it impossible to hire enough subs to replace them. Even the possibility of the rival union crossing the picket lines wouldn't provide enough staff.

A unilateral decision by the school board to shorten the school year and cut pay by ten percent sparked the first strike. Chronic underfunding contributed to the second three years later. The 1970 strike was a gutsy move, done in the face of a harsh no-strike law. The board's refusal to negotiate about prep time and a low salary offer fueled the walkout. Having struck three times, the district remained working during the tumultuous 1981 negotiation period.

Although rarely willing to go through it again, were the strikes worth it? An analysis of the 1981 strikes concluded that both the Minnesota Education Association and Minnesota School Board Association, ". . . reported bargaining results in a manner calculated to make their performance look good to their constituents." Looking beyond the spin, the professors concluded that seventy-two percent of the economic strikes resulted in settlements which were favorable to teachers.[16]

Despite this seeming high rate of success during that first bout of sanctioned strikes in 1981, they were followed by only seventeen in the last thirty years.

---

1. *Howard Lake Herald*, Open Channels December 16, 1981, p. 1.
2. *The Daily Journal*, October 8, 2002, p. 4.
3. *Fargo Forum*, February 3, 1984, p. A1.
4. *Howard Lake Herald*, Open Channels December 16, 1981, p. 2.
5. *Coon Rapids Herald*, January 15, 2004.
6. Interview, Spring 2010.
7. *Rochester Post Bulletin*, March 24, 1992.
8. *Crookston Daily Times*, October 26, 1981, p. 2.
9. *Brainerd Dispatch*, March 3, 2005.

10. *Star Tribune,* January 17, 2006, p. 1B.
11. Interview with parent, Spring 2010.
12. Interview, Minnesota School Board Association, Spring, 2010.
13. *The Proctor Journal,* October 22, 1981, p. 1.
14. *The Proctor Journal,* January 7, 1988 p. 1,3,5; January 14, 1988, pp. 1, 12.
15) Interview with union leader, February 2011.
16) Ley R., Wines W., "The Economics of Teachers' Strikes in Minnesota in 1981." *Economics of Education Review* 1985, pp. 57-65.

Chapter Six
Wants Versus Needs

Typically, there is a large difference between what an individual or group wants, and what they need. This is true as well in school districts. Management (the administrators and school board) and labor (in this case teachers) would each like a great deal of control. What they require in order to fulfill their role is much smaller.

Some of the motivations behind these desires include power, status, and the ability to control outcomes. The interplay between groups within a school district is typically known not only by staff, but the community as well. The public nature of what may become power struggles can exacerbate their intensity.

Distinguishing between wants and needs is crucial during negotiations. An issue that has been accurately perceived as a need is—by definition—worth fighting and striking for. A want on the other hand would be nice, but isn't worth the suffering it would take to get it. A number of 1981 strikes occurred when management was forced to give up what it thought were needs. In retrospect, they turned out to be things management wanted, but teachers felt they needed.

Managing district revenues is an essential school board function. Few teachers would invite the public's ire as instigators of a tax increase. Most are content to let their school board take the lead—and the heat—in determining tax rates each year as well as levy override and bond issue elections. Teachers may urge the board to begin those efforts and support their passage, but have little desire to take over that role. Each side would prefer to control—or at least significantly influence—most other district functions.

Management and labor would each prefer to decide:

- Who is hired
- Who is transferred, where and when
- Pay rates
- Work hours
- Discipline policies including how people are fired
- Leave policies and how they are applied
- Retirement rules including severance pay
- Length of the school day
- Assignment of tasks—classroom and extracurricular
- Creating, eliminating and reducing positions
- Setting the budget
- Performance reviews
- Student discipline
- Class size/workload
- Grievance procedures

School boards are obliged to carry out a number of functions, and carry the legal responsibility for doing so. In the broadest terms, these involve setting taxes, spending public money under a myriad of rules, avoiding going into debt and obeying labor laws; all in the name of educating their community's children. They must maintain some control of all district functions because they are responsible for them. Their needs then can be couched in terms of what they must do to meet the requirements they face.

Teachers as a group cannot unilaterally control any aspect of a school district's functioning. The question for them if their needs are not met is whether they will come back the next year. The issue was articulated clearly during legislative hearings in 1951 about a proposed anti-strike law for public employees. Referring to the ongoing strike in the Minneapolis schools, the president of the Minnesota State Federation of Labor charged that, "The school board's attitude that if you don't like your job you can quit is wrong."[1]

The two sides view needs in much different contexts. School boards feel they are acting on legal mandates. Teachers will only stay if conditions are acceptable.

While teachers' interests include all the items listed above, contracts agreed to between teachers and school boards don't include a direct role for teachers in setting budgets or taxes, and rarely allow teachers to negotiate about class size or work load. Adjusting class size and workloads is a crucial tool school boards use to control costs. If a district has ever agreed to include clauses in their teachers' contract setting class sizes or workloads, teachers may fight fiercely to maintain those limits. Not only do those decisions directly affect how much work teachers have to do, they impact the quality of service teachers can deliver. Given some control of this crucial feature of their work, teachers won't give it up easily.

Teachers needs include feeling safe and being treated fairly. Safety issues include a number of areas, such as who is laid off and the firing process. Involuntary transfers can place teachers with staff they don't know (or don't like) and place them at risk for failure. As the movement to make teachers accountable ties compensation and job security to student performance, assignment to an underperforming group of students can be threatening. Not at first seeming to be a contract issue, effective student discipline practices minimize risks of parental complaints, lawsuits and injuries to students or staff.

Fair treatment includes a standard set of rules that are known and followed. Who gets to take a personal leave day just before or after a holiday can be an important issue to the people involved. A specified application procedure and first-come, first-served rule simplify the process. A capricious process can lead to conflict between staff (How come you got to go when I asked first?), escalating into group conflict when staff side with one person or the other.

Unscrupulous administrators can use granting favors as a tool to reward supporters, creating opposing groups of "brown nosers" and "independents." While this can be done with issues as minor as who gets first dibs at the paper supplies, the more valuable the favor, the more intense the conflicts become.

Each of the rules and processes put into a teacher's contract regularize what happens, while at the same time limiting administrator's discretion. Those functions essential for teachers and administrators include:

Needed by school boards:	Needed by teachers:
• Determining budget	• Adequate pay & benefits
• Determining taxes	• Specified layoff process
• Deciding who is hired	• Specified transfer process
• Deciding who is fired	• Grievance procedure
• Number of positions	• Fair evaluations

It might seem that a school board must control teachers' pay, but those expenditures are only part of a bigger package. The board does need to keep the total expenditures from the general fund at a certain level. The amount paid for textbooks, secretaries, paraprofessionals, and principals will affect how much is left to pay teachers. In most contract negotiations, districts calculate their total cost for all the expenses involved in any proposal. For example, additional leave days mean more money for substitutes. Early retirement incentives could save or cost the district, depending on the details of the agreement and the number of people involved.

If the district can accept the total contract cost, there is a lot of flexibility about where the money goes. More in one portion will mean less in another. These days, health insurance costs may significantly reduce monies available for salaries.

This is not to say that districts aren't concerned about how money is distributed. Many are concerned about being able to offer competitive starting salaries to attract new staff. Insurance benefits are sometimes negotiated as part of teachers' contracts. In many districts health insurance costs and benefits are the same for all staff. How would the secretaries or principals react to a large increase in their insurance premiums?

After determining a total cost package, school boards have occasionally allowed the teachers' union to create a salary schedule. More often, salary schedules are hammered out in negotiations and have often been a point of contention. Should more money go to the new teachers, or those more experienced? Should steps—automatic raises for longevity—be collapsed at the bottom, or expanded at the top?

It can be confusing for the general public to witness ongoing disagreement after an average salary increase has been determined. That figure can readily be used to calculate total costs, but doesn't clarify where the money is going. Senior teachers, who no longer get annual step raises, may feel very strongly that they deserve a large portion of the increase. They get far smaller raises than newer teachers, and in lean years may have received little or nothing. Since their retirement pension is based on their five years' highest salary, they have a great deal riding on receiving a significant raise.

Teachers in Houston, Minnesota, felt strongly enough about this issue to strike over it in 1981. In the end, they settled for the same total amount offered by the district before the strike. Instead of all teachers receiving the same raise, more senior teachers received larger raises the first year, with everyone getting the same raise the next.[2]

Particularly in this time of declining enrollments and revenues, job security is a major concern of teachers and a focus of administrators. Given that some teachers from a certain area will have to be laid off, how is it decided who goes? Traditionally the answer is seniority, with the last person hired for that department or with that teaching license being the first to be laid off.

Seniority is popular with teachers and has been a part of almost all public school contracts, but is less common in charter schools. Critics of public schools say seniority results in districts laying off young, energetic "good" teachers while retaining those who are old and ineffective. Seniority is something most teachers who have it feel is a need, for it provides some measure of job security. Teaching becomes a less attractive profession if you can't count on being able to feed your family or pay your bills next year. Most teachers' unions would refuse to negotiate about seniority. Attempts to eliminate it run the risk of poisoning negotiations and would typically be grounds for considering a strike.

Tenure was first regulated by the Minnesota legislature in 1927. It basically states that for the first three years, teachers' contracts can be "non-renewed" without giving a reason. No formal evaluation or remediation process is required. After three years, teachers can only be fired for cause, which can include insubordination or poor performance. Typically, districts employ multiple observations and written remediation plans prior to a termination. Teachers can also be fired for violating a "morals clause" which can mean being convicted of significant crimes—including those that occur outside of school.

Tenure has also been criticized for retaining poor teachers. Governed under state law, altering it would be a matter for the legislative political process. While there is little that can be done locally about tenure, school districts, unions, and communities can work to ensure that performance processes are clear and followed. In addition to reassuring the public, it reassures teachers that a known and fair process will be followed. The union's only role in a discipline/termination is to ensure that the process is followed.

Critics of seniority and tenure point out that many people in the business world work in "at will" positions and can be laid off or fired at the whim of their employer. Teachers are professionals and expect to be treated as such. Job stability is one of the attractions of the field of education and is seen as a tradeoff for relatively low pay. This isn't enough to retain staff, with fifty percent of new teachers leaving the profession in their first five years. [3]

Needs by definition must be met and may well form the basis for a strike. Wants would be nice but are of less importance. The challenge comes in telling the difference. Each individual brings his/her own perspective to the question, based on personality, recent history, and expectations. What have been commonly held to be needs and wants in education have evolved over time.

In the early days, districts didn't negotiate with teachers, but dictated terms of employment. Everything was under the control of the administration and school board—length of the school year and day, workloads, transfer, layoffs, salaries and benefits. When I first began working in a school district, I remember talking with a senior teacher who reminisced about his early days. Each spring, every teacher had to go into the principal's office and ask whether they would have a job the next year, what they would be teaching, and how much they'd be paid. Two teachers with similar backgrounds and experience teaching in adjacent rooms could be paid differently, depending on how the principal felt about them.

In 1970, the Minneapolis Federation of Teachers had evolved to the point that they demanded a voice in district decisions. Their strike—despite at the time being explicitly illegal—was triggered in part by the board's refusal to negotiate about any policy matters, including prep time, student discipline or class size.[4] The strike settlement addressed all these teacher's concerns.[5]

When the balance of power shifted in teachers' favor with the right to strike, a number of school boards attempted to hold onto decisions that had been their prerogative. In Anoka, the district negotiator, faced with thirty-five contract language disagreements, said he had stubbornly resisted any contract language changes because they would erode the elected official's ability to manage the education program of the district.[6] Teachers received improvements in leave language and insurance benefits in the strike settlement, but acknowledged some over-reaching when they agreed to drop an "academic freedom" clause the district said would have allowed them to teach whatever they wished.[7]

In Jordan, the board's attorney categorized teacher's demands for prep time and pay for teaching a sixth period as sacrificing management rights.[8] The board in New Prague was steadfast in refusing to give up any of its or the administration's management rights.[9] They ended up agreeing to some new language, and to continue talks to settle others.[10]

Issues such as transfer language, extra duty pay, prep time, and number of leave days contributed to strikes in a number of other districts in 1981. School boards in those districts didn't initially want to meet teachers' demands for language changes, but after the strikes began were open to discussing them. Language issues were quickly settled in other districts, leaving salary as the only dispute.[11]

The seismic shift in power that occurred when Minnesota teachers were given the right to strike in 1980 illustrates the tension between wants and needs. Districts had been able to dictate terms, a situation viewed by some as absolutely necessary. There was no question in the minds of many administrators and school board members that school districts couldn't function if they had to negotiate about issues as basic as the length of the school year or assignment of duties.

In retrospect, those were issues that management wanted to control. Districts learned to deal with a shared decision making process. Management was now obliged to persuade the community and staff of the benefits of what it desired. Their needs—and the issues they were willing to strike for—turned out to be much shorter then they'd thought.

Unions found the limits of their power as well. If cuts have to occur, a seniority system written into the contract can determine which individuals within departments get laid off. It's entirely up to the school board to determine which area cuts occur in. Teachers—and the union—can feel strongly that the shop program should be saved and remedial reading teachers laid off, but that's a board decision.

Issues of management rights were not confined to early strikes. In 1991, an attempt by the Rochester district early in negotiations to lengthen the school year and work day angered teachers. Even after those proposals were dropped, teachers felt disrespected and were unable to reach agreement on the issue of subcontracting.[12]

The pendulum is showing signs of swinging back, with education reformers pushing to end seniority and tenure. There are those who believe that excellent schools require that administration have control and are seeking to remove teachers' right to strike. How the interplay of wants versus needs will evolve will depend on changes in state law and federal regulation and the ability of school districts to recruit and retain staff.

---

1. *Minneapolis Star,* January 26, 1951, p. 1, 9.
2. *Winona Daily News,* November 17, 1981, p. 1.
3. *Washington Post,* May 9, 2006.
4. *Minneapolis Tribune,* April 7, 1970, p. 1,9.
5. *Minneapolis Tribune,* April 21, 1970, pp. 1, 4.
6. *Anoka County Union,* September 18, 1981, p. 1.
7. *Anoka County Union,* October 23, 1981, p. 1.
8. *Jordan Independent,* September 17, 1981, p. 1.

9. *New Prague Times*, October 8, 1981, p. 1.
10. *New Prague Times*, October 22, 1981, p. 1.
11. *The Pioneer*, December 3, 1981, p. 1.
12. *Rochester Post Bulletin*, December 9, 1991.

Chapter Seven
Economics

Why do teachers strike? An obvious answer is to get more money. Given the potential costs of unpaid days off, are strikes an effective tool in getting more money? In the short run? In the long run?

Two professors thoroughly studied the Minnesota teachers' strikes of 1981 and developed some interesting conclusions. Their 1985 article in the *Economics of Education Review* rejected the way the MEA and the Minnesota School Board Association calculated whether strikes had benefitted teachers, saying both were misleading and construed in ways to look good to their constituents.

These researchers first compared striking and non-striking settlement increases. The strikes in 1981 were found to have gained striking teachers an average of $202 more than the average settlements of all teachers. This gross increase is misleading, for it doesn't take into account the cost of strikes. Striking teachers lost an average of 4.2 days' pay. Subtracting for lost days using the average teacher's daily salary, striking teachers received settlements of $270 less than the average of teachers in non-striking districts. Thus, when comparing the salary increases from one district to the next, it appeared that when the cost of lost days was included, strikes were a failure.

This same article included a more sophisticated measure comparing final settlements to the last pre-strike offer made by each school board. That analysis presented a more complex picture. They found that ten of the thirty-five strikes were dominated by non-economic issues. Defined by them as bad-blood strikes, financial gains were seen in only two of these non-economic strikes. The twenty-five remaining strikes were focused on money, and higher than average net economic gains were received in seventy-seven percent of these. The article concluded that economically motivated strikes were generally successful in gaining teachers additional dollars.[1]

What of the long-term economic consequences? Raises function similarly to compound interest. Each raise enlarges the base used to calculate the next percentage increase. A power point produced by Education Minnesota demonstrates the difference that accepting a $1,500 bonus instead of a $1,500 raise would make. The raise would serve as the basis for future increases, a bonus wouldn't. For a teacher currently making $37,937, the lost earnings during a career would be $26,633.[2] The double-digit settlements granted to teachers in the past made a great deal of difference in their eventual earning power and add additional support for the notion of striking for additional pay.

Calculating whether a particular strike was worth it is thus open to interpretation. Teachers in Howard Lake-Waverly, the longest strike in Minnesota, lost a great deal in the short term. Because substitutes were used, few days were made up and teachers lost fifty-four day's pay, calculated in 1981 dollars at $5,089.[3] Compared against their average salary after the settlement of $17,426,[4] this huge loss might seem to make it clear that they would never make up the difference. Those teachers who had only a few years left to work didn't make up the difference. Those who were beginning their careers did.

Teachers might feel that they are underpaid relative to other workers. Such feelings would contribute to frustration and a willingness to take stronger measures to gain pay. The American Federation of Teachers, using U.S. Census Bureau information, published a chart showing that from 1965 to 2007 teacher's earnings were exactly the same relative to other U.S. workers. During those forty-two years, teachers consistently made nine percent more than the average of all workers.

When calculated using inflation-adjusted dollars, teachers' wages increased from $40,777 to $51,009 during that same period. The increase relative to inflation wasn't even from year to year, and may have played a role in the 1981 strikes. Prior to 1973, teachers made consistent gains, receiving raises higher than the inflation rate. For the next nine years, their wages lagged behind inflation.

Legislative action to allow strikes in Minnesota thus coincided with a period of economic frustration for teachers. A number of striking unions cited figures showing they had lagged behind inflation for years as part of their rationale during the 1981 strikes, justifying their demands for raises in the range of thirty to forty percent.

Teachers do have a current grievance. U.S. Department of Labor statistics demonstrate that teacher salaries, compared to the average of twenty-three professions requiring similar educations, slipped further below average. Instead of earning only seventy-three percent as much as other professionals, teachers salaries went down to seventy percent between 2002 to 2007.[5] Teachers are losing ground relative to other professionals.

What are the economic factors from a district's point of view? The budget-setting process facing school districts in Minnesota presents a number of obstacles. Districts typically set budgets early in a calendar year for the school year beginning the following fall. This allows them to set payroll costs for the next school year. In tough times when revenues are contracting because of declining enrollment or a lack of funding, it will mean considering what programs to cut and how many staff to lay off. Staff are typically offered contracts in the spring—or are told they won't be receiving one—for the following school year.

This timeline provides an orderly process within each district, but is dependent on assumptions of how much revenue will be received. The legislature often waits until the end of its session in May to set state budgets, which in turn have to be calculated for each district. Thus, it's not until months after a school district has determined its expenses that they discover what their revenue will be.

All this is only for one year, while state law specifies that teachers' contracts must be for two years. If revenues from the state during the second year of the teachers' contract turn out to be less than expected, a district's only option is to cut staff. Teachers' raises for that year have already been determined.

It's surprising that more school districts in Minnesota don't go into debt. The importance of reserve funds and the reluctance of some districts to spend them down is understandable. Given political realities and the uncertainty of the state's resources, a more stable or predictable budgeting process is unlikely.

It is not only teachers who have to look at how much money they gain or lose during a strike. Depending on the state's funding rules for schools, districts could save or lose money during a strike. If the state provided funds for a strike day, and teachers weren't paid for that day, the district made money. If the state withheld money for that day because school wasn't held, the district would lose at least a little, because administrators, secretaries, and utilities would have to be paid.

State aid to school districts for strike days has varied over the years. During an illegal Minneapolis strike, the state withheld aid. The district appealed that decision, which was later reversed. During the Faribault strike the district wasn't sure whether it would be saving the $18,700 a day it wasn't paying teachers.[6]

For a number of years, the state paid on a per pupil per day basis, up to a maximum number of school days. This meant that districts weren't paid during strike days that weren't made up. A minimum number of days were required, with financial penalties if snow days (or strike days) shortened the school year below the minimum. There was no financial incentive to districts during a strike, and teachers could be fairly sure that some strike days would be made up rather than drop below the minimum.

Years later, the state dropped the requirement for a minimum number of school days in a year and provided aid on the basis not of the number of students attending each day, but the of number of pupils per year. This meant that during the Red Wing strike, state funding was uninterrupted and the superintendent said that the district was saving $50,000 a day.[7] The district had received state money for those days, but wasn't paying staff. Teachers on the picket line calculated how many days they would have to be on strike before the district had gained enough money to get out of the debt that the district had been in for years.[8]

Open enrollment played a factor in how more recent strikes affected districts. In the early days, students had to attend school in the district where their family lived. During a strike, parents only option for changing districts was to move or go to court and have relatives living in another district named their child's legal guardian. This enabled the child to change schools and enroll in the guardian's district. In 1988, the legislature enacted an open enrollment law, which allowed parents to place their child in any district.[9]

Three of the five strikes held since open enrollment was enacted lost students if the strike lasted longer than a week. International Falls lost forty-two of 1,500 students in 2002 which cost the district $200,000.[10] Red Wing lost forty-five students from a student body of 3,150, costing them $230,000.[11] The board chair in Crosby-Ironton announced shortly before the strike ended that the district had lost at least 200 students out of 1,300—a fifteen percent decrease. Plans were announced to lay off thirty-five percent of the teachers.[12]

At the height of the cold war, peace was maintained despite the United States and the Soviet Union's possession of nuclear weapons through MAD—Mutually Assured Destruction. Open enrollment produces a form of MAD applicable to districts and teachers' unions— Mutually Assured Damage. While Open Enrollment rules have been modified to require a January registration, currently 116 of Minnesota's 237 districts receive Statewide Integration Revenues and are open to enroll students at any time.[13]

As long as it remains the case that families are free to move their children to other districts, economic strikes lasting more than a week are an exercise in futility for both the union and management. The loss of revenue, teaching positions, and programs following the loss of students make it difficult to see how any stance but compromise is economically worthwhile for either side.

Teachers often resist facing the link between their salaries and layoffs, and adamantly reject the canard leveled by anti-union critics that "teachers' unions eat their young." The phrase refers to the layoffs of young teachers that can occur because large raises were provided. By seniority rules, the last staff hired in a department are the first to be laid off.

The link between high salary settlements and lay offs has been clear for a long time. Don Hill, the MEA president during the 1981 strikes, was asked by a reporter whether he was concerned that teachers would be fired to offset increased salaries. He replied, "That's always something we have to deal with. Bargaining for bodies is not pleasant. But the reverse is to ask the teachers to subsidize the system."[14]

A figure of $50,000 is sometimes used to calculate the cost of adding a teaching position. This might seem high, particularly for a beginning teacher, but includes benefits and costs associated with supporting staff—for example administration and supplies.

If a moderate sized district had fifty million dollarsto spend on teachers' salaries and spent an average of $50,000 per teacher, they could hire 100 teachers. If, however, those teachers would work for only $10,000 apiece, then the district could hire 500 teachers. Think of the additional programs and individual supports that could be put into place! On the other hand, if teachers struck and received a ridiculous settlement that cost $100,000 for each teacher, the district would only have fifty positions. Class sizes would be huge, and they'd be lucky to teach reading, writing and math.

That may seem like an absurd example, but a week after settling the Sauk Centre strike the board made plans to lay off twenty-two percent of the district's ninty teachers.[15] When the right to strike swung the balance of power in the direction of teachers, districts could no longer operate in ways they found economically advantageous. Low wages had meant funding surpluses. Some boards complained that dipping into their reserves as deeply as teachers desired would mean losing interest that was helping fund programs.

When teachers were relatively powerless, boards could operate as they saw fit. About the only constraint to offering low wages were difficulties in recruiting and retaining staff. Low wages meant lower local taxes and more programs for kids. The right to strike forced changes in the direction of higher salaries. Unable to immediately raise taxes, districts were forced to spend down reserves and/or lay off staff.

The economic milieu of the local community was also a factor. In outstate areas, teachers may be the largest group holding jobs that require college degrees. There are others in town with college degrees—business leaders, lawyers, ministers, health professionals—but teachers are usually the largest group of professionals paid by tax dollars. In many areas of the state, teachers' wages are higher than average local incomes. During the Bemidji strike, an editorial claimed that teachers were already earning almost twice as much as the average citizen of the school district.[16] In Wabasha, the claim was made that just the raise teachers were requesting equaled residents' average wages.[17]

The state of the local economy is important as well. Large plant layoffs or lower prices for local products depress all businesses in the area. Property taxes on businesses and farmers may not have dropped as quickly as their profits.

The Proctor strike of 1988 appears to illustrate what can happen when a local economy implodes but teachers continue to compare themselves to surrounding districts. The town was built to service Duluth, Messabi, and Iron Range trains. For years, the railroad provided relatively high salaries. By 1988, many of those jobs had disappeared and the school board said it could only afford to offer a six percent raise over two years. Teachers struck to gain parity with other Northern Minnesota Districts, settling for 10.2 percent after three days. The local paper called teachers the working elite, and said there was little support for teachers in the community.[18]

In these settings, it's not surprising that there may be little support for teachers' demands for higher wages. They're already among the best paid employees in town. If raises are linked in the public's minds to higher taxes or a lowered quantity of services for local children, sentiment may run very strongly against teachers. If those feelings are reflected in the actions of the local school board, teachers will indeed face difficulties. Proctor teachers appeared to residents to want additional pay, despite local hardships.

The Elk River district faced a much different funding milieu that same year. The school district had successfully lobbied the legislature for a funding increase of 13.4 percent to bring its income into line with metro schools.[19] Teachers felt that since funding had been successfully compared to metro districts, their pay should be increased to metro levels as well.[20] The superintendent said the board didn't want to put all the increase into teachers' salaries, but wanted instead to lower class sizes and offer more programs. After a seven-day strike, which included a substantial amount of hostility, teachers got 1.6 percent more than the district offered just before the strike.[21]

Teachers received a significant increase in power when they gained the right to strike, and were able to force districts to change priorities and place more emphasis on adequate salaries. Even during the heated 1981 strike season, a lack of state funding dashed cold water over the growth of salaries. On November 6th, the governor announced a projected state deficit and proposed cutting educational aids by eight to twelve percent.[22] Six strikes were settled in the week following the deficit announcement, none of which produced a short term economic benefit to teachers.[23]

As inflation subsided, so did expectations and raises. State funding has continued to erode in Minnesota. Long gone are the days of double digit raises—at least until inflation spikes again. The tide has been running against teachers' unions for some time. They face unrelenting criticism from those seeking quick, inexpensive (and anti-labor) solutions to America's education challenges. Year after year of budget deficits contribute to a public perception that those who "feed from the public trough" deserve very little. Whether individual union locals decide that strikes will be an effective means to their economic ends remains to be seen.

---

1. Ley Robert, Wines William, "The Economics of Teachers' Strikes in Minnesota in 1981," *Economics of Education Review* vol. 4 #1, 1985, p. 57-65.
2. "The High Cost of Zero," Education Minnesota Power Point, 2010.
3. Ley Robert, Wines William, "The Economics of Teachers' Strikes in Minnesota in 1981," *Economics of Education Review* vol. 4 #1, 1985 pp. 57-65.
4. *Minneapolis Tribune,* January 11, 1982, p. 13.
5. *Survey and Analysis of Teacher Salary Trends 2007,* American Federation of Teachers, 2008, pp. 10-12.
6. *Faribault Daily News,* December 19, 1975, p. 1.
7. *Red Wing Republican Eagle,* October 26, 2002, p. 1.
8. Interview by author, November 2002.
9. *Minnesota Revisor of Statues,* 1988 123.3515.

10. *The Daily Journal*, September 13, 2002, p. 1; November 19 2002, p. 1.
11. *Star Tribune*, October 15, 2002, p. 2B; *Red Wing Republican Eagle,* November 19, 2002, p. 1.
12. *Brainerd Dispatch*, April 2, 2005.
13. Minnesota Department of Education Q & A on Open Enrollment October 1, 2009.
14. *Crookston Daily Times,* October 22, 1981, p. 1.
15. *Sauk Centre Herald*, December 17, 1981, p. 2.
16. *The Pioneer,* November 5, 1981, p. 4.
17. *Wabasha County Herald,* October 9, 1981, p. 1, 2.
18. *Proctor Journal,* December 24, 1987, p. 12; January 14 1988, p. 4.
19. *Elk River Star News*, February 2, 1988, p. 1A.
20. *Elk River Star News*, February 24, 1988, p. 1A, 4A.
21. *St. Paul Pioneer Press*, March 3, 1988, p. 1A; *Elk River Star News,* March 8, 1988, pp. 1A, 2A, 3A.
22. *Granite Falls Tribune,* November 12, 1981, p. 1.
23. Ley Robert, Wines William, "The Economics of Teachers' Strikes in Minnesota in 1981," *Economics of Education Review,* vol. 4 #1, 1985, pp. 57-65.

Chapter Eight
Bad Blood

Teachers strike because of more than money. The Tracy strike appeared to be based on economic issues. It might never have happened at all if both sides had more clearly understood the new PELRA law. They believed that complying with strike filing deadlines was a necessary part of the negotiations process.[1]

After the union filed an intent to strike, the two sides stood at twenty-three percent from the district and 35.4 percent from the union. By the beginning of the strike, both sides had moved five percent closer to stand at 27.9 percent and 30.4 percent.[2] Having come this close, if they didn't feel they had to strike they might have continued negotiating.

The strike ended after five days after the district came up .9 percent and the union came down 1.6 percent. The superintendent said of the board's actions, "It was obvious that some type of compromise had to be reached and the sooner the better for the students." All strike days were made up. A teacher negotiator said there was no animosity during the negotiations and both sides agreed that neither would claim a victory.[3]

The Tracy strike was brief, civil and focused entirely on salary. Both sides were willing to participate in negotiations and compromise at each step. There was no attempt by the board to punish teachers through the use of substitutes or announcing that no days would be made up. There was no posturing by leaders on either side and no vilification of opponents.

What made this strike so different in tone from others, where parties were rarely able to sit down together or engaged in bizarre behavior like sitting for hours during negotiations and not saying anything? Some boards announced early in the negotiations process that in the event of a strike, subs would be used and/or no days would be made up. Superintendents and hired negotiators were quoted as seeking to "punish" teachers for striking. Union leaders spoke of seeking to win.

These strikes appear to be manifestations of the end result of an "us versus them" stance. Most school board members operate at a distance from teachers. They may personally know a few staff, but have only a limited feel for what goes on every day in classrooms and teachers' lounges. School board members rely on information they get from administrators.

The administration of a school district is heavily dependent on the leadership style of the superintendent, and tends to change with each new leader. Some superintendents are very collaborative, forging close bonds with staff in an atmosphere of trust. Others are authoritarian, enforcing their decisions with threats. Some Minnesota college instructors appear to foster an "us versus them" stance when teaching educational administration.[4] Staff in districts with authoritarian superintendents are often distrustful and resentments build with incident after incident that teachers resent.

Teachers get some of their information about their district leadership from union leaders. Administrators who treat union leaders in ways they find disrespectful or threatening can quickly influence the feelings of most teachers.

Negative feelings can build among staff, while school board members are oblivious. Unless they have developed their own effective lines of communication, reassurances by the administration that everything is fine may leave board members in the dark. A superintendent's desire to get "them" (the teachers) to do things differently can lead the board into a stance as opponents of, rather than partners with, teachers.

Board members can bring personal philosophies and agendas to their task of governing. It's not always possible to tell when a board member is acting as a spokesperson for the entire board, and when they're voicing their personal opinion. During the 1951 Minneapolis strike, the school board chair said she would actively work for passage of a no-strike law.[5]

It was reported that the board chair during the 1984 Sauk Rapids strike had been railed against by teachers and parents. They called her dictatorial, authoritarian and accused her of pushing a personal agenda. She responded that such attacks went with the job and that she was only representing what the board had decided.[6] The Sauk Rapids strike had been precipitated in part by the board's proposal to extend the school year by five days and add a sixth teaching period.

Unlike most strikes where the total cost of a settlement is the sticking point, the disagreement in Houston in 1981 was over how the agreed upon total would be distributed across the salary range. Despite this seemingly minor difference, the strike proceeded with the board advertising for subs and publishing their proposed raises in the local paper *by teacher's names*.[7] These were hard-ball negotiating tactics.

One reason for strikes mentioned in an analysis of the 1981 strikes was "bad blood," defined as grudges caused from earlier confrontations.[8] St. Cloud provides an example of negotiation difficulties that can build. During the 1979 negotiations, St. Cloud teachers picketed, refused to carry out voluntary activities and filed an unfair labor practice lawsuit, charging that the district was refusing to bargain on some issues.[9] They struck two years later during the next round of negotiating.

Another example of festering resentments occurred in Cambridge. Teachers had reluctantly accepted a fourteen percent raise in 1979 as part of a settlement that added a day to the school year. Shortly after that, administrators were given *annual* raises of up to seventeen percent because they had been assigned extra responsibilities and had to work additional hours. Teachers responded with what was described as a bitter letter writing campaign to the school board, creating an atmosphere of mutual distrust between the teacher and board.[10] The stage was set for a strike.

In Duluth the day before their 1983 strike, the two sides came to within 1 percentage point. Displaying what can happen when a board that is out of touch with its teachers, a negotiator for the school board said, "I don't know why there is a strike. I can't believe it's over two day's pay. But I don't know the reason."[11] There were warning signs however that the labor/management relationship in Duluth had serious problems. Teachers had identified 120 instances over the previous two years of what they claimed were contract violations.[12]

Legal disputes between union locals and school districts preceded other strikes. Hermantown teachers had gone to court in 1973 claiming the district had committed unfair labor practices during a round of negotiations that ended in a strike.[13]

Ten days after Crosby-Ironton teachers voted to authorize a strike, an arbitrator ruled in favor of the union over a disputed year-old incident. The superintendent had changed a long standing policy regarding who paid substitute's wages for days union leaders attended mediation sessions. The arbitrator said that a superintendent couldn't unilaterally change a past practice or a term and condition of employment because these stem from a relationship between union and employer, not individuals representing those entities.[14]

From the point of view of most union locals, arbitration is a significant escalation in a dispute. First, a grievance is filed over a violation of the current contract. Grievances are internal, handled in ways developed over the years between each school district and its teachers. If that process doesn't produce a resolution, the next step is to file and have it heard by an arbitrator.

If the union loses in arbitration, it will have to pay a portion of the fees involved. Therefore, the local probably will put the decision to arbitrate to a vote of its governing body. Disputes taken to arbitration are thus an indication that local teachers feel strongly about an issue they deem important enough to spend money on. They also mean that the relationship between labor and management are strained enough that a compromise couldn't be found and outside help is needed to settle the issue.

Relationships with teachers can break down as a result of board decisions and superintendent leadership styles. Several of the most recent strikes illustrate how this combination of factors can lead to a strike. Rochester hired a dynamic change-making superintendent in 1987 who instituted a number of changes. He and the board decided early in the 1991 negotiations to push for a longer school day and year and reduced teacher planning time. Although later withdrawn, these proposals so angered staff that despite salary proposals coming within two percent of each other, teachers struck and picketed in wind chills of fifty degrees below zero.[15]

Red Wing was in statutory operating debt, with a new superintendent. Teachers had accepted low wages in a previous settlement to help the district get out of debt, only to see administrators get larger raises and better insurance than was offered to the rest of the staff.[16] At the beginning of the 2001-2002 school year, the board didn't provide teachers with the automatic step and lane raises called for in the old contract. The union charged in court that the district and superintendent had engaged in unfair labor practices.[17]

This aggressive negotiating tactic had been discarded by most districts years before. It's interesting as well that the union named not just the board, but the superintendent in the lawsuit. There was a rumor—widely believed by teachers—that the new superintendent had said at an administrator's conference that he was going to break the local union.[18]

The Crosby-Ironton school board sought to eliminate health insurance. The district had a history of rocky relations between administration and staff. Teachers had conducted a vote of no confidence against the previous superintendent, who then left.[19]

What's behind this bad blood between teachers and administration? It appears to often be a case of a strong leadership style on the part of a superintendent engendering resentment on the part of teachers, coalesced around issues they perceive as an injustice. Teachers' hostility toward superintendents can be seen in the coverage of the Rochester strike. The superintendent in Rochester was described as being, "often a personal target of teacher anger and frustration during the strike".[20]

The difference in tone between strikes involving bad blood and those centered on economics can be seen in the two strikes in International Falls. Teachers were angry during the first strike and wore buttons saying, "Recycle Roberts," referring to the superintendent. The union president was quoted, "We hope that someone from the board will come forward and provide the leadership that's been lacking from the superintendent in the last several years and hopefully this will be resolved in a speedy manner."[21] Ten years later, under a different superintendent, teachers' remarks were focused on disagreements about costs of proposed settlements.

Although no one was charged, trees in the Red Wing superintendent's yard were cut down during the strike.[22] Carrying their feelings forward, almost all members of the teachers' union in Crosby-Ironton voted that they had no confidence in the superintendent six months after the strike.[23]

School boards have the right to adopt any negotiating strategies they wish. Superintendents can operate in whatever style they—and their board—feel comfortable with. What they have to be prepared for are the natural consequences of their behavior; be that collaboration, or rebellion.

---

1. *Tracy Headlight-Herald*, September 10, 1981, p. 1.
2. *Tracy Headlight-Herald*, October 1, 1981, p. 1.
3. *Tracy Headlight-Herald*, October 8, 1981, p. 1, 2.
4. Phone interview, Spring 2010.
5. *Minneapolis Tribune*, January 24, 1951, p. 1, 14.
6. *St. Cloud Times*, January 11, 1984, p. 1A.
7. *Winona Daily News*, November 13, 1981, p. 1.
8. Ley, Robert, Wines, William; "The Economics of Teachers' Strikes in Minnesota in 1981," *Economics of Education Review*, 4, #1 p. 57-65, 1985.
9. *St. Cloud Daily Times*, November 16, 1979, p. 1.
10. *Cambridge Star*, October 28, 1981, p. 1.
11. *News Tribune & Herald*, December 2, 1983, p. 1A.
12. *News Tribune & Herald*, November 29, 1983, Teachers' union ad.
13. *News Tribune & Herald*, September 5, 1973, p. 1A.
14. *Brainerd Dispatch*, January 13, 2005.
15. *Post Bulletin*, December 4, 1991.
16. *Republican Eagle*, October 22, 2002, p. 1.
17. *Republican Eagle*, September 23, 2002, p. 1.
18. Phone interview with former teacher, Fall 2010.
19. *Brainerd Dispatch*, November 23, 2005.
20. Post Bulletin, December 18, 1991.
21. *Daily Journal*, February 14, 1992, p. 1.
22. Phone interview with former superintendent, summer 2010.
23. *Brainerd Dispatch*, November 18, 2005.

Chapter Nine
Preventing Teachers' Strikes

A NUMBER OF THINGS THAT AFFECT potential teachers' strikes are beyond the control of local districts. A prime example is funding. Districts receive some federal funds, but in Minnesota the majority come from the state. While large districts employ lobbyists, they can't alter the economy or state revenues and there's little they can do to influence state expenditures.

Districts can ask local voters for additional funds. If they fail to do so, teachers have grounds to complain that the school board is choosing to get by with less. Often, however, even if a board does an excellent job of trying to pass a levy over ride, it's rejected. Ironically, children's futures are the only tax voters can directly control in Minnesota.

There are things local districts can do however to reduce the likelihood of a teachers' strike. These include developing a mutually acceptable method of determining costs, negotiating competently and frequently, adopting non-adversarial negotiation methods, developing effective lines of communication between board members and teachers, avoiding using negotiations as a platform for major changes, and educating the public and teachers about issues relevant to the negotiations process.

A number of strikes were caused and prolonged by disagreements about how much money a district had to spend, and how much proposed settlements would cost. School finances in Minnesota are very complex. Most of the federal and state money coming into a district have strings attached, allowing them to be spent for only certain things. Depending on when it's received and spent, money can accumulate in the district's accounts.

Dollars designated for transportation can thus appear in a total of unspent money. Unless district financial staff have made an effort to educate the public and teachers, there can be a widespread belief that the district has lots of money available and could afford to give teachers a significant raise. Once the teachers begin negotiating by asking for far more than the district has available in appropriate funds, the administration is in a weak position and appears to be making excuses. School boards would be well served by the effort needed to provide not only amounts, but a clear explanation of what terms like "reserve funds" mean and what they are used for.

Strikes in 1981 that occurred in part because teachers didn't accept district figures on how much money was available for salary increases included Anoka, Chaska and Lake Benton. In Proctor, teachers thought the district was hiding money.[1] The use of computers made calculating proposals faster, but disagreements over dollar figures continue. The board and union clashed in public discussions of the cost of teachers' salaries prior to the Crosby-Ironton strike in 2005.[2]

It is crucial for the business office of any school district to understand precisely how much a proposed contract settlement would cost. These after all are binding agreements—bills—that must be paid. This is not as easy as it may seem, because there are many ways to calculate projected settlement costs. The Minnesota School Board Association provides a Teacher Salary Summarization Sheet. Education Minnesota uses a different method, as does the Minnesota Bureau of Mediation.[3] Strikes in Albany, Cambridge, Rochester and Winona were impacted by disagreements over what to include in costing proposals.

The largest misunderstanding teachers and the public have always had is the difference between built-in increasing costs and raises. Frequently, districts will put forth numbers based on total costs, while union locals talk only about raises. They may then go on to dispute the other side's figures. Rank and file teachers and the public don't know who to believe, and may conclude that someone is trying to be deceptive. What's happened is not deception, but spin.

The difference between the two sides arises because teachers get automatic raises for more years of service (step increases) and for earning additional credits toward a graduate degree (lane changes). Step increases are granted at the beginning of each school year, and lane changes can be granted whenever specified in the contract.

Typically these raises go into effect at the beginning of each school year, even though every other year most districts haven't settled their next contract. It's simply assumed that similar steps and lanes will be included in the new contract.

A raise is understood by both sides to increase the amount of dollars in each step and lane. This can be a uniform percentage, or differing amounts in various parts of the salary schedule. Some school boards want to put extra money into beginning teacher salaries to help recruit new staff. Unions in districts with many veteran teachers may want additional money placed on the top of the scale. Both sides present proposals during negotiations, each of which must be calculated for total costs over the two years of the contract.

The breakdown occurs because both sides are focused on different aspects of the financial adjustments. The district looks at the whole picture—automatic increases plus any proposed raise, as well as costs associated with benefits such as medical insurance. Even something as seemingly insignificant as teachers' leave days can increase costs significantly. If teachers get an extra day of leave, then more subs have to be hired. If sub pay increases with the new contract, even more money must be found.

Teachers on the other hand tend to focus on the increases in various parts of the salary schedule, using the average percentage increase as the most relevant number. This will be far smaller than the total increase the new contract will cost the district.

Both sides can thus be completely accurate when the district says they are offering X percent while the union counters that the actual figure is far smaller. Teachers will tend to accept their leader's view as accurate and the public will be confused. All this friction—which has contributed to a number of strikes—could be avoided if an accounting system acceptable to management and teachers' unions could be agreed upon before negotiations begin.

It would seem axiomatic that both sides negotiate competently. It's in their own best interest to do so. Such has not always been the case. Some districts had difficulty accurately determining how much money they had available. An example of a mistake caught early occurred in Winona in 1981.

Voters approved a tax levy increase in September of that year because the district administrators said it was necessary to balance the budget. They pledged to not spend the increase on raises, promising to not increase teachers' salaries more than fourteen percent. That pledge got stretched during negotiations to seventeen percent in the face of teachers' request for thirty percent. In November the district discovered that it had $129,000 they didn't know they had, and increased their offer to twenty percent. Negotiations were settled without a strike.[4]

Lake City struck in 1981 as a result of a lack of understanding of each other's 'informal' offers. Just prior to going out, teachers dropped their request to $5,000. After declaring that $4,679 was their final offer, the board indicated it would go as high as $4,900. Talks broke off the day before the strike with the superintendent saying he wasn't aware of the $5,000 figure from the teachers.[5]

Neither side seemed to understand the other's position even after two negotiating sessions had been held during the strike. The board felt that nearly everything had been agreed to, at the $4,900 level. When teachers repeated their request for $5,275, the board broke off talks and withdrew its salary and language offers, saying the teachers hadn't really negotiated. Teachers commented that in hindsight, they might do things differently.[6]

Negotiations in Spring Lake Park were hampered early on by differing expectations. Teachers complained that the salary percentages being offered by the district wouldn't bring starting salaries up high enough. The board chair was surprised that starting salaries were an issue, because the board planned on letting teachers determine amounts within the salary grid once the average increase had been settled.[7]

The breakdown in communications in Crosby-Ironton was clear when the superintendent was surprised that teachers had held a strike vote. Negotiations had been going on for over a year, but she felt the district had been negotiating in good faith. A board member claimed that the union hadn't been prepared to respond to compromises proposed by the district.[8]

Preparing for negotiations does take time, and an unusual skill set. Union locals typically get advice from the Education Minnesota field representative assigned to them. Districts often employ a lawyer as a consultant. Some districts go one step further, hiring a professional to serve as lead negotiator. In addition to their familiarity with the negotiating process, hiring a professional negotiator allows the superintendent to not be the "bad guy."[9]

The Popovich law firm represented fifty-nine school districts during the 1981 negotiations. Popovich commented that teachers' unions, "... obviously don't know how to handle the dynamics of collective bargaining. They take personal offense to perfectly sound labor practices."[10] According to the MFT president, these tactics included angering teacher negotiators and causing them to waste time refuting nonsense rather than presenting their side of the contract dispute. The Minnesota School Board Association worked with the Popovich firm to develop a handout titled, "Ten-day Strike Notice action Plan." The plan included the statement, "The strike is a win-lose situation which the district cannot afford to lose."[11]

If part of the goal of professional negotiators was to be the "bad guy," many succeeded. Teachers complained that they weren't available and were directing negotiations, a charge routinely denied by school boards. The 1981 strikes put a strain on the capacity of both the Bureau of Mediation and some professional negotiators, prolonging strikes because negotiation sessions were delayed. A number of locals attempted to talk directly with board members. Most districts stressed board unity during a strike, and such attempts were unsuccessful.

In contrast to the win/lose tone of the MSBA's 1981 advice to districts, non-adversarial bargaining seeks to develop mutually acceptable solutions. One example is Interest-Based Bargaining (IBB), developed by the Federal Mediation and Conciliation Service.[12] Interest-Based Bargaining allows negotiators to become joint problem solvers. It can generate options that neither side had considered.

Successful Interest-Based Bargaining requires management-labor cooperation, sufficient time, a willingness to share information and forgo power as the sole method of winning.[13] IBB has been found to produce contract language on non-economic issues that is easier to implement and more useful. It does not substantially affect the outcome of economic issues.[14]

An example of the need for Interest-Based Bargaining can be seen in the Crosby-Ironton strike. Using traditional bargaining, one of the major hang-ups they encountered involved health insurance for retirees. The board's position was that it could no longer afford to provide health insurance to retirees. The teachers felt that they had spent their careers paying toward and expecting health insurance when they retired. One side said no, the other said yes, and neither would budge. A staff member from Education Minnesota broke the deadlock by suggesting setting up a health care benefit trust.[15]

Interest Based Bargaining would have begun with the board saying we can't afford to continue as we have been, and teachers saying they needed health insurance when they retired. Both sides would then have gone out and searched for solutions. This is a marked contrast to spending weeks during a strike demanding that the other side give in. Minnesota districts interested in Interest Based Bargaining can receive training through the Bureau of Mediation Services.[16]

Interest Based Bargaining isn't a panacea, and requires a desire by both sides to develop a settlement. A lack of negotiating contributed to and prolonged a number of strikes. In Cambridge the two sides didn't meet during the first two weeks of the strike and in Prior Lake they let three weeks pass before their first session, meeting only three times during the six week strike.

Both sides were in court seeking injunctions against the other during the Howard Lake-Waverly strike. A district court judge rejected the claims saying, "Obviously neither party is making an effort, or intends to settle the strike."[17] No matter what method of negotiating is used, if the two sides aren't willing to meet together and have priorities other than a settlement, little progress will be made.

Contract negotiations may seem like the logical—in fact the only—place to discuss changes to the contract. While this is true for official discussions, time constraints during negotiations limit discussion between parties and the opportunity for a broad discussion with the entire staff and community.

Salary discussions can't be finalized until many other issues are settled, and must thus be part of the formal negotiations. Floating ideas for major changes in severance pay, insurance or leaves could take place months earlier. The extra time provides each side with opportunities to poll their constituents and develop positions. Of equal importance is the opportunity to educate the membership of the other side. A thorough understanding of the issues and each other's concerns provides a solid foundation for formal talks.

A number of strikes were caused by proposals for significant changes in contract language. The push and pull of language issues can be seen in the Cambridge strike of 1981. The board wanted teachers to agree to give up their right to take grievances to court and grant the board the right to suspend teachers without pay. Teachers wanted language changes that would make taking extracurricular assignments and transfers between buildings voluntary.[18]

None of these changes directly affected district costs, but were a reflection of the desire of each side for control. Feelings could run high about these issues. In Faribault, teachers struggled for much of the strike to hang on to language allowing them to grieve conditions relating to school operations, rather than accept the district's new language allowing grievances only about contract terms.[19]

Some changes tangentially involve money. A number of strikes involved conflicts over district proposals for teachers to work more—an extra class period or more days per year—and teacher demands to be paid more for additional work.

Significant changes in school districts take time for a consensus to build. It isn't reasonable to expect teachers to work for free—i.e. extend the school year by two days for no additional pay. It also isn't reasonable to expect the public to immediately support extending the school year with increased taxes or decreased staffing. A thorough presentation and discussion led by the district of the advantages of adding the days, followed by working with the community and teachers to develop a proposal, will be more effective than announcing the change during negotiations.

Some districts resorted to what appeared to be punitive measures aimed at pressuring locals to settle. The most common was withholding automatic raises until the contract had been settled. To up the ante, some districts declared that such raises wouldn't be retroactive back to the beginning of the contract period, but would begin when a new settlement was reached. Several cases went to court, but weren't settled before the strikes ended. Whether they were legal or not, such tactics infuriated teachers.

It isn't clear whether the Rochester district proposed language changes it intended to hold through the negotiations, or whether these were issues designed to be given away to keep other gains. Teachers reacted negatively to being asked to work longer school days and a longer school year. Even when the proposals were withdrawn, resentment lingered and contributed to the negotiations breakdown.[20]

Effective negotiations are part of an ongoing effort to build relationships between school boards and administrators, teachers and the community.

The public has a large and crucial role to play in the operation of school districts. Education comes down to the interaction of one child with an intelligent, knowledgeable adult who skillfully presents information in a way that the child can grasp. Study after study has commented on the importance of the bond between teacher and child. Teachers must not only be skillful, they need to be a predictable, caring presence in each child's life.

Unhappy workers may be able to mine coal or work on an assembly line. Teachers facing threats of job insecurity, capricious discipline or evaluations, intimidation or unfair wages will find it very difficult to be fully nurturing. Parents recognize the caring nature of teachers, and prize it. Who wants a teacher who is worried, preoccupied or scared dealing with their child every day? What kind of atmosphere would exist in those classrooms?

The clearest sign that relationships between the school board, administration and teachers have broken down are an inability to resolve disputes, resulting in arbitration or court suits. When these cases occur, the community should look deeper than the issues involved in that particular instance. Why are the teachers so upset? What mechanisms need to be put into place that would develop solutions to differences? Who is standing in the way of finding an acceptable middle ground?

An "us versus them" atmosphere condemns a school district to mediocrity. It makes little sense for an administration and staff to see each other as opponents—or worse yet, during and after a strike as enemies.

Bad Blood and Economics

Far better outcomes will be developed through collaborating as partners. If the school district strays from this course, an informed and involved public can push for change.

Unfortunately, public schools can become the focus of a distillation of differences within a community. Social issues such as civil rights or abortion as well as religious controversies like creationism have sometimes been fought out in local schools.

When the controversy involves wages and benefits for public employees, strikes can result. In the late 1970s, teachers' wages lagged behind a high inflation rate. Their new right to strike enabled them to coerce districts into shifting priorities toward higher wages and fewer staff. When the governor announced a budget shortfall, teachers saw the big picture and settled for less. Union locals appeared to be well aware of large economic trends and adjusted their expectations accordingly.

Problems continue to result from local economic downturns. Teachers, who may be relatively affluent compared to the local population, are often focused on their students and colleagues. They may be unaware and sheltered from economic events going on around them. Plant closings, low crop prices, rising property taxes or growing unemployment may not have hit them personally.

Well aware of what's going on in other districts; teachers may seek raises that appear unreasonable to many local citizens. Past settlements may play a significant part in teachers' outlook. They may have settled for very little in the past because the district was in financial trouble. Now, they think it's their turn to be compensated. Having traded a higher raise in order to protect a benefit, they may be loath to see that benefit eroded.

The strike in Crosby Ironton presented a worst-case scenario. Teachers had been angry with the previous superintendent, holding a vote of no confidence in him. They were angry with the current superintendent and had taken one of her decisions to arbitration. Teachers had been told their whole careers that they would have health insurance when they retired. Against this, the local economy was in tough shape. Teachers made more than many local citizens and had far better benefits. The district was experiencing declining enrollment and revenues and was in statutory operating debt.

When the school board took the negotiating position that it could no longer afford to pay retiree health insurance, an impasse was created. Many in the community were adamant that teachers should give up the health insurance. Many teachers were close to retirement and felt that they had earned that benefit. Moreover, teachers in other districts weren't having to make such large sacrifices.

The strike that ensued was a disaster for everyone. As local and larger economies change, so will teachers' compensation. How that will play out remains to be seen, but one thing is clear—compromises will be necessary.

Most strikes can be avoided when school boards communicate well with staff, superintendents create an atmosphere of respect and trust, negotiations are effective and aren't used for controversial initiatives and the community understands the issues. There will be times however when a school board and its teachers see an issue very differently.

In an ideal situation, the two sides can problem-solve together and create a new solution that is completely satisfactory to everyone. It's more likely that each side will have to compromise. For anyone holding strongly to a position, compromising can be painful and frustrating. If a magic solution can't be found, the choice is clear—compromise during negotiations; or strike and compromise after interfering with student's educations and having torn apart the school district and community, perhaps for decades.

---

1. *The Journal*, September 24, 1981, p. 1.
2. *Brainerd Dispatch*, January 21, 2005.
3. Interview, Minnesota Bureau of Mediation, Summer 2010.
4. *Winona Daily News*, November 12, 198,1 p. 3.
5. *Republican Eagle*, October 5, 1981 p. 1.
6. *Republican Eagle*, October 9, 1981 p. 1.
7. *St. Paul Pioneer Press*, December 16, 1991, p. 6B.
8. *Brainerd Dispatch*, October 20, 2004; January 19 2005.
9. Interview Minnesota School Board Association.
10. *Daily Times*, October 26, 1981, p. 1C.
11. *St. Paul Pioneer Press*, October 18, 1981, p. 8Metro.

12. Bohlander G and Naber J. "Nonadversarial Negotiations: the FMCS Interest—Based Bagaining Program," *Journal of Collective Negotiations* 28, 1999, p. 41-52.
13. Federal Mediation & Conciliation Service, Interest-Based Bargaining, www.fmcs.gov.
14. Klingel, S; Interest-Based Bargaining in Education, 2003 http://digitalcommons.ilr.cornell.edu/reports/16.
15. *Star Tribune*, April 7, 2005, p. 1B.
16. Minnesota Bureau of Mediation Website, February 2011.
17. *Wright County Journal-Press*, December 17, 1981 p. 1.
18. *Cambridge Star*, September 14, 11 g 12; October 1981, pp. 1,3.
19. *Faribault Daily News*, November 26 1975, pp. 1, 18.
20. Post Bulletin, December 9, 1991.

Chapter Ten
Right to Strike

Given what's happened in the past, should teachers have the right to strike? The question can be viewed in practical and philosophical terms.

The 1951 strike in Minneapolis—their second in three years—so angered the legislature that they passed a strict anti-strike law. A key component stated that anyone violating the law was terminated and wasn't entitled to any rights associated with that job until they were re-employed. In addition to putting any strikers into employment limbo, the law punished employees after they returned to work. They couldn't be given any raises for a year and lost tenure, being placed on probationary status for two years.[1]

Nearly twenty years later, Minneapolis teachers were fed up with negotiations. The school board continued to refuse to discuss providing preparation time for elementary teachers, limiting class size and revising the student discipline policy. The Minneapolis Federation of Teachers (MFT) went on strike, while the rival City of Minneapolis Education Association (CMEA) voted not to.

The district attempted to open schools during the first two days of the strike. Out of 3,400 teachers, only 1,040 reported for work, many of them in elementary schools. The lack of supervision in junior and senior high schools led to students going where they pleased, in some cases breaking windows and vandalizing rooms.[2]

School was called off the third day of the strike to allow non-striking teachers to plan. The CMEA had been urging its members to work, but changed its positions because of what it cited as unsafe conditions in under staffed buildings. Schools were closed, and the legal wrangling began.

The CMEA wanted its members' employment status protected and went to court to allow them to not work because conditions weren't safe.

They also claimed that the 400 members of their union that hadn't reported for work weren't striking. The CMEA hadn't voted to strike, and its members spent those days talking with community leaders about educational needs in the district. The MFT tried to claim that its members weren't at work the first two days of the strike because they were on personal leave. Whether teachers absent the first two days were on strike or on leave were crucial distinctions, determining if teachers were still employed and if they would be subject to sanctions after returning.

As disputes about teachers' status moved through the courts, the district and teachers sought a way to settle the strike. The board was willing to discuss language changes by the third day of the strike. Who they could negotiate with was unclear. The CMEA insisted in court that it be included in talks. The MFT said that they were the only union on strike and should have exclusive negotiating rights. PELRA hadn't been enacted, so that issue was unclear.

A citizen's group formed to plan a court action assuring that no-strike law provisions be followed.[3] The Minnesota Civil Liberties Union offered its services during a teachers' rally to defend teachers' constitutionally protected right to strike. The Minnesota attorney general offered the services of his office, but saw no way to resolve the dispute. Governor Le Vander said teachers should go back to work or forfeit "all rights to be teachers."

Teachers continued to search for solutions and requested state mediation services. The governor denied the request, saying that the meet and confer law didn't provide for mediation services for public employees. He then went on to say that teachers had no standing to request assistance, and wouldn't until they were re-employed and returned to work.[4]

At this point, finding a way out was difficult. From citizens to the governor, there was pressure to apply the no-strike law. If it had been strictly applied, the school board couldn't have dealt with the MFT, who represented the majority of teachers. Since they were no longer employees, they had no right to be at the negotiating table.

Getting rid of 2,000 teachers wasn't an option, so the school board had to proceed through a doubly difficult process. The issues needed to be resolved, without a proper mechanism to do so. The board essentially ignored MFT teachers' lack of status, and met with them. An agreement on contract terms was met, but the strike was prolonged by a week while solutions were sought for getting around the no strike law's punishments of returning teachers. What good was a raise, if it couldn't be paid? Why should teachers settle, if they weren't sure whether they'd be rehired or protected from retaliation?

The board found a way around these problems by ignoring the intent of the law. Raises negotiated during the strike would be paid in a lump sum, one year after settling. All teachers would be rehired. Five of the fourteen days out would be made up, and teachers would be paid for seven days of the strike. A judge ruled that the first two days of the strike could be considered personal leave, thus teachers didn't lose any pay.

The no-strike law's intent was largely flouted. Teachers not only kept their jobs and got a raise, they got paid for striking! The only consequence of the law that stuck was losing tenure. The law had served its purpose by preventing any strikes by teachers for almost twenty years. When a group of teachers that was too large to get rid of became frustrated enough to strike, the law caused chaos. The school board was put in the uncomfortable position of having to find ways around the law while under pressure from citizens, the attorney general and governor.

What if an anti-strike law could be written that avoided problems—the most prominent being having to replace all the staff because they defied the law. Should effective laws be written preventing teachers from striking?

School boards hold most of the cards during negotiations. The legal right to operate the schools is theirs, and they hold the purse strings. Teachers ultimately have few options when faced with unacceptable conditions—they can leave, strike or stay on as disgruntled employees. Of the three choices, only a strike—or the threat of a possible strike—has the potential to produce a well-run school district. Teachers need a counter-balance to the power unrestrained school boards and superintendents could wield.

School boards and administrators have behaved in ways that infuriate teachers. A local attempt in Walnut Grove to take away the right to strike after it had just been granted in a new state law provides an example.

Poisoned negotiations led to a number of other strikes. Several districts changed past practice by denying automatic raises during negotiations, other districts asked teachers to work extra days and/or extra hours for no pay. Some districts refused to talk about issues teachers felt were vital to their interests—preparation time, voluntary transfers and grievance procedures. Pre-strike relationships had deteriorated in some places so much that despite the expense and risk, unions turned repeatedly to arbitrators and courts for relief.

Fighting against injustice—which is how teachers saw many of these disputes—is at the heart of the American tradition. Strikes forced some districts to make concessions in contract language, teaching school boards that they could continue functioning, even if teachers had more control of their assignments. Other strikes taught teachers painful lessons about the layoffs involved when they were paid more and there was less money for programs.

There are those who wish to strip teachers of their right to strike, tenure, collective bargaining rights and even pensions. Sometimes, these same people support market forces as the primary reality in labor-management negotiations. We are already seeing the result of paying teachers too little, in the chronic shortages of math and science teachers. There is a shortage of some special education teachers because working conditions are so challenging. Approximately fifty percent of new teachers leave the profession in their first five years.

The most politically palatable response to the teacher shortage has been to seek cheap solutions. Alternate teacher licensing relaxes requirements for teacher training, providing access for more people to take math and science teaching positions. Other possible solutions languish for want of funding: tuition forgiveness, pay incentives for scarce positions, longer school years or days. As the electorate continues to chase the chimera of "better schools for less money" teachers will continue to feel the pendulum of support swing away from them.

Time will tell how the calls for "we want the best teachers in the classroom" and "we can't afford all this pay and benefits" will play out. Denying teachers the right to strike would drive the future in a different direction but may again yield contrary outcomes, if we let history repeat itself.

---

1. Session Laws of Minnesota 1951 Chapter 156, section 179.54.
2. *Minneapolis Tribune*, April 10, 1971, p. 1.
3. *Minneapolis Tribune*, April 15, 1971, p. 1.
4. *Minneapolis Tribune*, April 16, 1971, p. 1.

Part Two

Chronology of Teachers' Strikes in Minnesota

Chapter Eleven
The Early Strikes

1946 St. Paul Strike

THE FIRST ORGANIZED TEACHERS' strike in the United States occurred in St Paul in November of 1946. The St. Paul Federation of Teachers had been formed in 1918. The union was originally outlawed by the superintendent and members were denied promotions and wage increases that were instead granted to teachers belonging to "loyalty clubs."[1] Some union members were transferred to less desirable jobs and even dismissed.[2] Despite this early opposition, membership in the union grew. Although at the national level the American Federation of Teachers opposed strikes by teachers, by 1946 St. Paul teachers' frustrations came to a head.

St. Paul schools operated as part of city government. One of the City Council members was named Commissioner of Education, who then supervised the Superintendent of Schools. Budgets were submitted for approval to the City Council, which was constrained by a city charter that set severe taxation limits that could only be changed by the City Charter Commission, and required voter approval.

It was not unusual to have up to fifty students in classrooms designed for thirty-five. There was no money for textbooks. Teachers often bought texts for students whose families couldn't afford them. Buildings were substandard with some large schools containing only one bathroom apiece for boys and girls. Compared to communities of similar size, teachers' pay was among the lowest.[3]

In the absence of state laws governing the status of public employee unions, a formal negotiations process had not been established. Beginning in July, the Teacher's Joint Council met with the city Commissioner of Education, the City Council and city finance committee. These meetings did not result in opening a negotiations process.

Teachers' demands included recognizing the Teacher's Joint Council as the bargaining agent; an immediate $50.00 a month raise; long range salary improvements totaling at least $1,200,000 in 1947; additional staff, adequate health facilities, visiting teachers, modernization of equipment, adequate supplies and a long-term building rehabilitation and construction program aggregating a minimum of $1,700,000 annually.[4]

The teachers held a strike vote on November 13 and served a formal notice of intent to strike on November 25. The city council responded by naming a committee chaired by the Education commissioner to try to avert the strike. The teachers refused to meet with the group because it had no authority to negotiate a settlement.[5]

Governor Thye met with the city council five days before the strike date and urged them to make new efforts to find a basis for settlement.[6] The city council sent a letter to the teachers stating that it could not meet the teachers' demands without a change in the city charter or legislative action.

They requested teachers' help in getting a number of new taxes passed.[7]

The governor asked teachers to delay for a week so he could work out a solution. They refused, and also refused his request to delay the strike for twenty-four hours. They did agree to meet with the governor the first day of the strike.

The superintendent stated that the strike was a violation of the teacher's contracts.[8] The commissioner of Education threatened to fire anyone who struck, telling them during a mass meeting that they would be putting their tenure and teaching licensure in jeopardy.[9]

The strike was thus a very gutsy move on the teacher's part. Not only were they being threatened with severe retaliation, there was no readily apparent way to increase funding for St. Paul schools. Unlike future strikes were there was a government entity that had the authority and ability to make changes teachers wanted, in this situation the City Council accurately stated the situation—there was nothing they could do. If teachers had been willing to wait indefinitely, the governor could have led the legislature to produce some change. Teachers however had had it, and weren't willing to wait any longer. They could only hope that someone, somehow, could find a solution.

Teachers walked out on schedule. Despite the commissioner's threats, there was little talk about the legality of the strike once it began. Instead, the parties involved focused on finding a solution. Add the mayor, state attorney general and governor; all clamoring to reopen the schools, and it's not surprising that there was little interest in the side issue of whether teachers had the right to strike.

Elmer Andersen—who was later a governor—was the parent of a St. Paul student during the strike. He was quoted later, "I remember the strike keenly because it is inconceivable to people today what a shock it was then to have teachers go out on strike. It was just absolutely unheard of."[10] A picture of striking teachers cooking a turkey over an open fire ran in LIFE.[11]

The first day of the strike, the Minnesota attorney general authorized the finance committee of the Teachers Joint Council to be the bargaining agent for the teachers, and empowered the city council to negotiate with that committee. Teachers insisted that meetings be closed, and the first bargaining session was held.[12]

This was a unique circumstance in a number of ways. In the absence of any public employee statue covering the issue, the attorney general identified a labor bargaining agent. The group of teachers selected to negotiate had no authorization from union members to act on their behalf.

Efforts to settle the strike continued to be a multi-ring circus. Parents and groups of ministers pushed for a settlement. Students held protest parades. The mayor called on teachers to return to work.

City council members were unable to negotiate a settlement because they lacked a funding mechanism. The Charter Commission was independent from the City Council and wanted time to deliberate.

One solution to the impasse called for a charter amendment. The Charter Commission offered to support an amendment in exchange for an agreement that teachers wouldn't go out on strike again during the school year, no matter how the vote turned out. Teachers rejected this offer, but it appeared the Charter Commission legitimized the possibility of another strike.

The strike was settled on December 27th, when enough pressure was brought to bear to convince the Charter Commission to raise taxes.

Teachers agreed to return to work, hopeful that voters would approve the changes. The following year, the charter amendment passed, separating school funding from the rest of the city government and raising revenue for the schools. St. Paul teachers went from being among the lowest paid in the country, to among the highest. Beginning salaries increased from $1,500 to $2,400, with top salaries rising from $2,600 to $4,200.[13]

The length of the strike, measured in lost school days, wasn't recorded. It took place over the Thanksgiving and Christmas holidays. Assuming the district planned to give the Friday after Thanksgiving off, and all of Christmas week—the 25th was on a Wednesday—the strike lasted for eighteen school days. Classes resumed early, on December 30th, with only January 1st off that week. This could have provided four made up days.

Because St. Paul was one of very few districts governed under municipal home rule charters, the issue of the legality of teachers' strikes wasn't clarified. It could be argued that the attorney general and governor's recognition of the strike and willingness to negotiate legitimized teachers strikes. This precedent wasn't applied however to subsequent strikes soon to take place in Minneapolis.

1948 MINNEAPOLIS STRIKE

A TANGLE OF FUNDING CONSTRAINTS and nebulous negotiations led Minneapolis teachers to strike on February 24, 1948. Like St. Paul, Minneapolis school funding was tied to the city taxing authority. A vote was scheduled for March to change the city charter, allowing increased funding for schools.[14]

The promise of improvements to the city charter had been enough to settle the St. Paul strike two years earlier. The upcoming vote didn't deter Minneapolis teachers. Chronic under funding laid the foundation for the strike, but teachers felt betrayed by unilateral contract changes.[15]

In 1946, Minneapolis teachers had participated for the first time in direct negotiations with the school board. A strike was narrowly averted when Mayor Hubert Humphrey offered his services and office at the last minute.[16] Faced with a budget shortfall, in December of 1947, the school board voted to shorten the school year by four weeks, imposing what amounted to a ten percent cut in pay. Teachers objected both to the cut in pay and violation of the previous agreement.

The district's negotiating process appeared muddled. Just before the strike, the superintendent said he wasn't authorized to act for the board.[17] When negotiations between the superintendent and union broke down, the superintendent asked the board to become directly involved.[18] From that time on, the board and the superintendent met separately with the union. At one point, the board chair didn't accept a proposal because he felt the superintendent wouldn't agree.[19]

A parent inserted the issue of the strike's illegality by filing a lawsuit seeking an injunction against the teachers.[20] Her lawyer asked the governor, attorney general, and county attorney to intervene. They all declined. A judge ordered that the unions show cause why they shouldn't be restrained from striking and picketing.[21] The original lawsuit had included only the unions and was withdrawn. A new one was filed to include the school board. The parent's attorney declared that the negotiations are illegal because the teachers fired themselves when they walked off the job.[22] The issue went to trial, but wasn't resolved by the time the strike ended.

The status of non-striking teachers was also a factor. There were 1,100 members of the women's and men's American Federation of Teachers union. 1,300 other nonunion teachers represented by the Central Committee of Teachers Organizations didn't strike.[23] The second day of the strike, the board announced a 'no work, no pay' policy. With the schools closed, non-striking teachers who were willing to work, wouldn't be paid.[24] They responded by threatening to file a lawsuit seeking full pay for the duration of the strike.[25]

The nonunion teachers sought to have a voice in the negotiations. The chair met with the superintendent in an attempt to reopen negotiations, which would include the union teachers.[26] The union teachers met with the superintendent the next day, with no involvement reported by nonunion representatives.[27]

Nonunion teachers complained about being left out of negotiations,[28] and wrote a letter accusing the superintendent and board of not being willing to meet often and long to negotiate. The superintendent strongly rejected the charge.[29] A late district proposal called for expanding the school year to 11 months, coupled with the raises teachers were requesting. Non-union teachers objected, saying they wanted to be part of studying such a change.[30] The strike ended by a vote of the striking teachers. All teachers' salaries were raised.

The duration of the agreement was in dispute. The superintendent wanted to only include the current year, because future revenue was unknown. Teachers wanted to include the following year.[31] The final settlement included raises that went into effect in January, following a calendar rather than school year cycle.[32]

How to pay for the raises was also in dispute. Early in the strike, Mayor Humphrey called for changes in the city charter. He pointed out that voters had rejected a one percent city payroll tax.[33] The City Council cooperated by agreeing to allow the school board to renege on its promise not to borrow more money. In addition to the City Council's approval, five members of the school board would also have to approve. Only three did so, leading a teacher to say that the school board had "shot Santa."[34]

By March 11th, the school board was willing to consider borrowing money.[35] Ten days later, the strike was settled utilizing borrowed money. Nine of the nineteen school days would be made up. Teachers received an additional forty dollars per month and agreed to the addition of a preparation week at the beginning of the school year.[36]

Many procedural issues were left unsettled. Who was authorized to negotiate on each side, contract length and the legal status of strikers remained unclear.

1951 Minneapolis Strike

THE LACK OF LAWS REGULARIZING public employment meant that relationships between employee groups were determined by the groups themselves. During the threatened 1946 Minneapolis school strike, the superintendent anticipated that janitors would honor teacher's picket lines.[37] In 1951, janitors were the first to talk of striking. Just before the intended strike date, the members of the Minneapolis Federation of Men Teachers demanded a wage increase.[38]

Male teachers were asking for a $1,000 raise, for men teachers only. The school board went on record as supporting a single salary schedule for men and women based on the principal of equal pay for equal work. The board refused to discuss separate raises for male teachers.[39] This request illustrates the sometimes uneasy relationships between the three teacher groups within the Minneapolis schools—separate men's and women's unions that were part of the American Federation of Teachers, and the those affiliated with the Minnesota and National Education Associations.

The women Federation teachers had decided not to strike, but would honor the men's picket lines. When the board refused to negotiate, the women voted to join the strike.[40] Newspaper accounts don't speak to the issue of why the women teachers would be willing to support male teachers' requests for unequal pay.

The issue of the legality of public employee strikes was put to the test. A district court judge issued a temporary restraining order preventing the janitors from striking.[41] A hearing was held for an additional temporary restraining order against the men and women teacher unions. The judge suggested an "armistice," asking that the teachers delay striking. He scheduled a hearing for the following week, stating that the right to strike issue would probably be decided in the janitor's case before that court date. The teachers agreed to postpone their strike. [42]

The janitor union's lawyer based their right to strike on an existing law that prohibited injunctions in labor disputes unless there is evidence of violence or fraud. The city's attorney argued that the state constitution prohibited the strike, and that the anti-injunction law didn't apply to public employees.[43] During final arguments in the janitor's case, union lawyers pointed out that a 1939 opinion by the attorney general permitted public school janitors to strike.[44]

A district court judge upheld the janitor's right to strike, citing periodic public employee strikes over the previous 100 years. He stated that there is no clear language in the law which states that public employees have no right to strike. The school board directed the city attorney to appeal the decision to the state Supreme Court and to seek an injunction from them. The clerk's union had been waiting to see whether a strike would be legal, and filed a notice of intent to strike.[45]

The janitor's strike began the next day, January 23rd, closing the schools. The Minnesota Supreme Court acted quickly, holding hearings four days later. The city's attorney argued that the janitor's union actions were an unlawful interference with a unit of government. Calling striking janitors a "group of schizophrenics," he characterized their actions as a takeover of the schools. Union lawyers insisted that this was a labor dispute, and that to deny them the right to strike would be to compel them to work against their will.[46] The Supreme Court took the matter under advisement.

Utilizing the lower court decision legalizing strikes, the two teacher's unions announced on February 3rd that they had been on strike since January 30th.[47] Since schools were closed because of the janitor's strike, this odd circumstance meant that the teachers had been officially on strike for four days before they told anyone about it.

On February 2nd, the Minnesota Supreme Court upheld the lower court decision prohibiting issuing an injunction against the janitor's strike. The 1933 anti-injunction law was written to excluded policeman, fireman, and others in jobs related to public safety. These were the only public employees subject to strike injunctions. It also stated that the disagreement was a labor dispute. It didn't speak to the broader constitutional issue of public employees' right to strike. [48]

An unusual feature of this strike was the extensive involvement of the governor. The janitors' and teachers' unions asked the governor to intervene .The governor offered the services of the state labor conciliator on the second day of the janitor's strike.[49] The next day, the governor met with the conciliator and wrote a letter urging the parties involved to negotiate.[50] Two days later, the mayor also called for negotiations. The superintendent agreed to meet with the union and conciliator, but said that all available funds had been allocated.[51]

Negotiation sessions were held with both the janitors' and teachers' unions. On February 5th, the janitors stated that they would be willing to reopen the schools if the district requested additional funding from the legislature.[52] Things did not go as well with the teachers.

The next day the superintendent said a minority of teachers were keeping things stirred up by attempting to obtain bargaining rights and take control of the school system. He said things had reached an impasse and no meetings were scheduled. The conciliator described the situation as pretty dark.[53]

Teachers increased their wage demands.[54] The governor called all parties to his office the following Monday. During a daylong meeting, a compromise agreement was worked out providing additional raises of $100.00 for teachers, $22.50 a month for janitors and $12.50 a month for clerks. All days of the strike were to be made up.

The governor had made the agreement possible by assuring the school board that the legislature would increase funding. On that basis, the board agreed during the meeting to raise salaries. He had also met with non-striking teachers and the mayor. The janitors' and clerks' unions accepted the offer. Union teachers voted overwhelmingly to reject it. The governor said he was disappointed, and recommended to the superintendent that schools be reopened the following day.[55]

When schools opened the following day, union teachers picketed. Most janitors refused to cross the lines, following the same practice they had each day of their strike by providing only enough staff to keep the buildings from freezing. All the non-union teachers reported for work, allowing elementary schools to open. Middle and high schools were more heavily staffed by union teachers, and didn't open. When classroom temperatures stayed near forty degrees, all schools were let out early.

The superintendent withdrew the previous day's pay offer because the janitors hadn't complied. The governor concurred, saying that he had done all he could and that getting a tentative agreement had been almost a miracle.[56] Later in the day, the governor met with a member of the Central Labor Council representing the union teachers. They negotiated the final agreement which teachers ratified that night. Classes began the next day.

The strike lasted eleven school days with two thirds to be made up. Teachers received a $100 a year raise. Non-striking teachers objected to adding days to the calendar without pay.[57]

Governors were called upon in other teacher's strikes, and offered opinions, but this was the only strike negotiated in the governor's office. The tight relationship between the AFT and other unions can be seen in the Central Labor Council's involvement in negotiations. Thus both sides in the dispute saw themselves over ridden—the school board by the governor, and teachers by the Labor Council.

The Minnesota legislature was in session during the strike. A Minneapolis state senator and representative introduced a bill prohibiting strikes by teachers. The school board chair from Minneapolis testified in favor of the bill, which passed a month after the strike ended. There would be no teacher's strikes in Minnesota for almost twenty years.

1970 Minneapolis Strike

After enactment of the no-strike law in 1951, concerns about public employee labor relations continued in the Minnesota legislature. In 1965 an act was passed granting public employees' organizations recognition to meet and confer with employers. Teachers were the only group excluded from this process.[58]

Two years later, a new law granted recognition to teacher's organizations. In districts with more than one union, a five-member council was to be formed to meet and confer. If agreement couldn't be reached, a three-member adjustment panel would be formed. One member would be from the teacher's council, one from the district, and a third mutually agreed upon. The panel would attempt to develop an agreement, or release their findings to the parties involved and the commissioner of education.[59]

Formally recognizing teacher unions and organizing teacher's councils brought some clarity. Adjustment panel's findings were non-binding and strikes remained illegal. The relationships between teachers and districts remained ambiguous, and by 1970 the Minneapolis AFT was willing to risk the harsh penalties of the no-strike law.

Salary was a dispute during the negotiations, with teachers asking $8,000 to $13,000 for bachelor's degree and $8,800 to $16,100 for a master's. The district offered $7,400 to $11,695 for a BA and $8,060 to $14,465 for an MA.[60] The adjustment board had recommended a pay increase of ten percent, which was more than the district was offering. The adjustment board's recommendation was rejected by AFT leaders.[61]

What were termed "policy issues" presented more difficulties during the negotiations. Teachers wanted language dealing with elementary prep time, teacher assignments, discipline policy and class size. The district wanted only to talk about salaries, viewing these other issues as administrative matters.[62]

The Teacher's Council was utilized during the negotiations, comprised of three AFT and two CMEA (City of Minneapolis Education Association) members. The AFT had 1,800 members, the CMEA 1,600. When negotiations stalled, the AFT voted to strike in two days.[63] The CMEA didn't hold a strike vote, but did vote to give legal support to any of its members who took personal leave during the first two days of the strike to try and contact state legislators about the needs of city schools.[64] The superintendent criticized this plan, saying that he would consider that an abuse of the personal leave policy.[65]

The superintendent hadn't been part of the negotiations, but agreed to meet the day after the strike vote. He offered suggestions that he pledged to take to the school board for approval that evening.

The school board agreed with the superintendent's recommendations, approving offers of maximum class sizes of thirty-five, eighteen specialized teachers would be hired, liability insurance, an additional paid vacation day, one hour of preparation time and an additional step on the salary schedule. The board increased its salary offer by accepting the ten-percent salary increase recommended by the adjustment panel and described it as its final offer.

The offer was rejected by the Teachers' Counsel. The district suspended personal leave, making it dependent on the superintendent's discretion. The board authorized a request for an injunction, which was issued against the AFT as the only striking union. The injunction enjoined them from striking, interfering with school functions and picketing.[66]

AFT leaders spent the night in motels to avoid being served a summons.[67] School opened Thursday, the first day of the strike. 2,000 teachers didn't report for work, including 400 CMEA members. A restraining order was issued against the CMEA, enjoining them not to strike. The CMEA teachers who didn't report for work spent the day distributing 33,000 flyers in the community. Claiming they were not on strike but were engaged in a plan of action to engage the community in developing a settlement, they vowed to ignore the court order.

None of the junior or senior high schools stayed open all day. Students engaged in some vandalism, and some teachers left buildings after seeing the situation.

Numerous outsiders joined the dispute, including the ACLU which offered to represent teachers, the attorney general and president of the AFL-CIO. The county attorney called for a special legislative session to enact a fair teacher's bargaining law, and Governor LeVander advised teachers to go back to work or forfeit all rights to be teachers. The governor said, "A democracy cannot survive with teachers who teach anarchy."[68]

Fewer schools opened Friday. The district announced that schools would be closed beginning the following Monday so non-striking teachers could plan. They would reopen on Tuesday.

On Monday, it was announced that schools would also be closed on Tuesday. The superintendent said he was willing to work to change the no strike law. Teachers who had worked on Friday would get Monday as a paid holiday. He announced that the Board was willing to negotiate on language issues, but not on further salary concessions.

At a CMEA rally on Sunday night, Dr. James Connerton, the regional director for the NEA recommended that members not return to classes as long as the MFT strike continued. He told them, "The law does not require you to be strike breakers."[69]

The school board president and superintendent met with MFT leaders Monday night in a room the AFT had rented in the Park-Nicollet Hotel. When they broke for supper, two CMEA negotiators entered the room and refused to leave. The MFT ordered them out because only the MFT was on strike. The police were called, but refused to arrest anyone unless the MFT signed a citizen's arrest complaint. Instead, the MFT rented a different room and negotiations continued.

The primary issue discussed was how to get around the automatic sanctions of the no-strike law. The MFT suggested that the board grant the raises, with the rationale that by the time the issue was settled the teachers would have spent all the money. Board members feared they would be sued. This was a realistic concern because a citizen's group formed to work for court enforcement of the no strike law.[70]

Negotiations broke down on Tuesday and MFT leaders sent telegrams to the state Labor conciliator and the governor seeking help in settling the strike. The CMEA threatened legal action, stating that the meet and confer law granted them the right to be included in negotiations. David Durenberger, a spokesman for the governor, said there was some doubt whether the school board could legally negotiate with the teachers when they were no longer employees. The school board chair reiterated the no-strike law penalties and the citizen's group rallied support for their planned court action.[71]

Attorneys for the CMEA, MFT and school board appeared in district court. The board sought injunctions against both unions for striking. The CMEA sought a restraining order against the MFT and board for not including them in negotiations. There was a great deal of discussion about whether striking teachers were still employees. The judge said he would not rule until affidavits were filed.

The governor rejected the request for mediation services, saying that the meet and confer law made no provision for such service. He also said that striking teachers had no standing until they were rehired.

In the midst of all these efforts by those outside the district to deny teachers' rights, the school board and superintendent were making every effort to find a way around the provisions of the no-strike law. They explored honorariums as a way to increase teachers' pay, and retroactive sabbatical leaves to reclassify them as non-strikers. They were unable to find a solution.[72]

The Minneapolis Central Labor Union and state AFL-CIO called on the governor to call a special session to help resolve the strike. He refused, saying, "I have no intention of calling a special session to give amnesty to people who deliberately violate the law, breach their contract of employment and ignore court orders." Pressure began building to change the anti-strike law. The AFT invited the superintendent to join them in a demonstration at the state capital. State Senator Wendell Anderson, a candidate for the DFL governor's endorsement said all punitive provisions should be lifted from the no-strike law because it was a barrier to strike settlement.[73]

Progress was made in negotiations on Friday, but no decision was made on whether to open the schools. A judge granted the district's request for a temporary injunction against the MFT and CMEA, enjoining members from striking, interfering with running the schools, encouraging others to interfere or picketing. The injunction enabled the board to impose sanctions on teachers who violated the injunction.

While 2,000 teachers stood quietly on the steps of the Capitol, five teachers met with the governor, who repeated that he considered them to be unemployed. Teachers stated that they had no intention of reapplying under those circumstances. The Minneapolis mayor condemned the legislature for failing to provide for binding arbitration in disputes involving public employees. 150 parents organized to begin a voluntary school.[74]

Despite the apparent intractability of the situation at the state capital, negotiations between the school board and MFT were making progress. Agreement was reached on the majority of the language issues during a Saturday session, with another session scheduled the next day.[75]

On Monday, the court injunction against picketing meant teachers picketed only the administration building. The state level Minnesota Federation of Teachers, meeting over the weekend, voted to authorize its executive counsel to call a state-wide walkout in support of Minneapolis teachers, if the Minneapolis teachers requested it.[76] While this never happened, one can only speculate on the effect of having teachers throughout Minnesota "fired" for striking.

The board offered significant improvements in language, including preparation times beginning the next fall; limiting class sizes in kindergarten through third grade to twenty-nine students and fourth through sixth grades to thirty-five; and a discipline policy that strengthened teachers' hands. Their salary offer was 11.5 percent, held in an unpaid reserve until the law changed or enough time passed that teachers could receive a raise. Teachers rejected the offer as inadequate, and negotiations broke off. The board formed plans to reopen the schools within a week. A county judge ruled that the board must include the CMEA in negotiations.[77]

The next day, school officials met with CMEA members and briefed them on negotiations. During the meeting, they also discussed the role of CMEA members in reopening the schools. While nothing was decided, the CMEA decided to pursue a lawsuit declaring that during the first two days of the strike, CMEA members who hadn't reported for work had taken personal leave and were not on strike. Therefore, they are not subject to anti-strike provisions. The MFT reached out the CMEA, calling for a joint meeting to help understand each other's positions.[78]

The superintendent announced plans to reopen the schools the middle of the next week. Letters were sent to all teachers asking whether they would report for work. Included in the letter was a statement that teachers had a right to a hearing to establish their status regarding absences during the first two days of the strike.[79]

The board attempted to placate teachers by announcing that all teachers who returned would be rehired; that their loss of tenure would not be used to jeopardize their careers and that the board supported legislative efforts to modify the harsh no strike penalties. CMEA leaders urged members to reply that they would return to work only if the schools would be safe.[80]

MFT leaders rejected the tactic of teachers declaring they were on personal leave the first two days of the strike. The superintendent stated that he anticipated about 1,700 out of the district's 3,400 teachers would report for work on Wednesday.[81]

District plans for Wednesday's opening were reported. Most elementary schools would operate normally. The high schools, where many teachers were MFT members, would hold three period days, similar to a summer school schedule. In a potential delaying tactic, MFT leaders collected requests for hearings about the first two days of the strike, estimated to take up to eight years to complete on an individual basis.[82]

While formal negotiations were not taking place, numerous phone calls were exchanged and informal meetings with school board members were held, sometimes in board members' homes. The biggest obstacle to settling was the harsh penalties that would have resulted with those teachers declared "strikers" being treated differently from those found to be "on leave" during the first two days. The board agreed to a general "no reprisals" policy meaning that all returning teachers would be treated the same. The MFT leadership announced that a settlement had been reached, and recommended approval.

Of the fourteen days of school lost, teachers were to be paid for seven—one of very few instances where striking teachers were paid for days not worked. They could be paid for an additional five days, if they worked make-up sessions. Thus, they lost pay only for the first two days. A judge ruled that teachers could retroactively apply for personal leave for those two days, thus making it possible for no loss of pay.[83]

Looking down the long lens of history, the cause of this strike and the manner it proceeded in appear to reflect the failure of the harsh anti-strike legislation. It didn't provide for meaningful negotiations or a system of appeal when negotiations failed. The penalties—and unclear status of striking teachers—hindered a settlement.

This strike also influenced the legislature, but this time in favor of union concerns. During an extra session, the Public Employment Labor Relations Act of 1971 provided rights to organize and bargain and established grievance and arbitration procedures. The prohibition against strikes continued. Language prohibiting raises for a year were dropped, but placing strikers on two years probationary status remained. Any organization participating in a strike would lose its exclusive representative status.[84]

---

1. Stacy Mitchell, St. Paul Public School Administrative History, Minnesota State Archives, p. 6.
2. Winkels Henry, *Who We Are What We Stand For*, Minnesota Federation of Teachers 1966, p. 6.
3. Carlson Cheryl , Strike for Better Schools—the St. Paul public school teachers' strike of 1946, Union Advocate 1997.
4. *St Paul Pioneer Press*, November 23, p. 2.

5. *St. Paul Pioneer Press,* November 17, 1946 pp. 1, 2.
6. *St. Paul Pioneer Press,* November 24, p. 2.
7. *St. Paul Pioneer Press,* November 23, 1946, p. 2.
8. *St Paul Pioneer Press,* November 16, 1946, p. 1.
9. *St Paul Pioneer Press,* November 24, 1946, p. 2.
10. Cheryl Braunworth Carlson, Union Advocate, 1997, in workdayminnesota.org.
11. *Life,* December 9, 1946, p. 40.
12. *St Paul Pioneer Press,* November 26, 1946, p. 1.
13. *St. Paul Pioneer Press Dispatch,* December 6, 1989, p. 13.
14. *Time,* March 8, 1948.
15. Trimble, Steve, *Education and Democracy: A History of the Mpls. Federation of Teachers.* Mpls Federation of Teachers, 1979, p. 46.
16. Trimble, Steve, *Education and Democracy: A History of the Mpls. Federation of Teachers.* Mpls Federation of Teachers, 1979, p. 45.
17. *Minneapolis Star,* Feb 19, 1948, p. 1.
18. *Minneapolis Star,* March 8, 1948, p. 1.
19. *Minneapolis Star,* March 12, p. 1.
20. *Minneapolis Star,* February 25 1948, p. 1.
21. *Minneapolis Star,* February 26, p. 1.
22. *Minneapolis Star,* March 6, 1948, p. 1.
23. *Minneapolis Star,* February 23, 1948, p. 1.
24. *Minneapolis Star,* February 25, 1948, p. 1.
25. *Minneapolis Star,* February 26, 1948, p. 1.
26. *Minneapolis Star,* March 2, 1948, p. 1.
27. *Minneapolis Star,* March 3, 1948, p. 1.
28. *Minneapolis Star,* March 11, 1948, p. 9.
29. *Minneapolis Star,* March 17, 1948, pg1.
30. *Minneapolis Star,* March 13, 1948, p. 1.
31. *Minneapolis Star,* March 15, 1948, p. 1
32. *Minneapolis Star,* March 22, 1948, p. 1.
33. *Minneapolis Star,* February 25, 1948, p. 1.
34. *Minneapolis Star,* February 26, 2948, p. 1.
35. *Minneapolis Star,* March 11, 1948, p. 1.
36. *Minneapolis Star,* March 22, 1948, p. 1.
37. *St. Paul Pioneer Press,* November 23, 1946, p. 1.
38. *Minneapolis Star,* Jan 6, 1951, p. 1.
39. *Minneapolis Star,* Jan 6, 1951, p. 1.
40. *Minneapolis Star,* January 11, 1951, p. 1.

41. *Minneapolis Star*, Jan 6, 1951, p. 1.
42. *Minneapolis Star*, January 13, 1951, p. 1.
43. *Minneapolis Star*, January 13, pp. 1, 3.
44. *Minneapolis Star*, January 15, 1951, p. 13.
45. *Minneapolis Star*, January 22, 1951, pp. 1,7.
46. *Minneapolis Star*, January 26, 1951, pp. 1,9.
47. *Minneapolis Star*, January 1951, p. 1.
48. *Minneapolis Star*, February 2, 1951, pp. 1,6.
49. *Minneapolis Star*, January 24, 1951, p. 1.
50. *Minneapolis Star*, January 25, 1951, p. 1.
51. *Minneapolis Star*, January 27, 1951.
52. *Minneapolis Star*, February 5, 1951, p. 1.
53. *Minneapolis Star*, February 6, 1951, p. 1.
54. *Minneapolis Star*, February 7, 1951, p. 29.
55. *Minneapolis Star*, February 13, 1951, p. 1.
56. *Minneapolis Star*, February 13, 1951, p. 1, 6.
57. *Minneapolis Star*, February 28, 1951, p. 1.
58. Minnesota revisor of statutes, Session Laws of Minnesota for 1965, chapter 839.
59. Minnesota revisor of statutes, Session Laws of Minnesota for 1967, Chapter 633.
60. *Minneapolis Tribune*, April 7, 1970, p. 1,9.
61. *Minneapolis Tribune*, April 8, 1979, p. 1.
62. Robinson, Corinne Adams, The 1970 Minneapolis Teacher Strike, Mpls Federation of Teachers, 1995, p. 4.
63. *Minneapolis Tribune*, April 7, 1970, pp. 1,9.
64. Robinson, Corinne Adams, The 1970 Minneapolis Teacher Strike, Mpls Federation of Teachers, 1995, p. 6.
65. *Minneapolis Tribune*, April 8, 1979, p. 1.
66. *Minneapolis Tribune*, April 9, 1970, p. 1.
67. Robinson, Corinne Adams, The 1970 Minneapolis Teacher Strike, Mpls Federation of Teachers, 1995, p. 6.
68. *Minneapolis Tribune*, April 10, pp. 1,6.
69. *Minneapolis Tribune*, April 11, 1970, p. 1.
70. *Minneapolis Tribune*, April 14, 1970. pp. 1, 10.
71. *Minneapolis Tribune*, April 15, 1970, pp. 1, 17.
72. *Minneapolis Tribune*, April 16, 1979, pp. 1, 7.
73. *Minneapolis Tribune*, April 17, 1970, pp. 1, 10.
74. *Minneapolis Tribune*, April 18, 1970, pp. 1, 9.
75. *Minneapolis Tribune*, April 19, 1970, pp. 1, 15A.

76. *Minneapolis Tribune*, April 20, 1970, pp. 1, 12.
77. *Minneapolis Tribune*, April 21, 1970, pp. 1, 4.
78. *Minneapolis Tribune*, April 22, 1970, pp. 1, 6.
79 *Minneapolis Tribune*, April 23, 1970, pp. 1.
80. *Minneapolis Tribune*, April 24, 1970, pp. 1, 12.
81. *Minneapolis Tribune*, April 26, 1970, pp. 1, 12.
82. *Minneapolis Tribune*, April 27, 1970, pp. 1, 8.
83. *Minneapolis Tribune*, April 28, 1970, pp. 1, 4.
84. MN Laws 1971—Extra Session, Chapter 33, Section 1, 179.61.

Chapter Twelve
Legal Strikes Begin

1973 Hermantown

The 1973 legislature significantly changed the two year old PELRA law. It now read that a refusal by the employer to request binding arbitration when requested by the exclusive representative could be used to justify a strike. It also allowed unfair labor practices to be a legal basis for striking. The new rules went into effect in May, 1973, and were put to use in Hermantown the following fall.

Teachers had been without a contract for over a year. A state mediator had been involved in negotiations the previous November, culminating in a tentative agreement in June. That agreement didn't hold because of subsequent disagreements about retroactive pay, work hours, and grievance procedures.[1]

The Hermantown Federation of Teachers (HFT) voted on September 5th to strike, but set no time line. A court hearing was scheduled for September 13 by the HFT, seeking a restraining order against the board and superintendent for unfair labor practices. One of their allegations was that the board refused to submit to binding arbitration.

Throughout this strike, issues reported in the media were muddled. The board said that it had written to the Bureau of Mediation requesting binding arbitration. The board attorney stated that the only unresolved issue was work hours, and that the board had agreed to retroactive pay, a salary schedule and grievance procedure.[2]

The Bureau of Mediation responded that it did not consider negotiations to be at an impasse, and wouldn't accept a request for binding arbitration. A mediator joined the negotiations. Meanwhile, the board immediately filed a new request for arbitration, while the HFT announced that it had been informed by the Bureau of Mediation that it was now legally free to strike.

In court, the HFT charged that the district was engaging in unfair labor practices by circumventing the negotiating process through contacting teachers individually and by public statements. The district said they were exercising free speech.[3] Perhaps this was the basis for the Bureau of Mediation's approval of the strike. The board had agreed to binding arbitration, which left only unfair labor practices as a justification for striking.

Negotiations continued for a week and broke off. Salary issues were reopened as past agreements unraveled.[4] On September 24th, the teachers went out on strike. The board attorney said striking teachers would be replaced.[5] The strike affected 2,000 students and ninety-six teachers. Thirty-five of the teachers, members of the rival Hermantown Education Association, voted to honor the picket lines.

Buses picked up students the first day of the strike but they were returned home because only four teachers reported for work. Salary and the length of the work day were the remaining unsettled issues. The district contacted substitute teachers, but announced that school would be closed.[6]

Negotiations resumed with a state mediator. A district court judge issued a temporary restraining order enjoining the school board and superintendent from bargaining individually with teachers and refusing to bargain in good faith. The district had been claiming that scheduling the work day was a management prerogative and not subject to negotiations. The judge rejected that argument, stating as well that classroom assignments, preparation periods, lunch periods and other structured time assignment were conditions of employment and were subject to negotiations. The board attorney said the decision would be appealed.

Both sides laid out their positions in the newspaper. Salary offers were close. The HFT claimed that changes in salary steps meant that the board decreased its total offer, rather than the $8,000 increase the board said it was offering.[7]

A marathon negotiating session was held with the director of the Bureau of Mediation Services on Tuesday, the second day of the strike. All issues except salary were reported to be settled, with the difference in offers amounting to only $10.00 per teacher per year.[8]

Despite the progress made in negotiations by the beginning of the second week of the strike, the mediators declared the two sides at an impasse, and the binding arbitration process was begun. A board spokesman said they were willing to meet with anyone at any time, but felt that arbitration seemed the best way to settle the matter. The union hoped to put public pressure on the board to continue negotiating during the arbitration process. Teachers continued to work extracurricular activities, including sports and the school play.[9]

Some confusion resulted from the ruling that the dispute would go to binding arbitration. The HFT was reluctant to enter into it, and not certain whether they had to. The question of whether teachers could refuse binding arbitration once a strike had begun hadn't been tested under the new law.

A town forum format planned by the school board for Tuesday was changed drastically by the intervention of about 150 parents. Meeting first with the board, they persuaded them to resume bargaining. They then went to the HFT strike headquarters with the same proposition, getting an agreement by both sides to resume and stay in negotiations until a settlement was reached. Some parents talked of barricading the doors to keep negotiators in the building if they tried to leave.[10]

Parental pressure resulted in an all-night session Tuesday, but no agreement. Wednesday evening, the board announced that classes would reopen Monday for grades ten through twelve using administrators and non-striking teachers. It was announced that make up days for the strike and no-retaliation clauses were additional unresolved issues. The district dropped below the State's 175-day minimum school year.[11]

Negotiations continued, and a tentative agreement was reached Saturday. The contract wasn't written, but the agreement included five make up days, protection for employees who supported the strike and agreement on work hours and salaries.[12] School began Monday. It was announced that raises would be 6.5 percent for the first year and six percent for the current year.[13]

This was the first but wouldn't be the last time that the issue of retroactive pay appeared to contribute to a strike. Failing to reach agreement during the first year of a contract cycle, and then declaring that since that year was done, raises would only begin once the new contract was signed was a very aggressive negotiating tactic. In this, as in every subsequent case where it was tried and resulted in a strike, the issue was dropped before a settlement was reached.

There were many questions about management prerogative/contract language during these early negotiations. Now that teachers had the right to bargain collectively, many district's "take it or leave it" approach to negotiations wouldn't work. Defining what should and shouldn't be part of contract language would take years and a number of struggles.

The First Fruits of PELRA - 1975 Strikes

Nineteen seventy-five produced the third largest number of teacher's strikes. Some readers may question at this point the timing of the strikes. Prior practice had been for contracts to begin in January of even numbered years. The PELRA law of 1971 moved the contract starting dates to July 1. Revisions in 1973 specified that beginning in 1975, teachers contracts would be for two years, with the contract year beginning on July 1 of each odd numbered year.[14]

The Hermantown strike took place under the old calendar. They were in the second year of the contract period, and had negotiated for twenty-one months. The 1975 strikes took place in December, six months into the first year of the new contract cycles. Two districts—Winona and Howard Lake-Waverly—went out on strike the same day.

An additional difference can be seen in which unions went on strike. The Minnesota Federation of Teachers was involved in all the early strikes, while the Minnesota Education Association units didn't participate. Beginning in 1975, locals of the Minnesota Education Association took the lead in striking.

There was apparently some status in being declared the first District to strike. An employee of the state Bureau of Mediation said his office didn't consider the Hermantown strike legal.[15] Howard Lake-Waverly and Winona both went out on December 9, 1975, thus granting them claim to be the first legal teacher's strikes in Minnesota. Hermantown may dispute this however, since they felt they had approval by the Bureau of Mediation to strike two years earlier.

Howard Lake-Waverly

A BOND ISSUE TO REMODEL part of the school recently damaged in a fire and to add additional space passed 761 to 243, demonstrating the community's willingness to take on an additional tax burden. [16]

Three weeks later, the teachers requested arbitration. Ten negotiation sessions beginning in April and three mediation sessions had resulted in little progress. The Bureau of Mediation declared them at an impasse, and certified the dispute for arbitration. The primary disagreement was the placement of new money in the salary schedule.[17] The district proposed that teachers with the most experience receive smaller raises, which the union said had been the case for the last several contracts.[18]

The board unanimously rejected arbitration. The union salary demand was a 17.5 percent raise, claiming the average settlements in the area were twenty percent. The district offered fifteen percent.[19]

Teachers quickly voted to strike on November 10, setting a December 9 strike date. They said they hoped a settlement could be reached before then, and claimed that the district never submitted written proposals during the negotiations process. They say they had no option but to strike in the face of the district's 'take it or leave it' stance.[20]

A number of teachers attended a school board meeting, and presented their concerns. The board's hired negotiator did all the talking for the board, something that frustrated many teachers, who would have preferred to hear individual board members' views.[21] This issue of who is most effective in speaking for each group is a question that remains unresolved to this day.

A member of the teachers' Action Committee published a long letter to the editor. In it, he responded to criticisms teachers faced about their short work year, relatively high wages, and suggestions that if they don't like it in this district, they could move to another. The last negotiation session was held on October 22nd, with no more scheduled.[22]

In the face of an impending strike date, the tactic of refusing to hold negotiation sessions appears to bear a strong resemblance to standing on the railroad tracks and watching the train approach. It will be seen many more times. Perhaps one (or both) sides have given up hope that a settlement can be reached. Alternately, perhaps one (or both) sides believe a strike really won't happen.

The Friday before the strike date, a negotiation session was held. The district increased its offer to 15.75 percent. The teachers rejected it, citing the cost of living of ten percent per year and the continued small raises for the most senior teachers.[23] An all-night session Monday night in St. Paul with the deputy director of Mediation Services failed to reach an agreement.[24] Progress was made however, with a reported difference in total contract price per year between the offers of $1,500, or twenty-two dollars per teacher.[25]

The teachers struck on December 9 and schools were closed. They settled two days later, accepting one day's lost pay. The settlement thus cost the district less than its pre-strike offer.[26] It could be argued that the strike was an economic failure for the teachers since they received less total pay, but additional money was provided for teachers with the most experience.

Winona

The Winona School Board appeared more aggressive about the issue of retroactive pay. A letter was sent to teachers on August 15th that any benefits realized under the new contract would become effective on the date of signing, and would not be retroactive. Teachers filed a grievance when their September checks didn't include increases in longevity pay. The board denied the grievances, saying they hadn't been filed within the timelines specified in the contract, and that step increases were subject to negotiations. Teachers responded by filing a class grievance.[27]

Four mediation sessions had resulted in the Bureau of Mediation certifying that they were at an impasse on nineteen contract issues. The two sides remained far apart, with the board offering eleven percent and teachers asking eighteen percent. At the school board meeting, the possibility of raising the district's offer by $100,000 was discussed. It was stated that such a raise would necessitate program cuts and possible layoffs.[28]

The union voted to strike any time after the next week if the board refused arbitration. Four hours later, the board voted five to one to reject arbitration and called for another negotiating session. Board members were particularly upset that union leaders hadn't submitted the superintendent's offer of an additional $107,000 to their membership. Discussions were begun about possible budget cuts that would allow higher salary offers.[29]

The discussion during a negotiation session sought a mutual understanding of the district's financial status, the costs of each side's proposals, and the financial implications of additional salary expenditures. There was general agreement that the two sides were $200,000 apart, and that any additional offers by the board would be accompanied by budget cuts. A strategy suggested by board negotiators was to not replace retiring teachers.[30]

Now that the PELRA law required districts to negotiate, we see this dichotomy articulated for the first time. More salary for individual teachers could only be provided if there were fewer teachers. Fewer staff would result in program cuts, something school boards resisted. The Winona teachers responded by suggesting that a referendum could provide additional revenue, and that budget allocations could be changed without affecting staff or programs.[31]

Much of the next negotiating session was taken up with disagreements about how far apart the sides were monetarily, and the cost of a number of ancillary pay increases for such things as coaching. Board negotiators acknowledged that they were unable to accurately predict the district's expenses for the second year of the contract. They hadn't calculated the effect of declining enrollment and had no idea how many retirements might occur.

The discussion was complicated by an "informal" offer of an additional $100,000 that the superintendent had mentioned during the final mediation session. Teachers were frustrated because it was never formally offered. The board negotiator spoke of it as a possibility without board approval. Little progress was made on salary, but some language issues were discussed.[32]

Perhaps this "informal" offer was a product of inexperience. It provides an example of the problems that can occur when a negotiator makes an unauthorized offer.

The following bargaining session centered around district finances—whether the reserve was available and how much could be offered without deficit spending. Few figures were agreed to. Board negotiators formally put the additional $100,000 offer on the table. When that wasn't acceptable, they agreed to discuss whether larger offers could be made with the whole school board. The WEA executive board voted to strike on December 9th if no agreement was reached.[33]

At the school board meeting, members refused to offer an additional $226,000 identified during the last bargaining session as the difference between the two offers. Instead, they agreed to offer teachers an additional $126,000. The WEA president said she was saddened that they were being forced to strike because the board refused arbitration.

One board member noted that the school board had voted in the fall not to offer retroactive pay. Since this hadn't been listed as a negotiable item, it couldn't be changed. The board would seek a legal opinion. This discordant note, occurring a week before the strike date, couldn't have sat well with the union.[34]

The union established strike headquarters in a former movie theater two days later. Because of illness, the board negotiator hadn't attended a bargaining session. Instead, the board was represented by the superintendent. A union news bulletin asked whether the board wanted a strike and was finished negotiating.[35]

Both sides agreed to meet with a state mediator the Saturday before the strike. The board's chief negotiator defended his absence at the last session due to illness, and called union members crude for calling the superintendent a messenger boy, claiming that he had full authorization to speak for the board.[36]

The mediation session resulted in no agreement. The WEA set a rally for Monday night, opened its strike headquarters and sent letters to the public explaining their position, urging citizens to contact board members. The president of the student senate for the Winona Area Vocational-Technical Institute announced that 300 out of 400 students were expected to attend a rally on Tuesday protesting against the strike. While they felt supportive of their faculty, they were concerned about the financial and educational hardships a strike could cause vocational students. The district formulated strike plans, calling for opening schools if enough staff crossed picket lines and substitutes could be hired. Extracurricular events would be determined on a daily basis.[37]

Teachers held a rally the night before the strike, led by MEA president Don Hill. Teachers from seven other districts attended in support. A last-minute negotiating session lasted all night, ending at 5:50 A.M. December 9, with the two sides $39,000 apart.

Teachers began picketing at 6:30 A.M. All buildings but two classes at the vocational school were closed. About seventy-five vocational school students counter-protested along with teacher picketers. They reported that students attending on the GI bill had already stopped receiving checks, and were concerned about the effects of an extended school year.

Union leaders said only two full-time staff crossed lines, and that they understood that part-time teachers had to cross or lose their jobs. A district spokesman said as many as fifty-two teachers crossed. No negotiation sessions were scheduled, with the board saying they were willing to sit down at any time. Six days could be lost before reaching the state minimum of 175 days to receive foundation aid. A random survey of citizens by the local paper reported that fifty-nine percent were opposed to the teacher's strike. [38]

At a union rally the evening of the first day of the strike, it was proposed that teachers' salary demands increase with each day of the strike. This would provide compensation for lost days' wages.

A negotiation session was held during the second day of the strike. Fewer teachers crossed picket lines, where several incidents of egg-throwing were reported. While ministers called for an end to the strike, an ugly note was added by phone calls threatening the families of a member of the school board and the chief negotiator for the WEA.[39]

Teachers withdrew their previous offer at the negotiating session, replacing it with a package costing $26,000 more. They explained that they were concerned about the district's costing methods. Board negotiators complained about this "regressive" practice and rejected it. The superintendent announced that schools would remain closed during the strike, adding that parents who wished to enroll their children in parochial schools would encounter no problems in transferring their records. The local AFL-CIO voted to honor the strike. A UPS delivery had been stopped, and no more fuel oil would be delivered by members of the Teamsters Union.[40]

The superintendent announced at the beginning of the second week of the strike that administrators would supervise sports practices and attend "away" games with teams. A basketball game and wrestling match had been forfeited during the first week.[41]

On Wednesday, a seventeen-hour session was held with a state mediator, resulting in an agreement. Board members and the public had complained about the mediator's request that it be a closed door session. The teachers met at 7:00 A.M., voted approval, and returned to class at 9:30. Five of the seven lost days would be made up, including the following Monday and Tuesday—the first two days of Christmas vacation.

The board negotiator explained that the district was able to increase its offer because of the savings resulting from teachers not being paid for two days. The settlement provided a 14.7 percent salary increase and an additional $37,854.00 in benefits. The superintendent noted that he would have to come up with several days' extra pay for building principals.[42]

The board approved the agreement on a four to one vote, commenting that they felt more comfortable negotiating in open sessions.[43]

Roseau

Early negotiations were very amicable in Roseau. The union suggested a modest increase of 7.5 percent. The cost of insurance was an issue, as were language issues about the length of the school day, leave policy, and severance pay. The district and union's costing figures were drastically different, the union saying their request amounted to 10.55 percent, with the district countering that the actual cost of the union proposal was 15.7 percent.[44]

In early October, the board offered what it said was nineteen percent over two years, up to $250.00 on single-coverage insurance and a half hour longer work day. Teachers asked for insurance payments of $625 and $700 and two addition days of sick leave.[45] An all-day mediation session resulted in agreement about extra-curricular pay, and brought the two sides "pretty close" on the salary schedule. The union held firm on its insurance request.[46]

Up to this point, it might be viewed that things were headed for a settlement in a harmonious district. A hint that the relationship between labor and management was strained can be seen in the six grievances that were settled in mid-October. None were directly related to negotiations, dealing instead with placement on the salary schedule.[47] This large number of grievances from a small faculty demonstrated that a spirit of collaboration and compromise was absent.

Negotiations bogged down by early November. The mediator declared an impasse and the union requested arbitration, which had been used the previous year. The board refused, saying they felt it was not in their best interest to go to arbitration every year. Citing declining enrollment and diminishing state aid, the board felt it had offered its top limit in the September session. The union said it understood that they could go on strike at any time, but planned to wait and hoped to continue negotiating.[48]

At the board's next meeting, they set a levy for the upcoming year that didn't include extra money for teacher's raises.[49] While making tax payers happy, this move didn't contribute to opening a way to settle.

How to calculate insurance costs continued to be contentious, with the board insisting that it be included as part of a total package settlement, and the union contenting that it should be considered separately. They also disagreed with the board's position that paying for family coverage would discriminate against single teachers, since they would be receiving less pay for the same work. Hours of work and assignment to extra tasks continued to be differences. MEA president Don Hill came to town, telling teachers that, "If you feel justified in what you are doing you should feel proud of what you do and not back away." After his talk, teachers voted to strike on December 11.[50]

Two more negotiation sessions, the last ending at midnight before the strike, yielded agreement on the salary schedule but not insurance, the costs of which were being subtracted from salaries. Teachers struck on December 11th. The board published what each teacher's proposed salary would be in the local paper.[51] While not unique, it does display an aggressive attempt to garner public support for the board's position.

The strike ended after three school days by splitting the difference between the salary proposals and length of school day. None of the days lost were made up.[52]

Luverne

The teachers' strike in Luverne illustrates how hard-nosed small town negotiations could be. That fall, teachers didn't receive raises for longevity (steps) or increased course work (lanes). They were told by the board chair that they were still operating under the old contract, so no increases could be granted. He suggested that teachers take the issue to a grievance or discuss it under the "meet and confer" language in the contract.[53]

That answer doesn't seem to make a lot of sense. If the board believed they were prohibited from granting automatic raises, then why offer a way to resolve the issue? And if they thought that granting the raises was permissible, then choosing to deny them was a sure way to anger the teachers.

The teachers responded by requesting a class-action grievance over the issue that was turned down by the board.[54] This must have cast a pall on the ongoing negotiations.

During an all-day mediation session on October 21st, agreement was reached on about half the language issues. The mediator declared talks to be at an impasse and teachers filed for arbitration the following Monday.[55] Because the class-action grievance had been denied, many teachers filed individual grievances about the lack of automatic raises. If not resolved within fifty days, each could go to arbitration. Teachers contacted the board, asking for more negotiations.[56]

The board responded to the request for negotiation by setting up a mediation session for December 2nd—two weeks away. The board said it felt that more could be accomplished with a mediator than face to face negotiations. During a regular board meeting, they set the tax levy for the maximum allowed, $56,372.00 more.[57]

When the board rejected arbitration December 9, teachers voted later that same night to strike on December 12. A key issue was extra-duty assignments. Previous contracts had included the phrase "by mutual consent" and the board wanted that changed to allow them to assign teachers without their consent. If the teachers would agree to this language, then the board would submit the other unresolved issues to arbitration.

Teachers responded that they would accept the district's language in return for a nineteen percent raise, an amount the board felt was totally unacceptable. The board continued to insist the new contract not provide salary increases until signed. The board published a rationale for why they had refused arbitration and their proposed salary schedule in the local paper.[58]

The mediation session was unsuccessful. An all-night negotiation session was held the night before the strike. The teacher's final position was 18.55 percent and dropping the mutual consent provision, or a 17.5 percent increase and retain mutual consent. The board's final offer was 16.31 percent and dropping mutual consent. In one of the more bizarre incidents in Minnesota bargaining history, in the middle of the night both sides sat across the table from each other and no one spoke for an hour and seven minutes.[59]

Teachers struck Friday, December 12. Busses picked up students, but they were sent home. The superintendent said he asked children to report to school as usual to "see where we stand," and announced the intention to open school the following Monday.[60] The local paper published a list of existing teacher salaries by name. The board began hearing the individual grievances teachers filed about the lack of automatic pay raises. Strike plans for the district included a statement that lost work days wouldn't be made up. A lengthy editorial called for making teacher's strikes illegal.[61]

The strike was settled during a twelve-hour mediation session in Minneapolis. It lasted for six school days, three of which would be made up. The average raise of seventeen percent split the difference between the pre-strike positions of 18.55 percent and 16.31 percent. Raises were based on the full two year contract, providing for retroactive pay. The settlement included gains in insurance benefits and a compromise on the mutual consent language allowing the district to assign "reasonable" non-teaching services. One basketball game was forfeited and other games were rescheduled. [62]

The language struggle in Luverne was unique. It was common in the early days for districts to hold the right to assign extra-duty tasks to teachers, often without pay. Many strikes included teacher's efforts to make assignments voluntary and compensated. In Luverne, extra duty assignments had been already been voluntary. Despite a strike, teachers lost that language.

---

1. *Duluth News Tribune,* September 7, 1973, p. 2.
2. *Duluth News Tribune,* September 5, 1973, p. 1.
3. *Duluth News Tribune,* September 14, 1973, p. 2.
4. *Duluth News Tribune,* September 22, 1973, p. 1.
5. *Duluth News Tribune,* September 24, 1973, p. 1.
6. *Duluth News Tribune,* September 25, 1973, pp. 1, 11.
7. *Duluth News Tribune,* September 26, 1973, pp. 1, 4.
8. *Duluth News Tribune,* September 27, 1973, p. 2.
9. *Duluth News Tribune,* October 2, 1973, p. 1.
10. *Duluth News Tribune,* October 3, 1973, p. 2.
11. *Duluth News Tribune,* October 4, 1973, p. 1.
12. *Duluth News Tribune,* October 7, 1973, p. 1.
13. *Duluth News Tribune,* October 9, 1973, p. 1.
14. Laws of Minnesota for 1973Chapter 635, MN revisor of statures.
15. *Winona daily News,* December 8, 1975, pp. 3, 8.
16. *Howard Lake Herald,* October 9, 1975, p. 1.
17. *Howard Lake Herald,* October 30, 1975, p. 1.
18. *Howard Lake Herald,* November 20, 1975, p. 1.
19. *Howard Lake Herald,* November 6, 1975, p. 1.
20. *Howard Lake Herald,* November 13, 1975, pp. 1, 6.
21. *Howard Lake Herald,* November 20, 1975, p. 1.
22. *Howard Lake Herald,* November 27, 1975, p. 1.
23. *Howard Lake Herald,* December 4, 1975, p. 1.
24. *Winona Dailey News,* December 9, 1975, p. 1B.
25. *Howard Lake Herald,* December 11, 1975, p. 1.

26. *Howard Lake Herald*, December 4, 1975, p. 1.
27. *Winona Dailey News*, November 18, 1975, p. 3.
28. *Winona Dailey News*, November 18, 1975, p. 3.
29. *Winona Dailey News*, November 19, 1975, p. 3.
30. *Winona Dailey News*, November 23, 1975, p. 3.
31. *Winona Dailey News*, November 23, 1975, p. 3.
32. *Winona Dailey News*, November 25, 1975, p. 3.
33. *Winona Dailey News*, November 28, 1975, p. 3.
34. *Winona Dailey News*, December 2, 1975, p. 3, 10.
35. *Winona Dailey News*, December 4, 1975, p. 3.
36. *Winona Dailey News*, December 5, 1975, pp. 3, 11.
37. *Winona Dailey News*, December 8, 1975, pp. 3, 8.
38. *Winona Dailey News*, December 9, 1975, pp. 1, 3, 11, 1B.
39. *Winona Dailey News*, December 10, 1975, pp. 3, 1B.
40. *Winona Dailey News*, December 11, 1975, p. 1, 3.
41. *Winona Dailey News*, December 15, 1975, p. 3.
42. *Winona Dailey News*, December 18, 1975, pp. 1, 3, 13.
43. *Winona Dailey News*, December 30, 1975, p. 3.
44. *Roseau Times-Region*, September 25, 1975, p. 1.
45. *Roseau Times-Region*, October 2, 1975, p. 1.
46. *Roseau Times-Region*, October 9, 1975, p. 1.
47. *Roseau Times-Region*, October 16, 1975, p. 1.
48. *Roseau Times-Region*, November 6, 1975, p. 1.
49. *Roseau Times-Region*, November 13, 1975, p. 1.
50. *Roseau Times-Region*, November 27, 1975, p. 1, 3.
51. *Roseau Times-Region*, December 11, 1975, p. 1, 3.
52. *Roseau Times-Region*, December 18, 1975, p. 1.
53. *The Star-Herald*, October 15, 1975, p. 1.
54. *The Star-Herald*, October 22, 1975, p. 1.
55. *The Star-Herald*, October 29, 1975.
56. *The Star-Herald*, November 5, 1975, p. 1, 3.
57. *The Star-Herald*, November 12, 1975, p. 1, 2.
58. *The Star-Herald*, December 10, 1975, p. 1, 9, B12.
59. *The Star-Herald*, December 17, 1975, p. 1, 8.
60. *The Star-Herald*, December 5, 1975, p. 1.
61. *The Star-Herald*, December 17, 1975, pp. 1, 2, B2.
62. *The Star-Herald*, December 24, 1975, pp. 1, 2.

Chapter Thirteen
Faribault—The Strike That Nearly Failed

There was a history of labor unrest in the Faribault District. The previous year, an impasse had been reached and the board refused arbitration. The union voted to strike and set up headquarters. The dispute was settled at the last minute. Only three months later, a new round of negotiations began.

By November, a mediator had declared an impasse on thirteen items because he said the two parties "had done little on their own to settle outstanding items." No additional mediation sessions were scheduled.[1] The grievance policy would prove to be a thorny issue. The union sought to keep current language which permitted grievances relating to school operation. The district wanted them limited to contract issues only (which would be common today).

Some fairly hard-nosed positions by the board included no retroactive pay unless contracts were settled by December 1. They wanted sick leave for family members used only for critical illnesses, complaining that teachers were taking days off to stay with their children who only had routine sicknesses. The board also wanted to be able to set the hours of the work day as needed.[2]

Teachers quickly decided to request arbitration.[3] The board rejected arbitration and called for continuing negotiations, several members saying they didn't want to abdicate their responsibility to settle the contract locally.[4]

The district had hired a professional negotiator who also worked for other districts. This limited his availability, because negotiations in other districts were also encountering crises. Faribault teachers repeatedly requested sessions directly with board members and offered to meet on a daily basis. An assistant superintendent explained that from the beginning, each side had indicated who their negotiators would be, and that to have two sets of negotiators would be a disaster.[5]

All teachers' contracts are negotiated in the same time frame across Minnesota. This was the first, but wouldn't be the last time that professional negotiator's availability would be problematic.

Teachers voted on December 11 to strike December 18, despite the fact that this would disrupt Christmas programs planned for the week before winter break. One negotiation session was scheduled before the strike date, and teachers said they were willing to negotiate all through Christmas vacation.[6]

Prior to the negotiating session, vocational students presented a letter saying the Student Senate would urge students to attend class on December 18, the first day of the scheduled strike. They were concerned about the hardships a strike could cause for vocational students.[7] The negotiation session yielded little movement. A subsequent session on Monday produced few results. The board developed strike plans, including keeping schools open and continuing extra-curricular activities. A mediation session was scheduled for the next day and the board voted to suspend further negotiations if an agreement wasn't reached. Teachers offered to continue to meet.[8]

None of the thirteen disputed areas were resolved during the mediation session and the board declared they would not meet until after the holidays. Teachers sent the board president a telegram offering to meet on Wednesday—the last day before the strike. Teachers didn't comment on the merits of the board's offer of 9.07 percent and six percent salary increases. They rejected the offer because it was tied to language that would give away rights they'd had for several years.[9]

MEA President Don Hill addressed teachers the night before the strike, and joined the picketers as the strike began December 18. Most students reported for class, but schools closed by 9:30, having been operated with administrators, aides, and parents. Five teachers crossed the lines.[10]

There were several incidents of water balloons thrown at picketers in the below-zero cold the first day of the strike. A committee of students at the vocational school called the governor's office asking for mediation sessions. The mediator was helping settle the Luverne strike, and didn't intend to call any sessions in Farbault until after the holidays.

The financial impact of the strike on the district was unclear. Not paying wages to teachers, aides and cafeteria workers saved over $20,000 per day. If the district met the 175-school-day minimum, whether the state would provide payment for days during a legal strike was unclear. The State Board of Education did pay Minneapolis state aid for strike days five years before, when district attorneys appealed an earlier rejection.[11]

Both sides published statements outlining their rationales in the local paper over the weekend. The board explained that the union's grievance language would allow an outside arbitrator to decide such management issues as curriculum, scheduling or deleting programs. This would in effect allow the teachers to manage the schools. Both sides agreed that the grievance issue and salary were the main stumbling blocks. In an occurrence that would not happen again in any teachers' strike, the paper published the names of teachers crossing the lines, thus holding them up to the scrutiny of the entire community.[12]

In a talk to the Chamber of Commerce, the FEA president explained that teachers felt strongly about the grievance language because since the superintendent started two years ago, he had been setting numerous policies without teacher input.[13] The local state senator, Clarence Purfeerst (DFL) said that it wasn't his responsibility to solve the strike. He suggested that perhaps the legislature should move up the deadlines for collective bargaining.[14]

Teachers contacted the board the day after Christmas requesting a meeting. The board declined, saying they would wait until the next mediation session scheduled for January 2. The board requested an opportunity to explain its position to the Chamber of Commerce.[15] During the meeting, the Chamber president noted that there seemed to be mistrust between teachers and administrators, and called for effective teacher evaluations.[16]

Two days of mediation in early January brought some narrowing of the differences in salary, but no agreement on grievance language. The mediator suspended talks, saying both sides were locked into their positions. No additional sessions were scheduled.[17]

A session was held on January 8th, but produced no results. The vocational school director met with students to discuss VA benefits, which allowed payments for only ten strike days. A number of veterans had families, and would be seriously impacted by a termination of their benefits. Health occupation students could become ineligible to take state board exams, delaying their entry into the job market by six months. Students contacted US senators Mondale and Humphrey to try to get a change in VA regulations.[18]

A fourteen-hour mediation session dealt with only two proposals on the grievance issue. Both were rejected, with the board charging teachers with a lack of sincerity and the union responding that the board was trying to beat down teachers.[19] Teachers held a "buying power project" and spent over $2500.00 at a local grocery store to demonstrate the positive economic impact teacher spending had on the local economy.[20]

Things got more personal when a group of parents picketed the savings and loan where the board chair worked, one parent blaming him for the impasse in negotiations. The board approved mid-year graduation for twenty-eight seniors, and was met with catcalls and jeers during a board meeting when they didn't discuss the strike. Without announcing why, the VA reversed its decision to terminate educational benefits for vocational students.[21]

An elementary school was opened January 19th with administrators, three subs, and two teachers who had been crossing the lines.[22] During a seventeen-hour mediation session that day, significant progress was made when the teachers accepted the district's grievance language if they could get adequate protection in other areas of the contract. Teachers proposed a reprimand policy. A new dispute surfaced, with teachers proposing that they lose only three days, while making up sixteen.[23]

The board modified teachers' proposals on a reprimand policy, school calendar and personal leave. Salary proposals remained apart at 16.3 percent offered by the board and teacher's request of 18.3 percent. Two additional elementary schools opened with subs and an undisclosed number of non-striking teachers. Subs were paid $60.00 per day, rather than the usual $27.00[24] A fourth elementary school opened on Thursday.[25]

The state board of education ruled that teachers must certify that a student has completed course work and is eligible for mid-year graduation.

This halted the board's efforts to allow some students to graduate mid-year. Both sides stepped out of a mediation session to accuse the other of holding students hostage in negotiations. A total of nine subs were being utilized in the four elementary schools that reopened.[26]

An eleven-hour session Friday and sixteen-hour session Saturday produced broad agreement. The board accepted teachers' reprimand language and salary request of 18.33 percent. Teachers proposed extending the school year in June and making up sixteen of the twenty-three lost days. The board offered nine, which wouldn't provide the required minimum 175 school days.[27]

The following Monday, six grades opened in the remaining elementary schools and four vocational classes resumed. Teachers filed an injunction in District Court protesting the use of uncertified substitutes. Teachers voted to accept losing ten to twenty-five days. This was rejected by the board president, who said there was, "no precedent for makeup of strike pay in the private sector and therefore no sound basis for teachers receiving special treatment in this area." He added that teachers "are starting to reap the logical consequences of their actions."[28]

The judge ruled quickly, determining that an administrator had taught a kindergarten class for five days without a kindergarten license. Since he had subsequently been replaced with an appropriately licensed substitute, there were no grounds for a restraining order. Classes reopened at three more schools and one more vocational school class. Nine teachers were crossing the lines.[29]

The director of the vocational school announced plans to open all classes, utilizing instructors certified on an emergency basis. Students receiving veteran's benefits had to return immediately, or they would lose their benefits.[30]

During a mediation session, the board refused to budge from its offer of nine make up-days. The number of teachers crossing the lines had grown to twenty one, and the district had hired subs to open more classes.[31]

The involvement of State Senator Purfeerst broke the stalemate. Citizens had asked him to intervene, and he decided to lead a Sunday morning negotiation session. The board chair felt that this would violate the state's open meeting law, and he arranged the state mediator to hold a session beginning at 1:00 A.M. Sunday morning. By 8:00, an agreement had been reached. Teachers agreed to make up thirteen student days, two of them without pay, losing pay for sixteen days. Schools opened Monday. The district lost eight days of school aid.[32]

News reports didn't indicate the rationale of the increasing number of teachers willing to cross picket lines. Were they motivated by financial concerns? Frustration with a strike that wouldn't end, despite resolution of all contract issues except make up days? Who those teachers were, and why they quit striking isn't clear, but the trend is. Had the strike continued, all the schools would have opened. The strike could have failed, which would have set a significant precedent for future teacher's strikes.

The Faribault strike provided examples of much that could happen during a strike. Aggressive bargaining and a strained relationship with the superintendent poisoned relationships with teachers. Teachers learned the limits of their input in school operations. Board members were surprised when the conflict spilled over into their business lives. Many outsiders were called upon—the governor, state and US senators, a district judge. Ultimately, the strike itself created new obstacles. Vocational students and mid-year graduating students were caught in a bind.

A lack of trust was a major contributor to this strike. Teachers had seen the board and superintendent act in ways that threatened teacher's pay and voice in decision making. The union's effort to develop far-reaching grievance language covering almost all school functioning was the result. What they asked for was beyond anything provided to any teacher's union because it usurped the basic responsibilities of the board. Not surprisingly, the union proposal was a stumbling block to settling.

What was needed was an effort to develop ways for each side to get their needs met. A compromise was eventually found that provided teachers with an acceptable procedure for reprimanding staff while allowing the board to run the district.

Perhaps because they were clinging to a model of private sector strikes, the board stuck to the position that strike days wouldn't be made up. Critics of unions say that teachers put their own needs above that of students when they strike. Prolonging a strike by working to punish teachers—which is what happened in Faribault—is an example of the board putting their priorities above students.

Extending missed days was not only harmful for students, it resulted in additional lost income for the district. The 'win-lose' and 'us against them' scenario that is often a part of strikes can lead to such lose-lose strategies.

Sauk Centre

Talks in Sauk Centre bogged down in January over the issue of work hours. Teachers had been teaching five hours with two hours of prep time. The district wanted to switch to one hour of prep time and one study hall. Teachers were concerned that this would lead to staff reductions, and suggested five and one-third hours of teaching. The board agreed to submit all but work hours to arbitration. While teachers made plans to strike, the district placed ads for substitutes in the local papers.[33]

Schools closed January 6. Six substitutes reported, but were too few to keep the schools open. Subs were paid $44.00 per day, the regular teachers' base pay. No plans were made to open kindergarten or special education classes.[34] MEA President Don Hill walked the picket line, saying, "I am trying to organize teachers to stand up for their rights."

Fourth, fifth and sixth grade classes opened the second day of the strike with subs and two teachers who crossed. One teacher was said to be a member of a religion that prevented her from joining a union, and the other was about to retire and was concerned about his retirement benefits. Extracurricular activities were cancelled. Picketers spent only forty-five minutes on the picket lines in the twenty-five below zero cold, alternating with forty-five minutes of warming up. The paper published primarily negative comments about teachers from parents and community members.[35]

The MEA got directly involved in the strike when it filed a restraining order over the issues of using unlicensed subs and not providing the names of subs.[36] A district court judge quickly ruled that the list of subs must be provided.[37] The school board refused to comply, citing concerns about subs being harassed and intimidated. The issue was scheduled to be heard in court in five days. A thirteen-hour mediation session over the weekend produced no movement and no more sessions were scheduled. A board negotiator said that missed days would not be made up and any state aid lost would be deducted from the teacher's settlement. Seventh grade classes opened.[38]

A week into the strike, a special education class opened.[39] An informal contact between a board and union negotiator progressed to a full negotiation session. A compromise was reached, calling for teachers to give up a prep hour for half of each school year. The agreement was ratified the same day by the board and union. The strike lasted seven days with no mention of make-up days.[40]

MINNETONKA

UNLIKE THE SAUK CENTRE STRIKE which was only about language, the Minnetonka strike was all about money. Teachers complained in mid-August about the slow pace of negotiations. The lack of a proposed school calendar hampered them from following the negotiation outline suggested by the legislature. Teachers proposed a cost of living adjustment every six months but the board hadn't offered a proposed settlement package.[41]

The Minnetonka Teachers Association (MTA) voted to employ "work to contract," a seldom-used tactic calling for teachers to complete only those tasks that fit within official work hours. They said they wanted to inform the public about how many extra hours teachers put in to complete tasks. The union president conceded that the district faced tight money conditions.[42]

In early November, the union requested arbitration over issues of salary, the calendar year and association days. The union asked 10.5 percent the first year and a cost of living raise the second. The board offered 5.5 percent and four percent.[43] The board rejected arbitration and the union responded by threatening to strike. The board reacted by developing plans to keep the schools open during a strike with subs.[44]

A tentative agreement was reached. The executive board of the MTA accepted it, but it was rejected by the general membership.[45] An audit report in late December utilizing a new procedure indicated that the district had a larger than expected budget surplus. The board stated, however, that it was anticipating expenditures to exceed revenue in the second year of the contract. Teachers felt there was enough money for raises and improved programs. The board wanted to reduce expenditures to avoid deficit spending.[46]

In January, the union threatened to strike. During a negotiating session, the superintendent agreed to lift a ban on teachers distributing negotiation literature on campus.[47] Although details of this issue weren't reported, it would have been unusual for teachers to be distributing union literature to students. If they were sending it only to other teachers, the administration chose to directly interfere in union functioning.

A mediation session failed and teachers voted to strike. Teachers asked for 16.9 percent, the board offered 15.9 percent. The district announced plans to keep the schools open, paying subs $43.00 a day instead of the usual $27.50. Teachers published a statement suggesting that parents keep their children home for their 'health and safety'.[48]

A session lasting until 1:30 A.M. failed to produce an agreement, and teachers struck on Thursday January 22nd. The superintendent decided to keep schools closed because there weren't enough subs to open all the schools at any given level. Parents reacted to the teacher's published statement about student's health and safety, fearing that crossing the picket lines would endanger their children. The board refused to offer more money because it would result in program cuts.[49]

Union negotiators accepted an offer by the board during a Saturday session, only to see the membership reject it on Sunday.[50] In an unusual move, negotiations then continued on Sunday between the board chair and a teacher who had not been part of the negotiating team. Instead, he was the leader of the union's 'settlement task force'. An agreement was reached by 4:30 A.M. and was accepted by teachers two hours later. Classes began two hours late that morning. One of the two days lost was made up.

Balancing a slight gain in salary against a lost day's pay and caps on the number of credits earned each year, teachers calculated that they gained $9,000 (that's the total divided between 387 teachers) over the offer rejected on Sunday. Teachers felt the strike was worthwhile because their higher salaries put them in a better position for future negotiations.[51]

The local paper published an open letter from the superintendent praising teachers' efforts in classrooms and calling for words of encouragement.[52] All in all, this was a brief, civil strike marked by some posturing by the board prior to the deadline.

An unusual feature was the insertion of a new person into the negotiations, which appeared to contribute to a settlement. The strike was also unique because the negotiating team reached agreement, only to see the general membership reject it—twice. In a number of other strikes, the union negotiating team agreed to bring a proposal to the membership for a vote—without the endorsement of the negotiators. It was unheard of for the rank and file to repudiate the efforts of their own negotiators, necessitating the involvement of another member of the union.

---

1. *Faribault Daily News*, November 11 1975, p. 1.
2. *Faribault Daily News*, November 26 1975, p. 1.
3. *Faribault Daily News*, December 2 1975, p. 1.
4. *Faribault Daily News*, December 2 1975, pp. 1, 10.
5. *Faribault Daily News*, December 11 1975, pp. 1, 14.
6. *Faribault Daily News*, December 11 1975, p. 1.
7. *Faribault Daily News*, December 15 1975, p. 1.
8. *Faribault Daily News*, December 16 1975, p. 1.
9. *Faribault Daily News*, December 17 1975, p. 1.
10. *Faribault Daily News*, December 18 1975, pp. 1, 18.
11. *Faribault Daily News*, December 19 1975, pp. 1, 10.
12. *Faribault Daily News*, December 20 1975, pp. 1, 2.
13. *Faribault Daily News*, December 23 1975, p. 1.
14. *Faribault Daily News*, December 24 1975, p. 1.
15. *Faribault Daily News*, December 26 1975, p. 1.
16. *Faribault Daily News*, December 30 1975, pp. 1, 8.
17. *Faribault Daily News*, January 5, 1976, p. 1.
18. *Faribault Daily News*, January 12, 1976, p. 1.
19. *Faribault Daily News*, January 15, 1976, p. 1.
20. *Faribault Daily News*, January 16, 1976, p. 1.
21. *Faribault Daily News*, January 18, 1976, p. 1.
22. *Faribault Daily News*, January 19, 1976, p. 1.

23. *Faribault Daily News,* January 20, 1976, pp. 1, 10.
24. *Faribault Daily News,* January 21, 1976, p. 1.
25. *Faribault Daily News,* January 22, 1976, p. 1.
26. *Faribault Daily News,* January 23, 1976, p. 1.
27. *Faribault Daily News,* January 26, 1976, pp. 1, 10.
28. *Faribault Daily News,* January 27, 1976, pp. 1, 8.
29. *Faribault Daily News,* January 28, 1976, pp. 1, 12.
30. *Faribault Daily News,* January 29, 1976, pp. 1, 14.
31. *Faribault Daily News,* January 30, 1976, pp. 1, 12.
32. *Faribault Daily News,* February 2, 1976, pp. 1, 10.
33. *Faribault Daily News,* January 5, 1976, p. 1.
34. *St Cloud Daily Times,* January 6, 1976, pp. 1, 2.
35. *St Cloud Daily Times,* January 7, 1976, pp. 1, 2.
36. *St Cloud Daily Times,* January 8, 1976, p. 1.
37. *St Cloud Daily Times,* January 10, 1976, p. 1.
38. *St Cloud Daily Times,* January 12, 1976, p. 1.
39. *St Cloud Daily Times,* January 13, 1976, p. 1.
40. *St Cloud Daily Times,* January 15, 1976, pp. 1. 2.
41. *The Maverick,* August 13, 1975, p. 1.
42. *The Maverick,* October 15, 1975, p. 1, 12.
43. *The Maverick,* November 5, 1975, p. 1, 8.
44. *The Maverick,* November 19, 1975, p. 1, 9.
45. *The Maverick,* August 26, 1975, p. 1.
46. *The Maverick,* December 24, 1975, p. 1, 7.
47. *The Maverick,* January 14, 1976, p. 1, 6.
48. *The Maverick,* January 21, 1976, p. 1, 7.
49. *Minneapolis Tribune,* January 23, 1976, pp. 1A, 4A.
50. *Minneapolis Tribune,* January 26, 1976, p. 5A.
51. *Minneapolis Tribune,* January 27, 1976, pp. 1B, 2B.
52. *The Maverick,* February 11, 1976, p. 1.

Chapter Fourteen
The Late 1970s

The next round of negotiations brought another spate of strikes, scattered across the two years of the 1977 through 1979 contract period.

Lake Benton

First up was Lake Benton, a small district with big relationship problems between the Board/administration versus the staff. The district faced serious financial difficulties because of declining enrollment and the School Board increased the tax levy by 13.8 percent.

In mid-October, teachers requested arbitration. Unresolved issues included leave, the school calendar, retroactivity and salary. The board offered twelve percent while teachers asked for sixteen percent.[1]

The board rejected arbitration, not wanting an outsider to determine how District money was spent and concerned about the cost and length of the arbitration process. Teachers dropped their request to fourteen percent, then voted unanimously to strike the next week, November 16.[2]

At a session the Monday before the strike, the union decreased its demands, offering to give up language requests. The two sides were a total of $5,435 over two years. That's not the amount per teacher, but the difference in total cost of each package. Despite this tiny difference, the strike proceeded on Wednesday, November 16th.

Schools opened that day, staffed with subs and two teachers who crossed the picket lines. Subs were paid $55.00 per day, rather than the usual $25.00. This represented more than the daily pay of beginning teachers, and was defended by the board as the recommendation of the Minnesota School Board Association. MEA President Don Hill walked the picket lines. In a letter to parents, the union said it was, "asking to be treated as humans."[3]

An informal session was conducted with the union's chief negotiator and one board member. Described as the first sincere and unified effort to work together for a compromise, it resulted in a salary offer acceptable to the board. Teachers rejected it, however, because it didn't include any make-up days or a clause calling for non-reprisal against teachers or their children.

The sheriff issued warnings against verbal harassment of subs and teachers crossing the lines. All subs were said to be certified, or have applied for certification. A district court judge issued a temporary injunction against the board. He ruled that denial of retroactive pay couldn't be an issue in negotiations; subs couldn't be paid more than beginning teachers, subs couldn't discuss negotiations with their students, and any abuse of children of striking teacher must cease.[4] The judge in this case was very sympathetic to the union's issues. What prompted concerns about non-reprisal isn't clear, but feelings must have run high when the well-being of teachers' children was in question.

A subsequent court hearing resulted in a different outcome. The union had requested a restraining order prohibiting the district from hiring uncertified subs. That was denied, the judge ruling that the law allowed districts to operate as they see fit. He also ordered that harassment of non-striking teachers be stopped, and reversed his earlier decision, saying subs could be paid $55.00 per day.[5]

A mediation session resulted in no movement. The board saw no reason to grant make-up days because school was in session, and refused to place a non-reprisal clause in the contract because it could then be grieved. They believed that issue was adequately covered by laws defining unfair labor practices.[6]

The board offered additional money, tied to a requirement that the union drop all lawsuits. The local was unable to accept the offer, having no control over the parent MEA organization.[7]

After twelve lost school days, the strike was settled. The board agreed to an increase of $41,386. The agreement didn't include any make-up days or a non-reprisal clause. The local union agreed to drop all lawsuits, but the MEA stated it would continue its lawsuit over hiring unlicensed subs. An editorial in the local paper cited poor communication between teacher and board negotiators, and quoted teachers as saying they went on strike because they were tired of being pushed around by a power-hungry board and a deaf administration.[8]

Board members believed the strike occurred because of MEA involvement. Acknowledging that there might have been some hard feelings once in a while, a board member felt that they weren't serious enough to result in a strike. Reflecting on the aftermath, another board member said, "It leaves a scar in the community. It takes years to get the feelings out. Hopefully we can get back to normal, but we all know it will take a while."[9]

There was no intractable language issue, and only a miniscule amount of money separated the two sides just prior to the strike. It's clear the district put a great deal of effort in the days leading up to the strike in keeping the schools open. This is the only instance where schools opened with subs the first day of the strike. Teachers' comments that it was only during the second week of the strike that meaningful negotiations began, and their frequently expressed frustration with how they were treated makes this appear to be a case of poor relationships resulting in a strike.

LAKEFIELD

LAKEFIELD PRESENTED QUITE a different picture. Teachers voted to strike after the board refused arbitration. Lakefield was in statutory operating debt. The board at first offered no raise, but agreed to an additional $100.00 per teacher the first year. Teachers asked $200.00 for a total cost difference of $4,000.[10] School closed November 30 and students were sent home at 9:00 A.M. The superintendent talked of hiring subs from out of state, citing the court case in Lake Benton, and of opening schools later in the week.[11]

A mediation session lasted only two hours before being called off, with both sides hardening their positions. Additional subs were hired, but not enough to open schools.[12]

Then Santa Clause showed up. An anonymous gift of $4,200.00 was received by the teachers' union, covering the difference between the two sides. The teachers voted to accept the board's offer, and the strike was over after two days.[13]

This was a unique settlement solution, made possible by the small total separating the two sides. The influence of one strike on another can be seen in the Lakefield superintendent's plan to hire unlicensed subs, based on the recent court ruling in Lake Benton. The motivation behind the MEA plan to pursue that lawsuit even after Lake Benton settled is also clear.

BUHL

TEACHERS IN A SMALL TOWN on Minnesota's Iron Range were the next to go out. All thirty-four teachers struck on Monday, April 3. Students had reported for school that morning, but were soon sent home. Extracurricular activities were cancelled, and no negotiation sessions were planned.

The board's final offer was an $1,800.00 average increase over two years.[14] Apparently thinking of a long strike, the district asked whether students could be promoted on the basis of their schooling thus far in the year. The State Commissioner of Education informed them that teachers had to give grades before they could be promoted or graduate.[15]

A mediation session settled the strike after three weeks, providing an average of $2,100.00 per teacher and twelve make up days.[16] The board approved the contract on a split vote, with the minority publishing a letter saying the majority sold district residents down the river. They were most angered because teachers were able to make up all but three days. In part, they blamed the mediator who they said would settle strikes by any means he could.[17] A spokesperson for the majority of the board countered, lambasting the two complaining members who they said contributed little to finding a solution.[18]

DISTRICT 916

SIX NORTH-METRO DISTRICTS had combined vocational and special education services into a special school district called District 916, employing 200 teachers. A merit plan had been in place for six years, providing thirty-seven percent of salaries, an average of $2406.00 per person.[19] Teachers objected to how the merit plan was being implemented, citing differences between departments.[20] Questions were also raised about how well it worked with special education staff.[21]

Teachers said a compromise on the merit pay system was the major stumbling block that lead to an impasse. The board offered a 15.1 percent raise.[22] The superintendent met with vocational students, telling them that school would remain open if possible. If they did not attend for fifteen days, state law required that they be dropped from enrollment. He acknowledged that some students were members of unions, and wouldn't be allowed to cross picket lines.[23]

The strike began May 3rd, latest in the school year of any Minnesota strike. The superintendent expressed concern about the scholarship status of many vocational students.[24] One special education school remained open with administrators and four teachers who crossed the lines. Another special education building remained closed. Parents of special education students sided with teachers, saying it was difficult to find teachers willing to work in special education.[25]

Both sides agreed in court to a limit of eighteen pickets at each site after two incidents of teachers being struck by cars in the first seven days on the strike, in one instance by the district's personnel director. Ten out of fifty vocational programs were open, using administrators and two teachers who crossed the lines. The superintendent said that no negotiating sessions were scheduled because the district was waiting to hear the teachers' response to their latest offer.[26]

Vocational students rallied at the state capital. Governor Rudy Perpich refused to get involved, calling it a local matter. His staff was investigating a tuition waiver and sought an opinion from the attorney general on whether students could retain their scholarship and grant money during the strike. The president of the student union said that students had already lost over $25,000.00 in the first week of the strike.[27]

A mediation session was held eight days into the strike, the first since it began. The teachers' new proposed pay plan and fringe benefit changes were rejected. Instead, the board voted to lay off forty-one teachers and aides. Teachers were upset, claiming the timing of the announcement was linked to the strike.[28] The superintendent defended the layoffs, saying they were necessary because a number of special education students had returned to their home districts because of the strike. Teachers responded by increasing their salary demands and pushing to drop merit pay entirely.[29]

Layoff announcements during other strikes led to settlements. Here, they triggered a response from teachers that set negotiations back.

At a board meeting two weeks into the strike, many parents of special education students were very critical about the lack of services their children were receiving. Daily negotiation sessions were held, with few results.[30]

The following weekend, negotiations began in earnest.[31] A compromise on merit pay was reached, reducing it to twenty-five percent of the salary and introducing the use of objective criteria and evaluation of teachers by central administrators, not immediate supervisors. Average raises were set at $2,300.[32]

The strike was over after thirteen days. None of the days were made up.

Settlement pay was reported in a manner that was unclear. Prior to the strike, the district was offering an average raise of $2,406. Teachers settled for a minimum salary increase of $2,300. While the exact figures of the settlement can't be discerned from newspaper accounts, when the thirteen days' pay was subtracted, teachers clearly lost money. Teacher's frustrations with a merit pay system that determined a substantial percentage of their pay, without adequate criteria and subject to the whim of immediate supervisors, made the strike worthwhile.

BURNSVILLE

NEGOTIATORS IN THE BURNSVILLE district continued to struggle through the summer. Despite talking for over a year, disagreements remained on fifty issues—more than in any other strike. Teachers earlier had asked for binding arbitration, but were refused by the mediator. On August 17, the mediator certified that an impasse existed on thirty-three items, and the teachers requested arbitration. The board agreed to submit only the economic issues, saying the language issues 'covered a vast area of management rights'.

Issues listed in the paper include many that are in large district contracts today, including transfer language, lane changes, posting of vacancies, calendar, and transfers. Workloads (class size) was the only identified issue that many districts continue to maintain is exclusively a management right.[33]

Teachers voted September 5th to strike, but didn't set a date.[34] On September 17th, they voted to strike two days later. Financial discussions between the two sides were marked by large differences in understandings. Teachers were asking for a twenty-two percent raise and the board offered 15.2 percent. Teachers claimed the board offer amounted to only 9.25 percent.[35] The two sides were $1.3 million apart, and the teachers said the district could fund the difference through its four-million-dollar reserve. The board said that no strike days would be made up.[36]

The strike began September 19th, with no negotiations scheduled. Teachers said they were seeking parity with other conference districts. The board claimed that teachers' requests would result in deficit spending—something the union says the district could afford because of its large reserve.[37]

A seventeen-hour mediation session the first weekend of the strike was unsuccessful. The two sides couldn't even agree on how much disagreement remained, with the teachers saying significant progress had been made, and the board replying that only minor language issues had been discussed. The board chair blamed the impasse on teachers 'continuing irresponsible and excessive demands' and said an early end to the strike was unlikely 'in view of the teachers' rigid and unbending posture.'[38]

The board defended lower salaries in Burnsville, citing the more senior staff in surrounding districts. It also claimed the surplus wasn't what is seemed, with $1.5 million tied up in accounts payable, inventory, and delinquent taxes. Teachers wanted a settlement comparable in average dollars to surrounding districts, even though it represented a higher percentage than those districts had settled for.[39]

By the beginning of October—with the strike nine days old—parents got involved, holding rallies and marches demanding a quick settlement.[40] Disagreement continued after a settlement was reached on October 5th, with the district saying teachers got a sixteen-percent raise, teachers saying it was fourteen percent. The difference occurred because the district used increases in payments for insurance when computing the higher figure. Teachers were scheduled to make up six of the fourteen school days lost to the strike.[41]

Despite the difficulties in transferring between districts, 126 students left the district during the strike, forty-eight of them to non-public schools.[42] Non-public schools in small towns often refused to accept public school students during a strike, or only if parents agreed to a long-term placement. No such understanding existed in this suburban district.

Albany

THE NEXT CONTRACT CYCLE brought only two strikes. The Albany school district was a tinderbox of labor unrest waiting for a spark. Seven wage-related grievances had gone to arbitration in recent years, three of them involving former union presidents. The district won one of them. Teachers filed a lawsuit charging board members and administration of harassing union officials, but dropped it when it interfered with negotiations.[43]

The district sought to begin a merit pay system, offering six percent each year and $22,000.00 in merit pay. Teachers asked for fifteen percent the first year and ten percent the second, and rejected a merit pay system, saying they knew of no other district in the state with such a system. The mediator certified an impasse, and in mid-October, teachers requested arbitration.[44]

It's worth noting that the Albany teachers—and apparently the administration and school board—weren't aware of the merit pay system in District 916. While that district was an unusual amalgamation of vocational and special education programs, its merit pay system had been at the heart of a strike just the previous spring.

The board dropped the merit pay system when an impasse was declared. The two sides remained far apart on salaries, with the board offering sixteen percent over two years. Teachers said they were requesting 19.3 percent, but the board said that figure was really twenty-two percent. The strike began November 12th. The superintendent said all schools would be closed during the strike and no negotiation sessions were scheduled. Residents' feelings about the strike split along age lines with younger people being more sympathetic to the teachers, and one older man saying teachers should be run out of town.[45]

During a session held the fourth day of the strike, the two sides agreed on how to compute salary costs. The biggest disagreement continued to be how to distribute the additional money. The district proposed creating two additional steps, providing raises to the most senior teachers.[46] That proposal was dropped during the second week of the strike.[47] Three days of negotiations resulted in a proposal offering 17.78 percent over two years that satisfied both negotiating teams. Teachers voted to reject the proposed contract because it didn't provide for any make-up days. A board spokesman responded, "Lost wages are part of the risks of a strike. We (the board) didn't go out on strike. The calendar is set. We're not going to change our minds."[48]

After picketing for another week, teachers met and accepted the same agreement they'd earlier rejected. While it didn't include any make-up days, teachers said they had unofficial, verbal agreements with some board members about making-up days. Students were out of school for thirteen days.[49]

Rather than resolving issues, the settlement created a long-running conflict. The board didn't grant any make up days. Teachers took the issue to district court, saying board members had agreed to some make up days. The court ruled that the contract had not been violated, but an arbitrator should decide the issue. The Minnesota Supreme Court agreed with the lower court decision.

An arbitrator ruled that teachers should have been paid for the 180 days specified in the contract, and had been paid for only 167. Thus, they were entitled to be paid for all thirteen strike days.[50] The arbitrator's decision changed what had been a poor move on the teachers' part—staying out an extra week over the issue of no days being made up—into a victory. This, along with the 1970 Minneapolis strike, are the only examples of Minnesota teachers being paid for picketing.

Labor/management relationships within this small town's schools continued to be bitter. The union filed many grievances in the two years following the strike, with district legal fees exceeding $65,000. The union president described the situation as a "personal fight between teachers and school board members."

A former board member said that the current superintendent had been hired to break the union, something he denied.[51] The superintendent was described by teachers as authoritarian, favoring teachers who always agreed with him, and having limited interpersonal skills. It was reported that the board attempted to buy out his contract in an effort to entice him to leave.

In the midst of all the other unrest, negotiations were hindered by the lack of agreement on how to compute costs. It shouldn't take four days of a strike to settle on an accounting method.

The relationship between the two unions in Albany was uneasy. With a majority of teachers, the Albany Federation of Teachers led the strike. Eighteen months after the strike, the Albany Education Association called for elections to see whether teachers would choose them as the primary representative. AEA members said that the AFT's "hard line approach" had outlived its usefulness. The AFT won decisively.[52]

This alignment reflects the original positions of the two unions—with the AFT being more militant. All but the Albany strikes occurring after the PELRA law went into effect were led by Minnesota Education Association locals, and this trend would continue. Albany teachers were thus an anomaly, without realizing it.

Audubon

Midway through the school year, all but a work load issue had been settled in Audubon. The previous contract had specified a five-period teaching load for high school teachers with an additional $400.00 for teaching an extra class. The board wanted that increased to six hours without any additional pay, and rejected arbitration.[53]

A negotiation session the day before the strike brought a compromise. The board agreed to keep current language, but would pay the extra only if an audit showed the district would not be deficit spending. Teachers voted to reject the offer.

Bad Blood and Economics

It was reported that a car tried to hit teachers during a pre-strike bannering rally, so police were on hand during April 2nd, the first day of the strike. Nonetheless, a city fire truck that was washing the street hosed down a group of teachers, and were warned that if the incident was repeated, those on the truck would be arrested.[54]

The board sent a letter to parents stating the MEA persuaded teachers not to accept its offer. Teachers responded that the union only provided financial consultation. The elementary school opened the fourth day of the strike, with all twenty-eight regular teachers on the picket lines. The district announced plans to open the junior and senior high by the end of the week.[55]

The strike ended after five school days, the board saying it had capitulated because some students had picketed with teachers, and substitutes were being harassed. No make-up days were planned. The superintendent called for reconciliation, saying a war had been fought, and now the hardest part would be to make the peace.[56]

---

1. *Lincoln County Valley Journal*, October 19, 1977, pp. 1, 3.
2. *Lincoln County Valley Journal*, November 9, 1977, pp. 1, 3.
3. *Lincoln County Valley Journal*, November 16, 1977, pp. 1, 2.
4. *Lincoln County Valley Journal*, November 23, 1977, pp. 1, 2, 3.
5. *Lincoln County Valley Journal*, November 29, 1977, pp. 1.
6. *Lincoln County Valley Journal*, November 30, 1977, pp. 1, 2.
7. *Lincoln County Valley Journal*, December 5, 1977, p. 1.
8. *Lincoln County Valley Journal*, December 7, 1977, pp. 1, 3, 4.
9. *Lincoln County Valley Journal*, December 9, 1977, pp. 1, 3.
10. *Worthington Daily Globe*, November 29, 1977, pp. 1, 3.
11. *Worthington Daily Globe*, November 30, 1977, pp. 1, 3.
12. *Worthington Daily Globe*, December 1, 1977, p. 1.
13. *Worthington Daily Globe*, December 2, 1977, p. 1.
14. *The Tribune-Press*, April 4, 1978, p. 1.
15. *The Tribune-Press*, April 11, 1978, p. 1.
16. *The Tribune-Press*, April 25, 1978, p. 1.
17. *The Tribune-Press*, May 2, 1978, pp. 1, 16.
18. *The Tribune-Press*, May 9, 1978, p. 11.

19. *Pioneer-Press-Dispatch*, May 23, 1978, p. 1.
20. *White Bear Press*, April 27, 1978, p. 1.
21. *Pioneer-Press-Dispatch*, May 9, 1978, p. 11.
22. *White Bear Press*, April 27, 1978, p. 1.
23. *White Bear Press*, May 4, 1978, p. 2.
24. *Pioneer-Press-Dispatch*, May 6, 1978, p. 3.
25. *Pioneer-Press-Dispatch*, May 9, p. 11.
26. *White Bear Press*, May 11, 1978, p. 6.
27 *Pioneer-Press-Dispatch*, May 11, 1978, p. 17.
28. *Pioneer-Press-Dispatch*, May 12, 1978, p. 2.
29. *White Bear Press*, May 18, 1978, p. 1.
30. *Pioneer-Press-Dispatch*, May 18, 1978, p. 2.
31. *White Bear Press*, May 25, 1978, p. 1.
32. *Pioneer-Press-Dispatch*, May 23, 1978, p. 1.
33. *The Sun, Burnsville*, August 23, 1978, p. 1.
34. *The Sun, Burnsville*, September 13, 1978, p. 1.
35. *Minneapolis Tribune*, September 18, 1978, p. 1.
36. *Minneapolis Tribune*, September 19, 1978, p. 1B.
37. *The Sun, Burnsville,* September 20, 1978, p. 1.
38. *Minneapolis Tribune*, September 25, 1978, p. 1B.
39. *Minneapolis Tribune*, September 28, 1978, p. 1, 4A.
40. *The Sun, Burnsville*, October 4, 1978, p. 1.
41. *Minneapolis Tribune*, October 6, 1978, p. 1,10A.
42. *The Sun,* Burnsville, October 25, 1978, p. 1.
43. *St. Cloud Daily Times*, November 12, 1979, p. 10.
44. *St. Cloud Daily Times*, October 18, 1979, p. 1.
45. *St. Cloud Daily Times*, November 12, 1979, pp. 1, 10.
46. *St. Cloud Daily Times*, November 24, 1979, p. 1.
47. *St. Cloud Daily Times*, November 26, 1979, p. 1.
48. *St. Cloud Daily Times*, November 27, 1979, pp. 1, 8.
49. *St. Cloud Daily Times*, December 3, 1979, p. 1.
50. *St. Cloud Daily Times*, October 24, 1981, p. 1.
51. *St. Cloud Daily Times*, September 9, 1981, p. 1.
52. *St. Cloud Daily Times*, September 10, 1981, p. 1.
53. *Detroit Lakes Tribune*, February 28, 1980, p. 6.
54. *Detroit Lakes Tribune*, April 3, 1980, p. 1, 3.
55. *Detroit Lakes Tribune*, April 10, 1980, p. 1, 4.
56. *Detroit Lakes Tribune*, April 17, 1980, pp. 1, 12.

Chapter Fifteen
Factors Contributing to the Strikes of 1981

Thirty five teachers' strikes occurred in Minnesota in 1981. A convergence of union activity, economics and changes in the law created conditions encouraging strikes. Prior to having a right to strike, districts could dictate terms including salaries, length of the work day, number of work days, insurance, grievance procedures, leaves and severance pay. There was little teachers could do. About their only choice was to change districts or professions.

The right to strike dramatically changed the power balance between school boards and unions. Like two neophytes at their first dance lesson, both sides had to learn new moves during negotiations. Some districts clung to the old ways with tactics such as denying retroactive pay or demanding longer work days, extra work for no pay and the right to assign extracurricular duties. In some cases, these positions were held by school boards well after strikes began. They were rarely successful.

Districts varied widely in the tone of negotiations. Some sought to maintain harmony, with both sides speaking of goodwill throughout negotiations and even after strikes began. Other school boards threw down the gauntlet from the beginning of strike talk, saying there would be no days made up and subs would be hired.

Power shifted in economic terms as well. Districts had been able to largely control the balance between paying staff more versus providing more programs. Market forces required districts to pay enough to attract and retain staff, but if a school board was comfortable with the salaries it was offering—even if they were low—teachers were faced with the choice of "take it or leave."

The economic condition of districts ranged from being flush with reserve funds to some that were significantly in debt. Interest rates were high. Some districts were able to fund programs just with the interest received from investing their reserve and were loath to give that up by spending reserves. A number of districts passed levy over-rides to stave off budget cuts, and didn't want to see those increases only go into teacher's pockets.

Union locals didn't always seem to realize what their new found power could do. Massive—and predicted—layoffs and tax increases followed some strikes. It could be argued that these occurred in places where districts had held wages down in favor of hiring more teachers. Higher wages garnered from a strike resulted in layoffs of twenty-two percent of the staff in Sauk Centre.[1] That must have been sobering both to teachers and the community.

The union's success in achieving wage increases varied as well. Some came out after striking much better than others. Calculating $100 a day in lost wages for strike days not made up, some teachers lost money over the course of the two year contract.

Lessons were certainly learned. News accounts of preparations in 1981 sometimes made it seem that strikes were simply a part of the normal negotiations process. They often turned out to be painful and traumatic and only one of the districts that struck in 1981 ever did so again.

Changes in the Law

The first PELRA law of 1971 had guaranteed the right to union representation and required that districts negotiate with unions. This resulted in uniformity within districts. Grievance procedures, leaves, fringe benefits and salaries were written into contracts and applied to all teachers. Teachers no longer had to go in individually to talk with their principal to find out what they would be paid the next year.

Changes to PELRA law in 1973 allowed strikes for the first time, but only in cases where the teachers agreed to binding arbitration, but the employer refused.

The Minnesota legislature significantly changed the PELRA law in 1980, making it much easier for teachers to strike. An opening clause permitted strikes when a collective bargaining agreement had expired. Written notification at least ten days prior to the strike was required. Because it played such a large part in the timing of events, a copy of part of the law is included below.

Subd. 1a. STRIKES AUTHORIZED: TEACHERS. Except as otherwise provided by section 31, teachers employed by a local school district, other than principals and assistant principals, may strike only under the following circumstances:

(1)(a) The collective bargaining agreement between their exclusive representative and their employer has expired or, if there is no agreement, impasse under section 31 has occurred; and

(b) The exclusive representative and the employer have participated in mediation over a period of at least 60 days, 30 days of which have occurred after the expiration date of the collective bargaining agreement… and

(c) Written notification of intent to strike was served on the employer… .and

(d) A request for binding arbitration has been rejected… [2]

Language in current law similar to the first part of section (1)(a) is interpreted as meaning that notification can be sent to a District any time after a contract has expired. In 1981, a few locals and school boards misunderstood the new law so thoroughly that they felt obliged to begin planning for a strike if a settlement hadn't been reached by June 1st.

Teachers' contracts across the state expired on July 30. The MEA filed over 370 requests for mediation on July 1, 1981—the earliest day possible under the new rules—beginning the strike timelines.[3] The state mediation bureau must have been completely swamped.

This left a thirty-day period after the contracts expired, followed by a forty-five-day "cooling off" period that was part of the mediation process. The first day locals could file an intent to strike was September 15th.[4] One hundred ninety-one did.

One provision of PELRA that significantly changed negotiations gave districts permission to hold closed door meetings to discuss negotiations.

Operating under the old open meeting law, some districts passed negotiation strategy on to board members one at a time. Now, information could be shared and discussed as a group, keeping board members better informed.[5]

Union Strategy

Don Hill, the MEA president, said the teachers' union was seeking to toughen bargaining positions by filing intent to strike notices, with the goal of getting entry-level salaries up to $16,000 plus full medical benefits in all districts.[6] He acknowledge that some districts didn't have the money but said close to 100 districts could afford it but weren't paying. He identified those as potential strike sites. A spokesman for the Minnesota School Boards Association didn't think there would be many strikes.[7]

There was a stark difference between the strategies of the two teachers' unions in Minnesota. The Minnesota Federation of Teachers, which had traditionally been more militant, didn't send out any early strike notifications in 1981 and boasted of quietly settling large raises for senior teachers. One of MEA's criticisms of MFT's strategy was that districts wouldn't put all their money on the table until threatened with a strike.[8]

In its early years, the Minnesota Education Association had avoided calling itself a union and opposed collective bargaining. During the six years Don Hill had been president of the MEA, he traveled the state urging teachers to fight for better working conditions. He readily admitted to orchestrating the mass filing of 200 intent to strike notices on the first day possible.[9]

In mid-October, Don Hill announced that he was a candidate for president of the National Education Association. Some editorials claimed that he was using the strikes to help his campaign.[10] He did little to campaign however, using his candidacy as a platform to speak at the NEA level about the value of strikes as a bargaining tool.[11]

In an ironic side note, employees of the Minnesota Education Association avoided a strike by voting for binding arbitration. They had struck two years ago, but a strike in 1981 would have crippled the MEA's efforts to support locals during a critical time.[12]

At the beginning of the MEA convention on October 15th, twenty districts were on strike. Striking teachers who attended the convention were seated in a place of honor.[13]

Economics

INFLATION WAS LOW DURING THE 1960s, rising from 1.7 percent in 1960 to 5.5 percent in 1969.

It heated up in the 1970s, hitting eleven percent in 1974 and 1979. In 1980, it reached 13.5 percent.[14] Since teacher's contracts were for two years, keeping up required settlements in the mid-twenty-percent range.

Differences in wages between districts fueled teacher dissatisfaction. The disparity between metropolitan and rural wages was $8,000. This may not seem that great, but the top salary for a teacher in Fairmont with a master's degree was $20,970.00 compared to St. Paul's $29,200.00.[15] Looked at from Fairmont's perspective, a forty-percent discrepancy could be enough grounds for a strike.

The lack of a consistent mutually accepted manner of calculating proposed settlements hampered negotiations. Disagreements included what costs should be included—insurance increases, extracurricular pay, subs needed to cover for leave days, severance pay.

Compounding these disputes were different understandings of district surpluses. Teachers tended to look at the total amount, and felt that it could all be applied to reaching a settlement. Boards typically sharply reduced the amount available, citing the many restrictions represented in the total. Many boards were reluctant as well to engage in deficit spending.

State funding is always a crucial factor in determining future school funding. A two-year contract forces districts to factor in what changes are in state funding are likely to occur during the second year. On November 6, 1981 the governor called for a special session to begin December 6th to deal with a budget shortfall of over $700 Million. He said there would be no 'sacred cows' when considering spending cuts and announced that December payments to school would be postponed.[16]

In the ten days following the governor's announcement, six teachers strikes were settled—none of them providing economic benefit to teachers. When losses for unpaid days are included, teachers generally received additional monies during strikes settled prior to the announcement, and didn't afterwards.[17] Only five strikes began after the governor's announcement.

Both sides prepared for negotiations. The Minnesota School Boards Association provided a pamphlet titled, "Tricks Labor Plays on Management." It advised that unions would attempt to organize parents to lobby for their side.[18] The Minnesota Education Association provided a contract negotiation manual titled 'Settlement Task Force General Management.'[19]

The strikes are presented here in chronological order. Some strikes affected others, and a group of 'scabstitutes' emerged that traveled from district to district as strikes began and were settled. Some strikes were brief and almost friendly. Others include the longest teachers' strike in Minnesota history, and bitterly divided communities.

---

1. *Sauk Centre Herald*, December 17, 1981, p. 2.
2. Minnesota Revisor of Statutes, *Laws of Minnesota for 1980*, Ch 617, p. 1591.
3. *Mesabi Sunday News*, September 13, 1981, p. 9.
4. *St. Cloud Daily Times*, September 14, 1981, p. 1.
5. *Anoka County Union*, October 23, 1981, p. 20.
6. *Mesabi Daily News*, September 15, 1981, p. 2.
7. *Mesabi Sunday News*, September 13, 1981, p. 9.
8. *Mesabi Daily News*, September 15, 1981, p. 2.
9. *Brainerd Daily Dispatch*, Sunday October 11, 1981, p. 9.
10. *Anoka County Union*, October 16, 1981, p. 2.
11. Interview with Don Hill, Spring 2011.
12. *St. Cloud Daily Times*, September 14, 1981, p. 6.
13. *Mille Lacs Messenger*, October 21, 1981, p. 7.
14. American Federation of Teachers, Survey and Analysis of Teacher Salary Trends 2007, p. 10.
15. *Mesabi Sunday News*, September 13, 1981, p. 9.
16. *Winona Daily News*, November 6, 1981, p. 1.
17. Ley Robert; Wines, William; "The Economics of Teachers' Strikes in Minnesota in 1981," *Economics of Education Review* 4, 57-65, 1985.
18. *St. Cloud Daily Times,* January 19, 1984.
19. *Prior Lake American*, September 2, 1981, p. 1.

Chapter Sixteen
1981 Strikes Begin

Paynesville

Both sides agreed to request mediation in mid-August. During their own negotiations, the board offered 21.7 percent, while teachers countered with an offer the board costed at 58.6 percent. Part of the difference in figures was the additional money teachers wanted if elementary class sizes were over twenty. There were many language issues as well, including hours of service, length of school year, teacher discipline and insurance.[1]

A mediation session in early September resulted in agreement on six language issues. The mediator suggested that total package dollars be negotiated first, followed by determining where the money would be placed—salary or benefits. Teachers said they would consider that.[2]

The board set a budget including $480,000 of deficit spending for 1981-1982, based on a ten percent raise for teachers. The superintendent said the district collected more money and spent less than anticipated the previous year and anticipated that happening again.[3] This appears to be a less precise budgeting process than other districts, who stood more firmly behind their numbers.

Teachers voted to strike and the board responded by setting strike plans calling for schools to be closed. The union president said that language issues could be quickly resolved if salaries could be settled. A negotiation session was scheduled for the day after the vote. Most of the front page of the local paper was taken up with negotiation news and strike plans.[4,5] During a session, teachers reduced their request to a thirty-eight percent raise and the board requested binding arbitration. Each side rejected the other's position.[6]

The homecoming coronation was held Thursday night, and teachers struck the next morning, September 25. The district was given only twenty hours' notice that teachers were going out. The law stated that strikes couldn't begin until after a ten-day waiting period had expired, but didn't require prior notice after that.[7] Some districts worried that teachers might go out in the middle of a school day, but none did.

MEA president Don Hill walked the picket line saying, "This might prevent other strikes, if both sides are sensible and can settle." Teachers said they were paid fourteen percent less than comparable districts. This was the superintendent's first year in Paynesville and he said, "I don't think there are harsh feelings between the teacher and the administration. And I am grateful for that." Four residents interviewed were critical of teachers for striking.[8]

No talks were scheduled as of the second day of the strike. The board said it was waiting for teachers to request another session. The board's chief negotiator said that teachers needed to change their demands and that the board didn't feel it would be proper to change their position. Over the weekend, teachers set up neighborhood get togethers in homes.[9] Picketers at the high school discovered that someone had dumped piles of manure in the driveway.[10]

The state mediator requested a session, held on the sixth day of the strike. Teachers re-presented their salary proposal, which was rejected. The board didn't offer a counter proposal, saying the two sides were too far apart. The district's chief negotiator said, "I don't think we have to play that game of exchanging proposals anymore. There's not much more bluffing that can be done by either side because the worst that could happen has already happened—we have a strike."

An editorial in the local paper described the effect of the strike as a serious tear in the fabric of the community. It talked of anger, pain and wounds that may never heal, and offered its facilities as a gathering place for board and union members to gather and meet informally. The district published a list of all settlements in the state.[11] A week later, the union published a list of top salaries in other districts demonstrating that seventy-seven percent were paying more than Paynesville.

The third week of the strike, informal talks occurred between the two chief negotiators and a board member walked into teachers' strike headquarters for a talk.[12] Informal meetings continued for three days without the board's hired negotiator, leading to a settlement October 18. The teachers approved it by a vote of fifty-three to thirty-five, with some calling the settlement "lousy." They said the combination of a citizens' petition to get the two sides talking and word leaking out that a tentative settlement had been reached pressured teachers into voting yes. Five of the fourteen strike days were made up, with a raise of 29.66 percent.[13]

The following month, the board approved a twenty-seven percent increase in the local tax levy, the maximum allowed.[14]

Tracy

Tracy used the district attorney as a negotiator. Teachers complained that arranging a meeting with him was difficult and he was slow to communicate. Speaking of filing an intent to strike, a chief negotiator for the teachers said, "... there is a state law which practically mandates that teachers made certain decisions at prescribed times in order to keep the process of negotiations alive and viable."[15] This is an early example of a union confusing what the law allowed with what they should do.

Citing the district's $700,000 reserve, teachers requested 35.4 percent. Because of declining enrollment, the board believed the reserve could be depleted in as little as three years. Both sides said they were willing to compromise.[16] During several sessions the week before the strike, including meeting with a mediator, the district increased its offer to 27.9 percent while teachers were at 30.4 percent.

The strike began Wednesday, September 30, closing schools the week before homecoming.[17] The first session after the strike didn't take place until the fourth day of the strike. A mediation session lasted from Monday morning until 3:00 A.M. Tuesday morning, with a break in the afternoon. After five school days, the strike was settled at 28.8 percent, with all days made up.

The superintendent said, "It was obvious that some type of compromise had to be reached, and the sooner the better for the students." Union leaders said they felt no animosity during negotiations and that both sides had agreed not to claim victory.

The paper reported that the settlement was higher than most districts. An editorial chastised the union, saying the board's offer was reasonable. A survey conducted by the paper found that seventy percent of the respondents approved the board's position.[18] The board ratified the contract in a four to three vote.[19]

Despite the brevity of the strike, the board's willingness to grant all days back and the willingness of both sides to compromise, a local editorial spoke of the malice generated in the community.[20]

Saint Cloud

St. Cloud presented a much different picture from Tracy, illustrating the long-term effects of difficult labor-management relationships. The previous round of negotiations had been troubled, marked by a lawsuit brought by the union over unfair labor practices.[21] Teachers had picketed and withheld voluntary services.[22]

Teachers complained during the 1981 negotiations about the district's hired negotiator, saying he wasn't readily available. They didn't trust the district's financial projections. During the last three contract cycles, teachers had been told their requests would put the district in the red, only to see the reserve increase by forty-seven percent.

The board requested arbitration. Teachers rejected that request, saying they wanted to maintain local control of negotiations. The board offered seven percent each year, teachers asked for thirteen percent and twelve percent. The district developed strike plans calling for closing schools and not making up strike days.

The board set a budget based on seven percent raises for teachers each year. It called for deficit spending of $1.55 million out of the $2.9 million reserve fund. Plans were discussed to cut $2.2 million the following year.[23]

In the face of such a large amount of deficit spending, it would seem logical that the union would happily accept the board's offer. After all, many districts refused to go into deficit spending at all. Looking back years later, the board chair attributed the strike to bad feelings carried over from 1979. The union president said, "The credibility as far as the finances was low."[24] Whatever occurred during the earlier negotiations, everyone involved would pay a heavy price.

During a mediation session, the district offered one percent less than it had the previous month and proposed raising beginning salaries by eliminating the first two steps. This would mean that beginning teachers would receive the same salary for their first three years.[25] Teachers voted ninety-three percent to strike but didn't set a date. They agreed to give the district twenty-four hours' notice before walking out. Unresolved issues included class size, transfers, leave and hourly contracts for some employees as well as salaries.[26]

The strike began October 1, with teachers asking for 32.4 percent and the district offering 21.67 percent. Teachers wanted all strike days made up, the board chair said it was their firm position that none would be. Most non-teaching staff were laid off and all schools were closed.

The board adopted a conditioning rule that athletes would have to practice one day for each day of lost practice before competing, up to ten days. A member of the girls cross country team was a contender for a state title, and looking forward to winning a college scholarship. Vocational students faced potential difficulties with apprenticeship and loan requirements.

Members of the senior class drove by picketing teachers on their homecoming float, expressing their support for teachers. No mediation sessions were scheduled. The state mediator said the two sides were very far apart, and he would schedule a session only if there was a substantial change.[27]

MEA president Don Hill came to St. Cloud for a rally the first evening of the strike. He criticized the ninety-five locals that had "caved in" and settled early. Two teachers crossed the lines, one for religious reasons. A vocational school student picketed the teachers. The union sent the board chair a letter asking to sit down and bargain. The board contacted the mediator to request a meeting.[28]

Leaders of twenty building PTSAs led a petition effort that began the third day of the strike. The board chair defended their decision not to meet without a mediator.[29] The petition with over 2,500 signatures was delivered to both sides and students—many of them athletes—held a rally at the administration building.[30] The two sides participated in a local radio debate the fifth night of the strike. The inclusion of hourly teachers—many of whom had fluctuating schedules—into the regular contract emerged as an issue.[31]

Comparisons with other districts' settlements were not straightforward. St. Cloud had considered Rochester a sister district. Rochester settled for 21.5 percent—just under the percentage offered in the St. Cloud district's last offer. While that would seem to argue that teachers should have accepted the board's offer, Rochester started from higher wages, justifying a larger percentage to catch up.

The Catholic schools in St. Cloud announced a policy of not accepting students during the strike, unless they had just moved into the community.[32] At a ten-hour mediation session held after seven strike days, both sides moved further away, teachers asking for a total of forty percent and the district withdrawing dental insurance.

Both sides did agree that the strike would probably last for weeks.[33] The newspaper published long statements from the union president saying teachers' wages had risen at half the rate of inflation, and the board chair talked of deficit spending and explained that state law prohibited closed door negotiations unless a mediator was present.[34]

Ten days into the strike, the board chair agreed to meet informally with teachers, saying that state open meeting laws prohibited more than one board member from participating.[35] The two sides agreed on how to calculate costs. The following day the mediator—who had been busy with other districts—found an opening in his schedule and called a mediation session.[36] Teachers lowered their salary proposal by $1000 per teacher, but the board didn't move from its position. The district's proposal for arbitration was rejected.[37]

In response to the failed mediation session, the district announced plans to hire teachers to be permanent replacements. Doubt was expressed that they could find 775 teachers and parents objected, saying they wanted a settlement with minimal bitterness on both sides. The board chair responded that with the number of teachers out of work because of declining enrollment, he believed they would find replacements at $100.00 per day, instead of subs usual $45.00. The MEA vowed to fight hiring permanent replacements in court. The PELRA law was mute on the issue of whether teachers could be permanently replaced during a strike.[38]

While subs were hired to temporarily replace teachers during a number of strikes, this is the only instance in Minnesota where it was suggested that teachers be permanently replaced. It's difficult to see its value. A tactic certain to anger teachers and with so many teachers to hire, it didn't serve as a realistic threat and didn't seem to shorten the strike.

The board chair and union president attended a public forum sponsored by a coalition of parent groups, whose leader charged that the strike had been caused by an "arbitrary and authoritarian management system." Coalition members criticized the board's decision to advertise for subs and called for immediate and continual negotiations.[39]

A hundred subs applied in the first two days.[40] The issue of how to calculate costs resurfaced, with the district using the number of teachers the previous year, and the union basing their figures on six fewer teachers in the current year.[41]

Seventeen days into the strike, both sides agreed again on how to calculate costs. The district discovered an error in state aid projections, giving them $313,000.00 more. Prayer services for an end to the strike were attended by 125 people. Fifteen vocational students met with the superintendent to voice their concerns. The county veterans' service officer expressed concerns about lost benefits to vocational students.[42]

Both sides voiced some optimism going into a mediation session- the third since the strike began. An agreement was reached including making up five of the eighteen days lost. The district had said from the beginning that no strike days would be made up, and held that position until the final mediation session.[43]

The union president said community pressure from the Parent Coalition, vocational students, and credit requirements for seniors contributed to settling.[44] Even after settling, the two sides couldn't agree on cost figures. The union said teachers would receive an additional $6,134.00 over two years while the district calculated the increase at $5,960.54. The paper reported a percentage increase of 26.38 percent, saying it was one of the largest settlements in the state.[45]

The following school year, state funding reductions and the contract settlement led to $1.1 million in budget cuts.[46]

Prior Lake

By mid-August, negotiators turned to mediation to get issues 'off dead center' according to a board member.[47] Teachers were requesting 67.7 percent while the board offered sixteen percent, and a strike began to be seen as a possibility.[48] The local paper provided a lot of space for teachers to express their salary concerns, focused largely on the discrepancy between their pay and nearby districts.[49] The board responded by pointing out that unlike districts being used for comparison, Prior Lake had to deal with declining enrollment. Citing districts that had settled for twenty-one percent, the district was frustrated that teachers hadn't accepted an earlier similar offer.[50]

The mediation session, held in early September, produced some movement. The district increased its offer to twenty-one percent; the teachers lowered theirs to fifty-seven percent, calling the board's offer an insult. A second mediation session was planned in two weeks.[51] In the interim, the union filed a notice of intent to strike on or after September 25—the day following the planned mediation session.[52]

In an unusual twist, the registered letter of intent to strike was received on September 11, three days before the timeline allowed by PELRA. The district attorney said that any teacher participating in what would be an illegal strike was subject to termination. Teachers placed a full page ad comparing their salaries, and the board made strike plans.[53]

The second mediation session was held on September 24th and resulted in a district offer of twenty-three percent versus a teacher request of forty-seven percent. The next session was scheduled four weeks away, well after a potential strike date.[54] Calling the month long delay between sessions unacceptable, the union went on strike October 1st. The board had gone into executive session the afternoon before the strike, but agreed to a negotiation session without a mediator too late to avert the strike.

The district's position was that even a twenty-five percent raise would quickly put them in debt. Teachers contended that the district could sell excess property and raise revenue. The district's business manager pointed out that revenue derived from the sale of property was restricted by law to capital expenditures.[55]

This was an example where teachers' lack of knowledge of district financial constraints led to unrealistic expectations. A thorough public discussion by the board of all the implications of their reserve funds would have cleared the issue of how much money the district had to spend.

The next mediation session took place on day seven of the strike. Teachers slightly reduced their salary demand and agreement was reached on several language items. The board didn't move from its salary offer. A minister sponsored a public meeting to discuss facilitating a strike settlement that was attended by 200 people. They developed a proposal that the two sides should keep talking and compromise. An editorial also called for ongoing negotiations.[56]

Several days later, the same minister was asked to lead a public meeting where the audience could ask questions of the board and union. It ended after an hour with many questions unanswered. The district began advertising for subs. The board chair wrote a letter to the editor telling teachers they were hiring subs to provide students with an education, but were willing to open schools with regular teachers if they would agree to settle in the near future.[57]

The board made what it felt were significant concessions during an all-day mediation session the fourteenth day of the strike. The union had been comparing itself to Shakopee wages, and the district agreed to a twenty-five percent raise, bringing salaries up to Shakopee's. The union rejected the offer, saying Shakopee's settlement included more money for beginning teachers and better insurance.

The district began interviewing subs with the intent to open schools November 2.[58] Things turned ugly when substitutes gathered in a parking lot in a neighboring town to be bused to Prior Lake for training. Tires on some sub's cars were flattened and they were the targets of obscenities.[59] Police escorted subs through the picket lines at the end of the day, and were called when teachers followed some subs home.

Grades one, two, three, and twelve opened November 3. No mediation sessions were scheduled, the state mediator saying he wouldn't schedule any until the two sides softened their bargaining positions. A petition was published in support of the board's position with over 800 citizen's names.[60]

The board increased the next year's tax levy by 17.8 percent. Grades four and five were scheduled to open on November 12.[61]

After thirty school days, the strike was settled when both sides agreed to submit the question of salary to binding arbitration. According to the mutual press release, "Both sides recognized a continuing impasse on the salary schedule and total dollar settlement." All language issues had been settled and the board agreed to six make-up days. Four more student days would be gained by using workshop days for student contact.[62]

The arbitrator ruled in February, giving teachers a 13.5 percent raise—the amount the board had been offering. Teachers were described as being bitterly disappointed.[63] No other teachers' union local would agree in the future to settle a strike through arbitration.

Deer River

The second district that went out October 1st was Deer River. About the same size as Prior Lake, the economics and atmosphere were quite different.

Mediation sessions were being held by the beginning of September, with the board offering an increase of $3,861. They described this as their final offer. Teachers requested $5,635.[64] Salary positions were reported in total dollar amounts, not percentages, during this strike.

In mid-September, teachers filed an intent to strike. Neither side had moved from their salary positions. The Board sent a letter to parents saying teachers' pay was in the top twenty percent of districts, and that their request would result in drawing down the reserve. Since interest earned from the reserve was helping pay salaries, the board was determined to be fiscally responsible. No strike days would be made up.[65]

Ten days later, a strike was authorized. Mediation had resulted in the board offering $4,500, teachers asking $5,400. Teachers said that their request would not lead to higher taxes or program cuts because the reserve was $1,579,612 and their request would decrease it by only $21,000 over two years. They pointed out that the superintendent and high school principal are highly paid compared to others in the county.[66]

The strike began October 1, after teachers again rejected arbitration.[67] Deer River was reported to have the highest per pupil fund balance of districts on strike—$1,349.00.[68] Seven days into the strike, teachers voted down a 'take it or leave it' offer of $5,000 and making up half the strike days. The board then reverted to its offer of $4,500. An all-day session over the weekend resulted in a board offer of $4,700 and all days made up, which was also rejected. Rival parent groups formed, one supporting the teachers, another the board.[69]

The two sides met twice the following week and exchanged proposals.[70] Agreement was reached October 20th, after eleven school days. Six would be made up and teachers received $5100.00.[71]

Once the strike was a week old, both sides appeared willing to compromise, submitting a number of proposals and negotiating regularly.

---

1. *Paynesville Press*, August 19 1981, p. 1.
2. *Paynesville Press*, September 9 1981, p. 2.
3. *Paynesville Press*, September 16 1981, p. 2.
4. *St. Cloud Daily Times*, September 23 1981, p. 1B.
5. *Paynesville Press*, September 23 1981, p. 1.
6. *St. Cloud Daily Times*, September 24 1981, p. 1.
7. *Paynesville Press*, September 30 1981, pp. 1, 1B.
8. *Paynesville Press*, September 25 1981, pp. 1, 8.
9. *St. Cloud Daily Times*, September 28, 1981, p. 1C.
10. *Paynesville Press*, September 30 1981, pp. 1, 1B.
11. *Paynesville Press*, October 7 1981, pp. 1, 4, 9.
12. *Paynesville Press*, October 14 1981, pp. 1, 2, 4, 7.
13. *Paynesville Press*, October 21 1981, pp. 1, 7.
14. *Paynesville Press*, November 4 1981, p. 1.
15. *Tracy Headlight-Herald*, September 10, 1981, p. 1.
16. *Tracy Headlight-Herald*, September 24, 1981, pp. 1, 2.
17. *Tracy Headlight-Herald*, October 1, 1981, p. 1, 3.
18. *Tracy Headlight-Herald*, October 8, 1981, pp. 1, 2, 4, 13.

19. *Tracy Headlight-Herald*, October 15, 1981, p. 1.
20. *Tracy Headlight-Herald*, October 8, 1981, p. 2.
21. *St. Cloud Daily Times*, November 14, 1979, p. 1A.
22. *St. Cloud Daily Times*, November 16, 1979, pp. 1A, 7A.
23. *St. Cloud Daily Times*, September 18, 1981, pp. 1A, 4A, 5A, 1C.
24. *St. Cloud Daily Times*, January 19, 1984, pp. 1A, 8A.
25. *St. Cloud Daily Times*, September 30, 1981, pp. 1A, 6A.
26. *St. Cloud Daily Times*, September 29, 1981, pp. 1A, 7A.
27. *St. Cloud Daily Times*, October 1, 1981, pp. 1A, 6A, 1D.
28. *St. Cloud Daily Times*, October 2, 1981, pp. 1A, 8A.
29. *St. Cloud Daily Times*, October 5, 1981, pp. 1A, 6A.
30. *St. Cloud Daily Times*, October 6, 1981, pp. 1A, 5A.
31. *St. Cloud Daily Times*, October 8, 1981, pp. 1A, 10A.
32. *St. Cloud Daily Times*, October 9, 1981, pp. 1A, 12A.
33. *St. Cloud Daily Times*, October 12, 1981, pp. 1A, 9A.
34. *St. Cloud Daily Times*, October 13, 1981, pp. 4A.
35. *St. Cloud Daily Times*, October 15, 1981, pp. 1A, 8A.
36. *St. Cloud Daily Times*, October 16, 1981, pp. 1A, 8A.
37. *St. Cloud Daily Times*, October 17 1981, pp. 1A, 6A.
38. *St. Cloud Daily Times*, October 19, 1981, pp. 1A, 7A.
39. *St. Cloud Daily Times*, October 20, 1981, pp. 1A, 5A.
40. *St. Cloud Daily Times*, October 21, 1981, pp. 1A, 6A.
41. *St. Cloud Daily Times*, October 23, 1981, pp. 1A, 13A.
42. *St. Cloud Daily Times*, October 27, 1981, pp. 1A, 6A.
43. *St. Cloud Daily Times*, October 23, 1981, pp. 1A, 13A.
44. *St. Cloud Daily Times*, October 27, 1981, pp. 1A, 6A, 8A.
45. *St. Cloud Daily Times*, October 29, 1981, pp. 1A, 7A, 1C.
46. *St. Cloud Daily Times*, January 19, 1984, p. 8A.
47. *Prior Lake American*, August 12, 1981, p. 2.
48. *Prior Lake American*, August 19, 1981, p. 1.
49. *Prior Lake American*, August 26, 1981, p. 1.
50. *Prior Lake American*, September 2, 1981, p. 1.
51. *Prior Lake American*, September 9, 1981, p. 1.
52. *Prior Lake American*, September 16, 1981, pp. 1, 12.
53. *Prior Lake American*, September 23, 1981, pp. 1, 8.
54. *Prior Lake American*, September 30, 1981, p. 1.
55. *Prior Lake American*, October 7, 1981, p. 1, 4.
56. *Prior Lake American*, October 14, 1981, pp. 1, 9.

57. *Prior Lake American*, October 21, 1981, pp. 1, 4.
58. *Prior Lake American*, October 28, 1981, p. 1.
59. *St. Paul Pioneer Press*, November 4, 1981.
60. *Prior Lake American*, November 4, 1981, pp. 1, 2, 9.
61. *Prior Lake American*, November 11, 1981, p. 1.
62. *Prior Lake American*, November 18, 1981, p. 1.
63. *Prior Lake American*, February 10, 1982, p. 1.
64. *Western Itasca Review*, September 1, 1981, p. 1.
65. *Western Itasca Review*, September 22, 1981, pp. 1, 6.
66. *Western Itasca Review*, September 29, 1981, pp. 1, 6.
67. *Western Itasca Review*, October 6, 1981, p. 1.
68. *Duluth News-Tribune*, October 9, 1981, p. 2A.
69. *Duluth News-Tribune*, October 14, 1981, pp. 1, 14A.
70. *Western Itasca Review*, October 20, 1981, p. 1.
71. *Western Itasca Review*, October 27, 1981, p. 1.

Chapter Seventeen
Strikes the Week Before MEA

Seven strikes began the week of October 5—five of them on Tuesday the 6th. Those five are listed here in alphabetical order. One was quite short. Another holds the record for the longest teachers' strike in Minnesota.

Anoka

Anoka was the largest district represented by the MEA, including 1,800 teachers and multiple high schools. It faced economic difficulties, having cut $1.2 million in the current school year, with plans to cut an additional one million dollars the next. Voters approved an operating levy on September 9th, staving off future cuts.[1]

The following Monday, teachers filed an intent to strike, seeking to tap into the just-approved funds. In two mediation sessions, the board had upped its offer from seventeen percent to twenty percent, then twenty-two percent. The union held firm at forty-one percent and said the district was "stonewalling" on forty-nine language issues. The board's negotiator acknowledged that he had stubbornly resisted language changes that "would in effect erode the elected official's ability and responsibility to effectively manage the education program of the school district." The board formulated strike plans.[2]

Two mediation sessions the following week produced no movement, and teachers voted on September 23 to strike, with no set date. A central issue was the district's omission of a salary schedule in their proposal. Teachers had been allowed to set the schedule in previous negotiations, based on total cost figures, and had been criticized by the superintendent.[3] Frequent sessions were held and the teachers presented a new total package. They jammed the next school board meeting, announcing an October 6th strike date. The board developed strike plans stating that activities would be held if there were staff and that no days would be made up.[4]

Prior to the strike, the board offered 27.9 percent while the union requested thirty-nine percent. Seventeen language issues remained unresolved. The board suggested utilizing a nonbinding fact finding panel or arbitration—either on single issues or the total package. Teachers rejected arbitration, continuing to call for more dollars and a salary schedule. The two sides couldn't agree on how the meeting the evening before the strike ended. Teachers said the board walked out, the board said the mediator ended the session 'after the two sides had sat and looked at each other for a while'.

The strike began on October 6. Twenty five teachers crossed the lines. Parents and students at one of the high schools—Coon Rapids—pressured to proceed with Friday's homecoming football game using an alternate coach, but it was cancelled. The evening of the third day of the strike, a late night session produced some movement. Teachers dropped their demand to 36.5 percent. The board presented two alternative salary schedules based on 27.9 percent with no language changes. The board asked that their proposal be presented to all teachers for a vote and teachers asked to speak to the entire board.

The district's reserve fund was a point of contention. Teachers sent letters out citing the entire reserve, while district officials pointed out that less than half of that total was available for salaries. They claimed that all the money from the general fund and more was being expended.[5]

The MEA president predicted that some strikes might last until after the first of next year. Negotiators in Anoka on both sides were pessimistic about an early settlement after sessions three days in row during the second week of the strike produced little movement. Teachers rejected the proposed salary schedule, saying it provided too little to veteran teachers. The district pointed out that beginning teachers salaries compared well to other districts, starting at above $16,000 the second year.

Students and parents picketed the picketers at two of the high schools. Students from Coon Rapids were particularly upset at having lost homecoming, and the disruption of the season for what they termed the best football team in the school's history. Alternative coaches had been found for six teams, but the superintent cancelled all extracurricular activities after receiving telephoned threats of violence if games proceeded. Students felt they had been lied to and cheated, calling it Black Friday.[6]

A compromise was reached in marathon sessions held late in the second week of the strike. Teachers received a 30.2 percent raise and made up three of the seven days. Settlement of language issues reflected compromise as well. Teachers received improved insurance and leaves but didn't get extra prep time or additional control of the calendar. Neither side was happy, and increased layoffs were predicted. An editorial stated that after wages lost for days not made up, teachers gained $50.00.[7]

The Anoka strike was characterized by its frequent negotiations—meetings occurred almost every day of the strike's second week. The parent booster club strategy of locating alternate coaches, only to have games cancelled led to very hard feelings.

Howard Lake-Waverly

Howard Lake and Waverly are two small towns in central Minnesota, and are an unlikely setting for the longest teachers' strike in Minnesota history. A member of the 1981 school board said there were strong personalities on both sides of the labor dispute.[8] The strike may have started because of the general move to use the new PELRA law, but descended into a textbook case illustrating how everyone loses during a prolonged strike.

The board announced in mid-September that the union had filed an intent to strike. If a strike occurred, schools would be closed.[9] Mediation sessions had begun September 1, and voters had just approved a mil levy increase. Although there were some language issues, money was identified as the main difference.[10]

A mediation session on September 24 was unsuccessful and October 6 was set as the strike date. The board set strike procedures including "Follow Murphy's law." No strike days would be made up, and leave would not accrue.[11]

The strike began as planned on October 6. Teachers asked $6,000, the Board offered $3,800.[12] Both sides sounded conciliatory, the board stating that it would be willing to cut programs to increase pay, and teachers acknowledging that the district didn't have a lot of money. No sessions were scheduled, and the superintendent said schools would remain closed.[13]

During the second week of the strike, teachers published a comparison of their salaries with other professions. The board published its proposed salary schedule. No sessions were scheduled and a large number of high school students demonstrated, requesting the two sides to resume negotiations.[14]

The mediator requested that the full Board attend a mediation session on October 17th. Teachers reduced their request to $5,985.00 but added new clauses into negotiations. They included no reprisal and making up all strike days. The board responded that it felt a duty to search out alternative ways to continue student's education. Teachers published a statement of their salary proposal and priorities.[15]

Two mediation sessions at the end of the third strike week produced movement but no agreement. Teachers agreed to accept the board's first year salary, if the board would accept their second year proposal. The board suggested going to arbitration.[16] During a mediation session held the following weekend the board increased its offer to $4,512.00 saying it was the most is could possibly offer. When it was rejected, the board convened in an emergency session and voted unanimously to begin hiring subs at $105.00 per day.

School opened with subs for grades one through three on November 4.[17] Both sides went to court, the district gaining a restraining order limiting pickets. The union requested an injunction prohibiting hiring subs, which was denied.[18] Kindergarten opened November 10, grades seven and eight on November 12th. Teachers published an ad questioning the board's motivation, pointing out that buses were running almost empty, the high cost of subs and money saved from those teachers who weren't working.[19]

A mediation session lasting twelve hours on November 13th produced a number of proposals. Teachers decreased their request to $5,350.00 and the board offered $120 more, contingent on no make-up days and no retroactivity. The board suggested arbitration. All proposals were rejected. By November 17, school was open for grades kindergarten through eighth. The

MEA placed an ad in the local papers from Don Hill, criticizing boards and administrators running schools with strikebreakers.[20]

While the board's position on no make-up days was rigid, it wasn't unusual for a district operating schools with subs. Denying retroactivity after a strike has begun was rare, presenting an obstacle no local would accept.

No formal proposals were presented during a mediation session November 21. Presenting an alternative to making up strike days, teachers stated that after November 30, they would be increasing their salary demands by $100.00 a day. Seniors returned to school November 24 and the district intended to open all classes by December 1st. Teachers placed two adds, once listing incidents of poor conditions in the reopened schools and one criticizing board members for not settling.[21] The teachers' tactic of threatening to add money to their salary demands complicated negotiations.

Teachers had started an alternative school on November 19th. The district threatened parents with criminal charges because their children were truant. The union went to court December 7th seeking an injunction to prevent enforcement of the compulsory attendance law.

The union also filed a suit questioning the basic condition of the schools being taught by subs and challenging the district's right to deny access to a Blue Ribbon committee's request to inspect the schools. Negotiators on both sides published a statement that they had agreed to a guarantee of mutual trust of silence on any item discussed during negotiations.[22] The judge denied all the motions, rebuking both sides for not making an effort to settle the strike.[23]

Events took a strange turn on December 11, forty-four days into the strike. During an eight-hour mediation session, a tentative agreement was reached providing an average $4,993.00 raise and eleven make-up days, with an additional four unpaid make-up days. The negotiators present, including two from the board, shook hands.

The full board, meeting the next day, unanimously voted to reject the agreement. The union held a ratification vote, passing the agreement forty-eight to ten. The teachers were left puzzled and angry, with no new talks scheduled.[24] The board explained its position, saying that the agreement was too expensive and included too many make-up days. Because they had opened with subs, only seventeen days had been lost, not forty-four. A group calling itself "Citizen's Right to Know" published a list of proposed teacher's salaries by name, and a long list of signatures to a petition supporting the board's position.[25]

The MEA filed suit against the board, claiming unfair labor practices and violations of the open meeting law. At the December 11th session, both sides had agreed not to disclose terms of the proposal until it had been presented to the teachers. The board met twice in closed sessions without proper notification or tape recording, and once in public before the teachers' meeting.

The judge ruled in favor of the teachers, assessing a $50.00 fine to each board member for violating the open meeting law. Citing their failure to follow agreed upon nondisclosure procedure, he also found that the district violated unfair labor practices statues, and enjoined them from refusing to bargain in good faith and from breaching agreements. Calling the strike 'unwholesome', he said the board, "has a duty to and is obligated to engage in good faith negotiations".[26]

The strike finally ended on January 10, after fifty-eight school days encompassing four months. Teachers received average raises of $4,803 with five days made up. The *Minneapolis Tribune* calculated that teachers lost an average of $4,456.77. Beginning as one of the earlier teachers strikes of 1981, it continued until it was the final settlement that contract year.

The state legislature cut aid to schools in a bill that became law on January 14. Districts were allowed to raise local taxes by two mils, which the Howard Lake-Waverly Board declined to do. Instead, the board chair said the district would have to make cuts to pay for the agreement.[27] Four days later, the board directed the administration to propose cuts for the next year.[28]

Three teachers resigned as a result of the strike, leaving to pursue other professions.[29] There were twenty-eight fewer students in the district after the strike, representing a loss of $45,322 in state aid per year.[30] The budget deficit for 1982-1983 was projected at $265,000.00.[31]

Splitting the pre-strike salary difference of $6,000.00 from the teachers and the board's offer of $3,800.00 would have resulted in a settlement of $4,900.00—less than $100 away from what was eventually agreed to.[32]

Lake City

This was one of the shorter strikes. The two sides were fairly close to begin with, and most problems seemed to be misunderstandings rather than firm positions.

Lake City teachers felt in early September that they were delivering a high-quality education for less than other area staff.[33] They filed an intent to strike notice on September 14.[34] A mediator was not utilized until October 3rd. The union said a strike date would be set if no agreement was reached during the mediation session.[35] Teachers decreased their demands from $5,375 to $5,000, but the board moved up to only $4,700.00, what it called a final offer.

Teachers voted the next day (October 4th) to strike on the 6th, providing little time to prepare the community. It was homecoming week, and the superintendent announced that all activities would be cancelled in the event of a strike. The district would not seek to reopen with substitutes. Some confusion was evident in the superintendent's lack of knowledge that the teachers considered $5,000 to be a minimum figure to prevent a strike.[36]

The board increased its offer to $4,900 the day before the strike was scheduled. Teachers cited the one-million-dollar reserve fund, saying giving them $5,000 would cost only $49,000 more. The superintendent confirmed the one-million-dollar figure, but said it would be spend down by $250,000 during the current school year. Both sides used different figures to compare salaries with other districts.[37]

The strike began October 6th. The next day, a five-hour session brought to two sides within $575.[38] Negotiations stumbled the following day. A number of language issues were agreed to, contingent on a total cost of $4,900. When the teachers later repeated their demand of $5,275, the board walked out, withdrawing its $4,900 offer.[39]

Negotiations continued the following evening and all through the weekend, culminating in a settlement.[40] Salaries increased an average $4,944 and all four days of the strike would be made up. Teachers gained increased insurance premiums and improved leave language. Secondary teachers would no longer be required to accept a class during their prep period.[41]

The willingness of both sides to meet every day and work through misunderstandings and setbacks brought a quick settlement.

Rockford

Almost identical in size to Lake City, the strike in the Rockford District would not find a quick solution. Pre-strike positions were $6,500 by the teachers versus $4,300 offered by the district. All activities would be cancelled.[42] No negotiation sessions were held during the first two weeks of the strike.[43]

A twenty-three-hour session held the after the fifth week of the strike resulted in an offer by the district of $5,500. It was rejected by the teachers, who held out for not less than $6,000. The board announced it would hire substitutes to reopen the schools.[44]

Five days later, an agreement was reached providing $5,600 and sixteen make-up days of the twenty-seven-day strike. The district announced that it would be spending $750,000 of its reserve, and would cut programs next year. Seventeen students left the district during the strike.[45]

Fewer negotiation sessions were a significant difference between the Rockford and Lake City strikes. Without a local daily paper, both sides had limited access to a public forum to make their positions known.

This may have been a case where the threat of hiring substitutes helped bring about an agreement. In the last week under that threat, the district came up only $100, while the teachers dropped $400.

Wabasha

The Wabasha school board clung tenaciously to its desire for arbitration. In vain.

The WKEA, like many MEA locals, filed an intent to strike on September 14. The board offered 11.6 percent and 10.3 percent while teachers were asking 18.9 percent and 14.9 percent.[46] The board urged binding arbitration beginning in early September as an alternative to striking. Teachers responded that they hadn't been treated fairly by arbitrators in the past.[47]

Teachers voted September 28th to authorize a strike with no date set. The board offered twenty-five percent, an average of $4,220—as much as it said it could afford—while the union sought 31.7 percent which would yield an average $5,668 raise. The district's fund balance stood at $500,000.[48] October 6th was set as the strike date. The superintendent announced that all activities would be closed and predicted that given the large differences, the strike would be a long one. No sessions were scheduled and he said the board, "should not go higher and does not intend to put any more money on the table."[49]

One of the sixty-three teachers crossed the line the first day of the strike, saying that he was nearing retirement and felt it was in his best interest to cross. The next session was scheduled for the beginning of the second week of the strike. The superintendent said declining enrollment would necessitate spending down the reserve.[50]

The paper published several statements by local residents calling the teachers "greedy." The superintendent said that the average per capita income in the county was $6,648 and the teachers' demand for nearly that much in a raise angered some residents.[51]

Urging by the public resulted in moving the negotiation session up from Monday to Friday, but no agreement was reached. The board renewed its offer of binding arbitration, saying that school could resume immediately if the union would sign an agreement to submit to arbitration. It refused to increase the cost of the total package, but added monies saved during the first four days of the strike. The teachers didn't offer any new proposals. The two sides used different figures to compare proposals with other districts. No sessions were scheduled for the second week of the strike. Teachers placed an ad including the home phone numbers of board members and the superintendent, urging citizens to call.[52]

Friday night of MEA weekend, a settlement was reached providing 26.3 percent, an average of $4,700 and making up five of the seven days. Even at this point there was no agreement on the figures, with the teachers saying the raises amounted to $5,100. The discrepancy involved monies saved during the strike and the teachers' agreement to accept only five instead of ten sick days.[53] The district projected deficit spending of $100,000 for the current year with cuts proposed for the second.

Twelve seniors on the football team quit, saying their season was lost. An editorial recommended ways to avoid further strikes:

1) Stronger working relationships between school board members, administrators and teachers including more frequent meetings between the parties;
2) Greater understanding of the other's needs and positions;
3) A continuing reminder of the need for uninterrupted education;
4) Continued reminders of the emotional effect of a strike.[54]

In late October, the board voted to increase the tax levy by eleven percent.[55]

The board appeared to have done fairly well during the strike, getting teachers to accept an agreement that split the difference much less than half way. Perhaps the strategy of infrequent negotiations, holding to a firm total package cost and repeating calls for arbitration was effective.

Eden Prarie

Eden Prairie didn't go out until two days later because of a union challenge and confusion about the new deadlines. Back in March, the Minnesota Federation of Teachers had mounted a challenge to become Eden Prairie teacher's exclusive representative. Some teachers felt—and the district's business manager confirmed—that during previous negotiations, salaries had fallen behind neighboring districts. The AFT utilized professional negotiators while the MEA relied on local committees. Under PELRA, there could be only one exclusive bargaining agent. They were chosen by vote and could be challenged when at least thirty percent of the teachers signed cards seeking an election.[56]

The MEA local maintained control during a vote that occurred late enough to throw off the strike deadlines followed in the rest of the state.

The earliest they could file an intent to strike was September 24th—ten days late.[57] At a session in mid-September, teachers dropped their request from 58.5 percent to 43.2 percent while the district raised its offer two percent to 24.9 percent.[58]

The board began developing strike plans in early October. The state Bureau of Mediation was contacted to determine the first legal day teachers could strike. Which day counted as the first day—when the letter was sent, or the next—and July having thirty-one, not thirty days for mediation - meant the Bureau settled on October 6th as the first legal strike day. Two mediation sessions were scheduled before then.[59]

Teachers informed the district on October 6th that the strike would begin the 8th. Neither side agreed on how to calculate total package costs of proposals presented during negotiations. Teachers suggested that the board hold a referendum to raise additional tax revenue. The board responded that the deadline for initiating referendums had already passed.[60]

The strike began October 8th. The superintendent said that days would not be made up and that the board's proposal would result in $500,000 in program cuts over the length of the contract. Teachers organized neighborhood coffee parties for informational purposes and a prayer line. They published an ad comparing salaries between neighboring districts. High school class officers formed a telephone tree to keep each other informed.[61]

The first mediation session since the strike began was held on the fifth day. Some agreement was reached on language issues, and the teachers slightly reduced their salary demand. The district held firm on its salary offer. Both sides reached some understanding on how to calculate costs.[62]

The next session was held a week later. Some language affecting costs was agreed to, decreasing the teacher's request to $12,667. The board again offered arbitration, which was rejected by the teachers. Teachers requested meeting without the mediator, saying his lack of availability hampered negotiations. The board wanted to stay with mediation because it provided for closed door sessions. Students spoke at a school board meeting of delayed college acceptances and missed scholarship applications.[63]

Saying they were responding to the communities' request, teachers reduced their demands substantially to $9,844 during a session held early in the fourth week of the strike. The board responded by moving money around without increasing the total cost. During a session held later that week, the board put more money on the table for the first time since the strike began, increasing its offer by $183 to $6,183. Concerned citizens picketed, calling for more frequent negotiations.[64]

A session held Thursday of the fifth week of the strike produced some language agreement. While that meeting was going on, the rest of the board approved a plan to reopen schools with substitutes.

All the remaining language issues were settled in a session held the following weekend. The two sides came closer together, at $9,010 and $6,210. For the first time, the two sides are costing proposals the same way. The union offered to split the difference in salary and make-up days, which had become a stumbling block. At a board meeting, a citizens group presented a petition calling for the use of local labor relations professionals to assist in negotiations.[65]

Optimism about a settlement was shattered the following week. Teachers again offered to split the difference in package cost but the board held its position. Substitutes were interviewed with plans to open grades one, two and twelve on November 22nd and all grades by December 14.[66]

Icy roads kept the schools closed on the 22nd, delaying the reopening until the 23rd. Many teachers hired were substitutes in other Twin Cities schools. All winter sports began practice with replacement coaches.

Three sessions were held the seventh week of the strike, producing significant change on both sides. Teachers proposed a package costing what the district had proposed before the strike, with most of the increases occurring during the second year. They felt that this would put them in an acceptable position for future negotiations. The board increased its offer to $6,543 with twenty-six make-up days and asked that the teachers take the offer to their membership. Teachers refused, saying beginning salaries were too low and it would not help them in future negotiations. The district placed an ad calling their offer the highest in the metro area.[67]

An agreement was reached during a session held one week later. Twenty six days of thirty-four would be made up and salaries increased an average of $6,291 over two years. This figure included the lost wages from eight days teachers weren't paid and was lower than the agreement rejected by teachers during the previous session. The salary schedules had been rearranged and a thirteenth step added to accommodate teachers with a doctorate.

Teachers felt that their settlement was comparable with neighboring districts, although it wasn't up to the average. The district announced it would have to cut $500,000 to pay for the settlement.[68] With estimated state reductions in aid payments, plans were formulated to deal with a deficit as high as $1,250,000.[69]

Infrequent negotiations, in part caused by the lack of availability of mediators and intransigence on the part of the board in not moving from their salary position until the strike was four weeks old contributed to lengthen the strike. By the end of the strike, teachers were in a losing situation. None of the days in the final week of the strike were made up, and they settled for less money than had been offered during a previous session.

Walnut Grove

Walnut Grove, a community with 756 residents on the banks of Plum Creek, cherished its idyllic image immortalized by Laura Ingalls Wilder. Pa Ingalls helped buy the bell in the Lutheran Church, where the current pastor was also a member of the school board. People from all over the world came to visit the Laura Ingalls Wilder Museum.

Residents thought a teacher's strike couldn't happen in their town. All five pastors in town gave sermons on forgiveness during negotiations.[70] It's ironic that the board held to some of the most draconian positions of any district in 1981 and voted to reopen school with subs after only four days.

Teachers voted to authorize a strike on September 30. The board offered $2,950 while teachers asked $6,000. The district suggested utilizing a mediator, but the teachers objected because a mediator wouldn't be available for nearly a month.[71] The following week the two sides met face-to-face. The board moved up to $4,000 and teachers came down to $5,350.[72]

Three language provisions were major sticking points. The board wanted no retroactive pay, so negotiated raises wouldn't begin until the contract was settled. A few other districts tried this, but quickly dropped it. The district also wanted to be able to negotiate salaries individually with teachers when hiring. Teachers felt that an adequate starting salary schedule would make this unnecessary. A uniform salary schedule was universally desired by teacher's locals. The district also proposed a "no strike" clause, asking teachers to forego the right PELRA had recently granted.

Just before the strike, the district made it clear that it was not interested in changing its stand on contract language.

The strike began October 9th. The board quickly began interviewing subs.[73] School reopened on the fifth day of the strike for grades one through nine. This was the first striking school in 1981 to open with substitutes.[74] Subs came from South Dakota and Iowa as well as the immediate area, attracted by the pay of $65.00 per day. One of the twenty teachers in the district crossed the lines. Teachers from six other districts and Dan Hill participated in picketing. A mediation session brought no movement from either side.[75]

A mediation session Sunday, November 1st produed some movement. Teachers gave up requests for severance pay, life insurance and bereavement leave and reduced their salary demand to $4,950. The board gave up the no-strike clause, raised its offer to $4,100 and said it would be retroactive if the contract was signed that day. One striking teacher resigned.[76]

An agreement was reached on November 8th, providing average raises of $4,500 and two of nineteen days to be made up. The mediator had presented a proposal that included dropping the no-strike and no-retroactivity clauses and allowed to district some flexibility when placing new hires on the salary schedule. The board unanimously approved it, while the teachers barely passed it in a ten to nine vote.[77]

This may be a case where the mediator's knowledge of common practices in other districts was helpful. The board's harsh positions may have worked prior to the no-strike law, but weren't tenable given teachers' newly acquired power. They did however result in allowing the district something no other striking district could do—place newly hired teachers higher on the salary scale.

1. *Anoka County Union*, September 11, 1981, p. 1.
2. *Anoka County Union*, September 18, 1981, pp. 1, 20.
3. *Anoka County Union*, September 25, 1981, pp. 1, 2.
4. *Anoka County Union*, October 2, 1981, p. 1.
5. *Anoka County Union*, October 9, 1981, pp. 1, 9, 18.
6. *Anoka County Union*, October 16, 1981, pp. 1, 2, 20, section 3, pp. 1, 4, 5.
7. *Anoka County Union*, October 23, 1981, pp. 1, 2.
8. Telephone interview, June 30, 2010.
9. *Howard Lake Harold*, September 17, 1981, p. 1.
10. *Howard Lake Harold*, September 9, 1981, p. 1.
11. *Howard Lake Harold*, October 1, 1981, p. 1.
12. *Wright County Journal Press*, October 8, 1981, p. 1.
13. *Howard Lake Harold*, October 8, 1981, p. 1.
14. *Howard Lake Harold*, October 15, 1981, pp. 1, 8.
15. *Howard Lake Harold*, October 22, 1981, pp. 1, 8.
16. *Howard Lake Harold*, October 29, 1981, p. 1.
17. *Howard Lake Harold*, November 5, 1981, p. 1.
18. *Wright County Journal Press*, November 12, 1981, p. 1.
19. *Howard Lake Harold*, November 12, 1981, p. 1.
20. *Howard Lake Harold*, November 19, 1981, pp. 1, 8.
21. *Howard Lake Harold*, November 26, 1981, p. 1.
22. *Howard Lake Harold*, December 10, 1981, p. 1.
23. *Wright County Journal Press*, December 17, 1981, p. 1.
24. *St. Paul Pioneer Press*, December 14, 1981, pp. 19, 27.
25. *Howard Lake Harold*, December 17, 1981, pp. 1, 8.
26. *Wright County Journal Press*, December 24, 1981, p. 1.
27. *Minneapolis Tribune*, January 11, 1982, p. 16A.
28. *Howard Lake Harold*, January 21, 1982, p. 1.
29. Open Channels, *Howard Lake Harold*, January 27, 1982, p. 1.
30. *Howard Lake Harold*, February 4, 1982, p. 1.
31. *Howard Lake Harold*, February 25, 1982, p. 1.
32. *Howard Lake Harold*, January 14, 1982, p. 1.
33. *Red Wing Republican Eagle*, September 10, 1981, p. 11.
34. *Red Wing Republican Eagle*, September 14, 1981, p. 1.
35. *Red Wing Republican Eagle*, October 2, 1981, p. 1.
36. *Red Wing Republican Eagle*, October 5, 1981, pp. 1, 16.
37. *Red Wing Republican Eagle*, October 6, 1981, pp. 1, 20.
38. *Red Wing Republican Eagle*, October 8, 1981, pp. 1, 2.

39. *Red Wing Republican Eagle*, October 9, 1981, pp. 1, 14.
40. *Red Wing Republican Eagl,e* October 12, 1981, p. 1.
41. *Red Wing Republican Eagle*, October 13, 1981, p. 1.
42. *Wright County Journal Press*, October 8, 1981, p. 1.
43. *Wright County Journal Press*, October 15, 1981, p. 1.
44. *Wright County Journal Press*, November 12, 1981, p. 1.
45. *Wright County Journal Press*, November 19, 1981, p. 1.
46. *Wabasha County Herald*, September 17, 1981, p. 1.
47. *Wabasha County Herald*, October 6, 1981, p. 1.
48. *Wabasha County Herald*, October 1, 1981, p. 1.
49. *Wabasha County Herald*, October 6, 1981, pp. 1, 12.
50. *Wabasha County Herald*, October 8, 1981, pp. 1, 2, 4.
51. *Wabasha County Herald*, October 9, 1981, pp. 1, 2.
52. *Wabasha County Herald*, October 15, 1981, p. 1.
53. *Winona Daily News*, October 17, 1981, p. 1.
54. *Wabasha County Herald*, October 22, 1981, pp. 1, 2, 4.
55. *Wabasha County Herald*, October 29, 1981, p. 1.
56. *Eden Prairie News*, March 12, 1981, p. 1.
57. *Eden Prairie News*, September 17, 1981, p. 1.
58. *Eden Prairie News*, September 24, 1981, pp. 1, 10.
59. *Eden Prairie News*, October 1, 1981, p. 1.
60. *Eden Prairie News*, October 8, 1981, p. 1.
61. *Eden Prairie News*, October 15, 1981, pp. 1, 9.
62. *Eden Prairie News*, October 22, 1981, pp. 1, 3.
63. *Eden Prairie News*, October 29, 1981, pp. 1, 10.
64. *Eden Prairie News*, November 5, 1981, p. 1.
65. *Eden Prairie News*, November 12, 1981, pp. 1, 12.
66. *Eden Prairie News*, November 19, 1981, p. 1.
67. *Eden Prairie News*, November 26, 1981, pp. 1, 8.
68. *Eden Prairie News*, December 3, 1981, p. 1.
69. *Eden Prairie News*, December 24, 1981, p. 1.
70. Daily Journal, International Falls, October 22, 1981, p. 6.
71. *Tracey Headlight-Herald*, October 1, 1981, p. 1.
72. *Tracey Headlight-Herald*, October 8, 1981, p. 1.
73. *Tracey Headlight-Herald*, October 15, 1981, p. 1.
74. *Duluth News-Tribune*, October 20, 1981, p. 2A.
75. *Tracey Headlight-Herald*, October 22, 1981, pp. 1, 9.
76. *Tracey Headlight-Herald*, November 5, 1981, p. 1.
77. *Tracey Headlight-Herald*, November 12, 1981, pp. 1, 2.

Chapter Eighteen
MEA Week

Eight districts went out in the three days of MEA week—October 12 through 14, more than any other single week. Some strikes were very brief, others more significant. They are presented here in alphabetical order by date.

Proctor

Mediation services were first utilized in mid-September, with the board offering 9.5 percent and 9.3 percent.[1] An intent to strike notice was filed on September 14, the union president explaining that they were following PELRA guidelines. Differences were focused on salary and fringe benefits, with the union asking for a tenty-eight percent increase. The superintendent said the district had a comprehensive strike plan and could "handle a walkout."[2]

In an effort to dispel rumors of hidden money and a large fund balance, the board invited union negotiators and MEA representatives to attend the state auditor's exit meeting, where they were allowed to ask any questions they wished. The district proposed arbitration and called for collapsing some steps to equalize increases and raise starting salaries. It was announced that in the event of a strike, all activities would be cancelled.[3]

Teachers rejected arbitration, saying it always favored school boards' positions. By late September, the board increased its offer to 10.1 percent and 9.7 percent and dropped its proposal to restructure the salary schedule, while continuing to deny there was hidden money.[4] District finances were discussed at the next school board meeting, which was attended by the state auditor. His findings wouldn't be ready for thirty days. After the meeting, he was closely questioned by teachers about whether there was a hidden fund balance. The district continued to insist that budget figures were being misinterpreted.

The newspaper reported that both sides were following plans of action set at state headquarters (MEA and Minnesota School Boards Association), making it difficult to gauge the preferences of those involved at the local level.[5] If true, this would be an extraordinary case of a local school board and union being dictated to by state level organizations. In every other instance, districts and unions insisted they were operating independently, and were only utilizing state organizations for consultation and support.

Before the strike, the board increased its offer to 12.8 percent and 9.38 percent, with the teachers asking for 15.6 percent and 12.4 percent.[6] The second day of the strike, negotiations were conducted in a "spirit of friendliness and understanding." In dollar figures, the district offered $4,234, with the teachers asking for $5,400 average raises.[7]

An agreement was reached early enough on Wednesday, the third strike day, for the conference-contending football team to play. Some speculated that pressure to enable the game to proceed contributed to the quick settlement.

Teachers settled for $4,700, which included improved insurance and more personal leave days.[8] No make-up days were part of the agreement. It was reported that when school resumed, it was as if nothing had happened. There was no animosity or polarization on either side. Board members expressed some concern that in two years, cuts might have to be made because the surplus would be depleted.[9]

Whether because of pressure to support a winning football team, or effective negotiations, this was one of the least painful strikes.

CAMBRIDGE

THE SECOND MEDIATION SESSION in Cambridge was held September 14th. It was unsuccessful, and the union became one of nearly 200 to file an intent to strike notice. During the meeting, the union came down significantly from asking for forty-eight percent down to thirty-two percent. The district came up as well to thirteen percent each year, tied to three regressive language items. These included sharply reducing accumulating sick leave, giving up the right to take grievances to court and new language that would allow the district to suspend teachers without pay. Teachers complained about the district's use of a professional negotiator.[10]

At the next school board meeting, a parent presented a petition with 500 signatures supporting teacher's efforts to receive a fair settlement. Several board members responded to her remarks by saying that the district did have money available, but needed to use the interest earned on it. No new mediation sessions were scheduled.[11]

Parents involved themselves in many strikes, including with petitions. This is the only instance where parents pushed not for a settlement, but for the teachers' position. Moreover, they did so immediately after the intent to file notice, before even a vote to strike had been taken. While administrators and board members in other districts spoke of the value of using interest earned from reserve funds, it was unusual for this comment to come up during an official board meeting. It provides a clear statement of the board's priorities.

Mediation sessions were held on October 2nd and 3rd. Teachers rejected an offer of 14.7 percent and 13.2 percent, asking instead for twenty percent and 16.7 percent. The board said that teacher's demands would cause cash flow problems and result in tax increases. Teachers rejected the board's figures and responded that they shouldn't have to bear the burden if the district experienced financial problems. Teachers voted to strike October 12. Language issues included teachers' requests that transfers and extracurricular assignments become voluntary. No new sessions were scheduled.[12]

Both sides said they were willing to meet but the mediator declined, saying he was waiting for either side to change their offer. Don Hill, the MEA president, attended a rally the night before the strike began.[13]

The first mediation session wasn't held until nine days into the strike.[14] The meeting was held in St. Paul at the Bureau of Mediation, just down the hall from a room where the St. Cloud district was reaching an agreement. Cambridge negotiators exchanged proposals, with the district calling for binding arbitration on most items and the teachers lowering their request by $700. Teachers rejected arbitration and another offer to tie raises to successful passage of a levy referendum.

Teachers hosted an information session at the community college. It was attended by 500 people who were mostly supportive of the teachers' positions.[15]

By the fourth week of the strike, a group of parents formed to picket homes of negotiators and push for a settlement. The ministerial association said the strike was dividing the community and damaging the ability of school staff to work together. They called for more frequent mediation sessions and a search for solutions.[16]

The strike lasted past the governor's call for a special session to deal with a budget shortfall. The board authorized the use of subs and began advertising for them. Informal talks between the superintendent and teacher negotiators led to an all-night mediation session in St. Paul, attended by the full school board. An agreement was reached providing for 16.2 percent and 15.5 percent with 11.5 of twenty-two days made up. Emergency leave language was broadened and teachers could withdraw from extracurricular activities, based on seniority.[17,18]

CROOKSTON

NEGOTIATIONS IN CROOKSTON took place against a background of financial difficulty. In late September, voters rejected by over two to one a levy override vote designed to maintain current programs. The district was faced with cuts that couldn't be planned until after salaries were determined.[19] The link between pay raises and cuts was thus laid out clearly and publicly.

Teachers voted September 30 to strike on October 13. Language issues were largely settled. Teachers asked 34.7 percent and the board offered 17.4 percent. Days before the strike, the board increased its offer during a mediation session to twenty-one percent and the teachers came down to 29.5 percent.[20]

During a one-hour negotiation session the night before the strike, the district proposed using "last best offer" arbitration. Teachers refused and stated they needed an offer of at least 26.68% before they would submit it to a vote. Board negotiators said the district had been deficit spending for several years and stuck to their twenty-one-percent offer.[21] The strike began October 13. Forty non-teaching employees were laid off the first day of the strike, the superintendent calling them the "real victims" of the strike.[22]

A negotiation session held the first weekend of the strike produced some agreement on insurance but no movement on salaries.[23] A mediation session the fifth day of the strike saw teachers come down to 28.72 percent while the board didn't move. Teachers said making up all days would be a settlement condition; the board said none would be made up. Don Hill was in town, saying the MEA was 'ready to do battle' to support local unions.[24]

During a session held the second weekend of the strike, the board proposed 23.9 percent increase. Teachers voted it down the following day and counter proposed twenty-eight percent with all days made up. The board called making up all days ridiculous.[25]

A mediation session on day twelve produced several proposals. Teachers came down to 27.5 percent with ten days made up, the board stayed at 23.9 percent. When little progress had been made, the mediator suggested going to binding arbitration with teachers making up half the days and school resuming Monday.[26] Talks continued, and the two sides settled at 24.85 percent with six of twelve days made up.[27] Later in the month, the board directed the superintendent to make recommendations of programs and staff to be cut next school year.[28]

Glenwood

By the beginning of the school year, the two sides had met together eleven times. Issues included salary, personal leave and an additional eight minutes of preparation time for elementary teachers, providing as much prep time as secondary teachers received. The district viewed prep time in the same light as class size—both were inherent managerial rights and weren't negotiable. The district offered fifteen percent while the union asked for thirty percent. Due to the lack of progress, mediation was suggested.[29]

Neither side seemed prepared for the new pace of preparations leading up to possible strikes. During their next meeting, the school board requested a mediator and voted to hold their first closed negotiation session.[30] The union filed an intent to strike on September 14. The first mediation session was held three days later.[31]

During the session, the board increased its offer to thirteen percent and ten percent and compromised on leave language while holding fast on existing prep time. The union felt the leave changes were regressive and rejected the offer. The district offered to go to arbitration, but the union refused. The union wasn't prepared to make a counter offer, and the district claimed that teachers didn't want to find a settlement.

A mediation session was set for October 1st. Union leaders said they were willing to delay a strike in hopes that meeting was successful.[32] A strike authorization vote was held on September 28. The mediation session had to be postponed until October 13th because the mediator wasn't available. Teachers were angered that the district withdrew its twenty-three percent offer after it was rejected, returning to their previous position of fifteen percent. Teachers ran an ad in the local paper explaining their position.[33]

During a negotiation session held without the mediator on September 30th, the district reinstated its twenty-three percent offer, while the union came down to twenty-eight percent. The union indicated later that it would be willing to come down further if the prep time issue was resolved. District officials continued to insist that they couldn't guarantee that many minutes a day. The district approved strike plans calling for cancelling classes and extracurricular activities. The union announced on October 3 that the strike would begin October 12 if no agreement had been reached.[34]

A negotiation session held October 10th was unsuccessful and the strike began on schedule. A mediation session held the second day produced some movement. The district increased its financial offer to 23.5 percent, proposed shortening the school year by two days and agreed to make elementary prep time an official board policy and pay elementary teachers a $200 bonus.

The union continued to insist that prep time be written into the contract, which they said could be done if the district hired additional part time music and physical education staff. The board complained that the union hadn't budged from its positions during the last three sessions. Teachers replied that they were looking for a total agreement, and wouldn't move on money until the prep time issue was resolved. It was discovered that the two sides had been using different numbers of teachers in computing total cost and increases per teacher.[35]

An agreement was reached during the third day of the strike, providing 25.9 percent and one and one-half days made up. Teachers agreed to a board policy stating that elementary teachers would be provided forty minutes of prep time the first year of the contract, and fifty minutes the second.[36]

At this point, all would seem to be well. Both sides compromised and a settlement was reached in only three days. However, a disagreement quickly surfaced. The board felt it had agreed to a $5,175 increase *per teacher*. The union felt that they had agreed to an increased cost total of $336,375. The dispute involved how many teachers should be included in the calculation. The district counted only the sixty-five teachers working in the current school year and multiplied the dollar increase by that amount. The union felt that the newly negotiated increase should be added to the total paid to teachers the previous year, and divided by the number of teachers working this year.

This would have distributed last year's wages of four former teachers among the current staff, raising their average increases to $6,300. The district disputed this method of calculation, saying it was not what they agreed to. The union claimed they were using a method that had always been used in the past and on October 29th filed an intent to strike.[37] With a second strike date set for November 14, a mediation session was held November 11.[38]

Teachers agreed during the mediation session to accept the $5,175 average increase based on the lower number of teachers working in the current year.[39]

This seems to be a strike influenced by some naivety on both sides. A mediator wasn't called in until just before the MEA suggested locals file strike notices. The board clung to prep time as "inherent management right" even though the new strike law had changed the balance of power. The union appeared to feel it had a great deal of power, forging ahead to a strike despite very small differences in money. Teachers held to a rigid negotiating strategy, providing few counter proposals. It's difficult as well to understand how teachers felt they could fold the salaries of previously laid off teachers into their raises.

Hill City

Hill City was one of the smaller districts to strike, with only twenty-six teachers and 360 students. They filed an intent to strike on October 2nd, several weeks after many MEA locals. Meeting with a mediator in mid-September, the board offered $4,039 while teachers asked $5,339. The district announced that in the event of a strike that extracurricular events could take place if advisors and coaches would be found. The union said that coaches wouldn't work and that local subs had also agreed not to work.[40]

There were a number of informal offers exchanged in a session on Monday, October 12. The board came up $700 and the teachers down $200. The two sides disagreed on how far apart that left them. The board suggested arbitration, the union offered item by item last-best-offer arbitration. Both offers were rejected.

The negotiation session ended, and a school board meeting was held. The board formalized its decision to offer standard arbitration. The union president announced that he had been ready to make another offer to avoid a strike. In light of the board's arbitration decision they would be on strike at 12:01 A.M. the next morning, the earliest minute they could.[41]

This was unusual on the union's part, both to move to a strike at the earliest day possible and to provide so little advance notice—only a few hours.

The long MEA weekend provided enough time to reach a settlement, with students missing only two days. Teachers received $4,800, an additional personal leave day and increased insurance payments with one day made up. The superintendent said school restarted with a 'forgive and forget attitude' and a teacher negotiator said they put everything behind them and picked up where they left off.[42]

This was another brief strike with few after effects.

Isle

Although only slightly larger with thirty-two teachers, Isle wasn't as fortunate, perhaps because there were a number of language as well as economic issues. Professional leave, extra compensation for a sixth period or over twenty-five elementary students and making extra duty assignments voluntary were unresolved.[43] Teachers followed MEA timelines and filed an intent to strike notice on September 14.

A union spokesman said teacher morale was high because negotiations had been running smoothly and now that there was a strike deadline, they expected the contract to be settled soon. Tying the threat of a strike to an anticipated settlement illustrates the thinking of some locals under the new PELRA law. The superintendent on the other hand felt it was ludicrous to file an intent to strike while negotiations were making progress.[44]

The board adopted strike plans calling for closing schools and all activities. The union utilized MEA's pre-strike contingency plans.[45] During a September 25th session, the board costed the teacher's request as a fifty percent raise, countering with 20.1 percent. Teachers said they would strike on October 1st unless the board offered a starting salary of $13,000. The board negotiator's explanation of why anything over a fifteen percent raise would result in spending down the reserve wasn't believed. Teachers accepted the board language for professional leave and neared agreement on other language issues.[46]

All language issues were settled during an open session held September 30th attended by most of the teachers and thirty students and members of the public. A mediator would be sought for future meetings, with the authority to close sessions. The money gap closed with teachers asking $5,575 and the board offering $4,550. Because progress was being made, the union postponed the strike date until October 13—the last day available under their current intent to strike notification. A citizens group formed to provide information about strike-related issues. About fifty people attended the first meeting.[47]

The day before the strike, the board increased its offer to $5000 but agreement couldn't be reached on how to spread that out throughout the salary schedule. After the meeting, teachers met and, after one indecisive outcome, voted to strike.[48]

The strike began on the 13th, and a member of the board met with a teacher negotiator for much of the first day developing a proposal. It was discussed by the board as a whole on Wednesday, but rejected because it placed most of the raise in the first year. Board members said it would end up costing too much. The board member who had persuaded the professional negotiator and superintendent to move up to $5,000 was "crushed" by the teachers' rejection of that figure and the board's rejection of the proposal he had informally developed. Saying there was little else he had to offer, he talked of resigning from the board or not seeking reelection.

Two teachers had never agreed with the idea of striking and refused to picket. Teachers on the line talked of citizen's lack of understanding of the issues. Teachers received scheduled paychecks at the end of the second day of the strike, but had to line up outside the door of the district building to receive them.[49]

No sessions were held the second week of the strike until Friday. In response to a request by teachers for an earlier session, the superintendent said only that the professional negotiator and board members would all be available on Friday. Teachers and some members of the public attempted to call a session for Tuesday, but no board members attended.

During the Friday session, the $5,000 figure was utilized to develop a salary schedule. When the district's Apple II computer wasn't up to the task, a math teacher used his calculator to develop the grid. In percentages, it amounted to 15.1 percent the first year, 15.47 percent the second for a 30.57 percent total. The raises were loaded more heavily the second year, and were in line with what the district proposed the day before the strike. Three of the seven days would be made up, with the board negotiator saying teachers had to be punished for calling a strike. Union negotiators stormed out of the meeting at that point, but returned around midnight recommending ratification because the losses weren't worth continuing the strike.[50]

This is a rare instance of a strike that failed to produce any gains for teachers. All language issues had been settled before the strike began, and the only remaining issue was money. Teachers ended up settling for what they had been offered before the strike began and lost four days' pay. The situation could be chalked up to a failure by the district to prepare a salary schedule that could be discussed during negotiations until the last day of the strike, when it was largely developed by a math teacher.

Fridley

Superintendents sometimes loom large in the records of strikes. That certainly wasn't the case in Fridley, which was in the process of searching for a new superintendent.[51] Teachers voted September 24th to strike, with no date set. Guaranteed elementary prep time, teacher work days and the right to refuse extracurricular assignments were unsettled language issues. The board offered an average raise of $5,667, a twenty-five percent increase, and announced that no attempt would be made to reopen schools in the event of a strike.[52]

Negotiation sessions were infrequently held during the run up to the strike, meeting once the week of September 28, and a mediation session October 12th—the day before the strike. The union president was quoted, "I think we have it straight in our minds that this (strike) is going to happen. No matter what the (district's financial) situation is, teachers didn't cause it and we should not have to pay for it." The district had been experiencing declining enrollment and subsequent layoffs. Teachers said beginning salaries were $700 less than the metro average.[53]

During the mediation session, the board increased their offer by $100 and teachers lowered their request to $6,300. The district business manager said the reserve had $1,830,141 in operating funds.[54] This was a large amount in a district with 3,434 students and 209 teachers.

During a mediation session held the second week of the strike, teachers held firm to their salary request and the district refused to budge on language issues. The board suggested arbitration and invited teachers to a meeting to clarify issues about the district's finances. Teachers sang Christmas carols while on the strike line and decorated a Christmas tree in strike headquarters to symbolize how long they were willing to stay on strike.[55]

The strike was settled on October 28th. Teachers received $6,213 and made up six of ten days. Elementary prep time was guaranteed, but extracurricular assignments were not voluntary. A day would be provided at the end of each quarter, split between time for grading and in-service.[56]

Thief River Falls

Teachers filed an intent to strike on September 14th, along with other MEA locals. The board was offering eleven percent and 10.1 percent which it said would zero out the operating budget balance. The district's proposed salary schedules appeared on the front page of the paper. [57]

Creative offers were exchanged at the end of September. Teachers offered to bring unresolved language items to binding arbitration after thirty days of negotiations. The board suggested that all items, including salary be submitted to binding arbitration. When that was rejected, they offered non-binding arbitration. The union wanted to use the average of raises granted in the first five districts in the region. The first mediation session was scheduled for early October because no mediators had been available until then.[58]

Don Hill was in town on October 2nd, and teachers voted to authorize a strike after his talk. The district formed strike plans including no make-up days.[59] An audit showed that the district's reserve dropped the previous year by $156,000 to $883,000.[60]

In a mediation session the first week of October, the district offered $4,500 and the teachers asked $5,600. An offer by the teachers to split the difference was rejected. The strike was set for the following Tuesday. No sessions were scheduled.[61]

The strike began on Tuesday with four of 217 teachers crossing lines. The carpentry class at the vocational school had voted to meet during the strike, and was open. The instructor explained that he felt he was applying his Christian beliefs in holding class. The director of the vocational school expressed concern about the potential for a number of drop outs resulting from the strike.[62]

Picket lines were peaceful with postmen, UPS drivers, and a food delivery driver refusing to cross. The district made arrangements to pick up mail and UPS deliveries and the food truck driver delivered his load early in the morning before picket lines formed. Wednesday night, someone smeared manure on the windows of teachers' strike headquarters. The board sent a letter to homeowners stating that acceding to the teachers' demands would put the district well into a deficit the second year.[63]

A nine-hour negotiation session held on day six of the strike produced little movement. Teachers came down to $5,495 while the district didn't move. The session had been held in response to pressure not to wait until the mediator was available.[64] When a nine-hour mediation session was held on day eight, it produced no results, each side saying the other needed to make a move. Students were being lost to non-public schools.[65]

More than 500 people attended a public forum held to discuss the strike. Teachers answered questions. Board members didn't attend. The board continued to hold their position during a session on day fourteen while teachers dropped their request to $5,353.[66]

By day seventeen, citizens formed a group to support a strike settlement, and the student senate at the vocational school organized picketers. Informal talks between the board chair and chief teacher negotiator yielded no results. The union wanted all days made up, the board refused to offer any make up days.[67]

On day twenty, teachers voted not to consider an offer brought to them without comment by their negotiating team. It offered $5,150 and seven of twenty days made up. A settlement was reached two days later on November 13 for the same money with eight of twenty-two days made up. Teachers explained that they had settled because of the difficulties facing vocational students.[68]

Twenty five K-12 and sixty-one vocational students were lost.[69] The teachers' offer to split the difference before the strike would have resulted in an agreement at $5,100. After a prolonged strike and the loss of many students, the final settlement was $5,150. The board appeared to lose this struggle.

Granite Falls

In August, the two sides were very far apart in salary requests, with the board offering twenty-two percent over two years while teachers wanted twenty-two percent for the first year alone. It was agreed that a mediator would be called in, and previous positions were reverted to—only six percent by the board and thirty-two percent for the first year by teachers.[70] The superintendent and principals received a one year nine percent raise. Some board members expressed concern about the size of the raises, citing the faltering rural economy.[71]

Teachers filed an intent to strike along with other MEA locals on September 14th. No progress was made in the first mediation session, the board reiterating its position of twenty-two percent and the teachers requesting forty percent. Board members said they couldn't go higher because their offer would already dip into the reserve fund.[72]

The second mediation session produced some movement. The board increased its offer to 23.5 percent, a raise of $4,350 while teachers came down to thirty-nine percent or $7,600. The board suggested binding arbitration, which was rejected. The board also agreed to hire a professional negotiator for the first time and developed strike plans. Schools would be open only if substantial numbers of teachers crossed the lines. Football would continue because those coaches weren't teachers.[73]

Formation of a strike plan by the board angered teachers, who voted to authorize a strike after an unsuccessful negotiation session.[74] The board had gone up to $4,800 while teachers came down to $6,800. Both sides cited comparison salaries to bolster their positions.[75]

The strike began October 14—the day before MEA—after the board provided what it called its final offer of $5,000.[76] The mediator called them together the second day of the strike. The board agreed to meet, even though their professional negotiator couldn't attend. The mediator said it was his practice to call parties together as soon as possible after a strike started because the issue of make-up days got bigger and bigger as time passed.

Picketing was peaceful, with teachers avoiding a school construction site and athletic events.[77] The peace was shattered the sixth day of the strike when the publisher of a local agricultural paper drove through the picket line without stopping. When he parked, a teacher asked him to honor the picket line and the publisher advised the striker that if they were in his way, he would run over them. When he left the building, he squealed his tires while accelerating at the picket line, leaving twenty feet of tire marks.

As he neared the pickets he slammed on the brakes but was unable to stop, knocking a teacher up onto the hood of his car.

The teacher rolled off and the driver left, shaking his fist at the picketers. He was charged with three misdemeanors—reckless driving, failure to stop at a picket line and hit-and-run driving. The teacher was bruised and suffered chipped cartilage in his back.

A mediation session on day eight produced some shuffling of monies, but both sides held firm to their total costs.[78] Teachers were down to $6,200 by day twelve of the strike, but the district continued to hold firm at $5,000, saying it was considering hiring subs. The driver who hit a picketer pled guilty to careless driving and failing to stop. He was fined $500 and given a suspended ninety-day jail sentence.[79]

The board voted on day fifteen to hire subs to be paid ninety dollars per day, beginning with grades one through three and twelve. A citizens group led by two ministers called a meeting attended by negotiators and forty people. Both sides explained their positions. The citizens' group then presented a compromise proposal that was rejected by both sides. The board approved a twenty-eight percent increase in the tax levy to make up for the state's reduction in funding.[80]

Classes for grades one, two, and twelve opened on day twenty-two of the strike. Two days later, grades four and eleven were added. The day before school reopened, teachers voted on an offer of $5,403 with five make up days. They turned it down four votes short of the two-thirds majority the local required for approval. While the money was acceptable, the limited number of make-up days wasn't. Teachers opened an alternative school for grades one through three, saying MEA lawyers assured them it had the same legal status as other private schools.[81]

The strike ended November 22 after twenty-six days. Teachers received $5,403 and made up eight days. The agreement included two "volunteer" days to help with school related matters with no pay. Union members weren't told of the two days until after they'd voted.[82] It's a good thing they voted to accept however, since in the last week of the strike they gained no increase in the salary offer and realized a net loss of another two days.

New Prague

Early in September the New Prague school district increased its offer to eighteen percent. Teachers countered with a request more than double that, at 37.9 percent. Saying they had no inclination toward striking, teachers moved ahead with other MEA locals to submit paperwork that would allow a strike.[83]

A new superintendent was hired in mid-September. At the same board meeting, strike plans were approved. The board had increased its offer to nineteen percent. Little progress was reported on language issues. Teachers worked to develop a distribution model for how raises should be placed on the salary schedule.[84]

Teachers voted on October 1st to strike on the 15th if an agreement wasn't reached. Language issues included preparation time, personal leave, extra pay for a sixth class, early retirement and severance benefits. The board's suggestion of mediation was rejected by teachers who said it would take too long to obtain one. Board members were surprised and bewildered by the strike vote because mediation hadn't begun. They felt the law intended that mediation be used prior to a strike.

Board negotiators said they were offering 23.7 percent while teachers were asking thirty-five percent. However, the board refused to give up management rights. Teachers said they were willing to meet any time, but the board wanted to stick to the original schedule of meeting every other week, with the next session scheduled October 12.[85,86]

Sessions were held the Saturday and Monday prior to the strike. The board wanted to focus on total costs while teachers were primarily concerned with how the raises would be distributed across the salary schedule. By Monday, teachers were willing to consider the use of a mediator.[87] There was no time to arrange for one before the strike deadline.

No agreement was reached during a twenty-five-hour session that began on Wednesday, so teachers began picketing on October 15. This was the first day of the MEA weekend so school had not been scheduled. Teachers picketed Friday as well, with negotiations beginning again on Monday. An agreement was reached the next day providing a $5,300 raise and both days made up. The district accepted teacher's proposals for how to distribute the raise. Language issues weren't settled, but it was agreed they would be discussed in meet-and-confer sessions to be held before the end of the school year.

The district said that the second year of the contract would result in $100,000 of deficit spending unless programs were cut and staff laid off, or a referendum was passed.[88] The next week, the board approved a tax levy increase of twenty percent.[89]

Both parties seemed a little naïve. The board in assuming teachers would utilize mediation before deciding to strike and that management rights that were formerly common could be held onto in an era that included the right to strike. Teachers picketed empty schools for several days, and agreed to settle with language issues unresolved.

Lester Prarie

No negotiation sessions were held between July 22nd and September 8th. In addition to salary, language issues included limiting elementary class size, prep time and insurance.[90] The lack of negotiation sessions became a factor when the union filed an intent to strike on September 14 along with other MEA locals. A mediation session the next day resolved language issues.[91]

Despite no strike date having been set, the board set strike plans which included no make-up days. The district offered $3798 while teachers asked $5,850.[92] During a school board meeting, the district made what it called its final offer of $4,150 . . ."today, tomorrow, next week, during a strike, or after a strike." The board said their offer would result in deficit spending and offered arbitration.[93]

These hard-nosed bargaining positions by the board were tempered a week later by their discussion of raising fees and making some minor cuts to provide money for a larger raise. Teachers suggested using capital outlay money, which could be done if approved by voters.[94]

A strike date was set for October 14 at 10:00 p.m.—after the football game.[95] At that time, the board was offering $4,200 while teachers asked

$5,250. The board disagreed with the teachers' method of calculating costs. The board discussed opening school with subs paid seventy dollars per day, if enough could be found.[96]

The strike began after the football game—an unusual gesture on the part of a local. During MEA weekend a long session was held during which the board offered $4,880. Teachers voted to reject the offer. The board rejected splitting the difference with the teachers' request of $5,070, which would have resulted in a settlement of $4,965. Both side reverted to their previous positions.

The following Monday—the first day school was out—the union's chief negotiator stepped down, saying he had done all he could to bring about a settlement. He continued on the committee, and a new head negotiator was named.[97]

The board began seeking subs, planning to reopen schools the week of November 2. During a board meeting, members of the public urged meeting without a mediator. The board replied that their professional negotiator had recommended meeting only with a mediator. During a mediation session after five strike days, the board offered $4,677 with one make up day while teachers made two offers—$5,071 with all days made up, or $5,335 with no make-up days.[98]

The strike ended November 1st with nine of ten days made up and $4,989.[99] The superintendent talked about planning budget cuts.[100] The school year was extended from May 27 to June 4 with four Saturday teacher workshop days.[101]

The board could have avoided any disruption and saved fourteen dollars per teacher if it had agreed to split the difference during the mediation session held after the strike began.

---

1. *Proctor Journal*, September 10, 1981, p. 1..
2. *Proctor Journal*, September 17, 1981, p. 1
3. *Proctor Journal*, September 24, 1981, pp. 1, 4.
4. *Proctor Journal*, October 1, 1981, pp. 1, 11.
5. *Proctor Journal*, October 8, 1981, p. 1.
6. *Duluth News, Tribune*, October 12, 1981, p. 1.

7. *Proctor Journal*, October 15, 1981, p. 1.
8. *Duluth News Tribune*, October 15, 1981, pp. 2A, 10A.
9. *Proctor Journal*, October 22, 1981, pp. 1, 11.
10. *Cambridge Star*, September 16, 1981, p. 1.
11. *Cambridge Star*, September 23, 1981, p. 1.
12. *Cambridge Star*, October 7, 1981, p. 1.
13. *Cambridge Star*, October 14, 1981, pp. 1, 2.
14. *Cambridge Star*, October 28, 1981, p. 1.
15. *Cambridge Star*, November 4, 1981, p. 1.
16. *Cambridge Star*, November 11, 1981, pp. 1, 4.
17. *Cambridge Star*, November 18, 1981, p. 1.
18. *Cambridge Star*, December 2, 1981, p. 1.
19. *Crookston Daily Times*, September 23, 1981, pp. 1, 2.
20. *Crookston Daily Times*, October 10, 1981, p. 1, 2.
21. *Crookston Daily Times*, October 13, 1981, p. 1.
22. *Crookston Daily Times*, October 14, 1981, pp. 1, 2.
23. *Crookston Daily Times*, October 19, 1981, pp. 1, 2.
24. *Crookston Daily Times*, October 22, 1981, pp. 1, 2.
25. *Crookston Daily Times*, October 27, 1981, pp. 1, 2.
26. *Crookston Daily Times*, October 30, 1981, p. 1.
27. *Crookston Daily Times*, November 2, 1981, pp. 1, 2.
28. *Crookston Daily Times*, November 10, 1981, p. 1.
29. *Glenwood-Pope County Tribune*, August 27, 1981, p. 1.
30. *Glenwood-Pope County Tribune*, September 3, 1981, pp. 1, 2A.
31. *Glenwood-Pope County Tribune*, September 17, 1981, p. 1.
32. *Glenwood-Pope County Tribune*, September 24, 1981, p. 1B.
33. *Glenwood-Pope County Tribune*, October 1, 1981, pp. 1, 2A, 4A.
34. *Glenwood-Pope County Tribune*, October 8, 1981, pp. 1, 2A.
35. *Glenwood-Pope County Tribune*, October 15, 1981, pp. 1, 2A.
36. *Glenwood-Pope County Tribune*, October 22, 1981, pp. 1, 2A.
37. *Glenwood-Pope County Tribune*, November 5, 1981, pp. 1, 2A.
38. *Glenwood-Pope County Tribune*, November 12, 1981, p. 1.
39. *Glenwood-Pope County Tribune*, December 3, 1981, p. 1.
40. *Aitkin Independent Age*, October 7, 1981, p. 1.
41. *Proctor Journal*, October 14, 1981, p. 1.
42. *Proctor Journal*, October 21, 1981, p. 1.
43. *Mille Lacs Messenger*, September 10, 1981, p. 8.
44. *Mille Lacs Messenger*, September 16, 1981, p. 2.

45. *Mille Lacs Messenger*, September 23, 1981, pp. 2, 5, 15.
46. *Mille Lacs Messenger*, September 30, 1981, pp. 1, 2.
47. *Mille Lacs Messenger*, October 7, 1981, p. 8.
48. *Mille Lacs Messenger*, October 14, 1981, p. 1.
49. *Mille Lacs Messenger*, October 21, 1981, pp. 2, 7.
50. *Mille Lacs Messenger*, October 28, 1981, pp. 1, 2.
51. *The Fridley Sun*, September 23, 1981, p. 1.
52. *The Fridley Sun*, September 30, 1981, pp. 1, 3.
53. *The Fridley Sun*, October 7, 1981, pp. 1, 6.
54. *The Fridley Sun*, October 21, 1981, pp. 1, 4.
55. *The Fridley Sun*, October 28, 1981, pp. 1, 3.
56. *The Fridley Sun*, November 4, 1981, pp. 1, 4.
57. *Thief River Falls Times*, September 14, 1981, pp. 1, 7.
58. *Thief River Falls Times*, September 30, 1981, p. 1.
59. *Thief River Falls Times*, October 5, 1981, pp. 1, 4.
60. *Thief River Falls Times*, October 7, 1981, p. 1.
61. *Thief River Falls Times*, October 12, 1981, p. 1.
62. *Thief River Falls Times*, October 14, 1981, p. 1, 18.
63. *Thief River Falls Times*, October 19, 1981, pp. 1, 4.
64. *Thief River Falls Times*, October 26, 1981, pp. 1, 4.
65. *Thief River Falls Times*, October 28, 1981, pp. 1, 3.
66. *Thief River Falls Times*, November 4, 1981, pp. 1, 3.
67. *Thief River Falls Times*, November 9, 1981, pp. 1, 3.
68. *Thief River Falls Times*, November 16, 1981, pp. 1, 5.
69. *Thief River Falls Times*, November 18, 1981, pp. 1, 3.
70. *Granite Falls Tribune*, August 20, 1981, pp. 1, 14.
71. *Granite Falls Tribune*, September 10, 1981, pp. 1, 16.
72. *Granite Falls Tribune*, September 17, 1981, pp. 1, 16.
73. *Granite Falls Tribune*, September 24, 1981, pp. 1, 14.
74. *Granite Falls Tribune*, October 1, 1981, p. 1.
75. *Granite Falls Tribune*, October 8, 1981, pp. 1, 20.
76. *Granite Falls Tribune*, October 15, 1981, p. 1.
77. *Granite Falls Tribune*, October 22, 1981, pp. 1, 16.
78. *Granite Falls Tribune*, October 29, 1981, pp. 1, 18.
79. *Granite Falls Tribune*, November 5, 1981, pp. 1, 18.
80. *Granite Falls Tribune*, November 12, 1981, pp. 1, 18.
81. *Granite Falls Tribune*, November 19, 1981, pp. 1, 16.
82. *Granite Falls Tribune*, November 26, 1981, pp. 1, 14.

83. *The New Prague Times*, September 10, 1981, p. 1.
84. *The New Prague Times*, October 1, 1981, p. 1.
85. *The New Prague Times*, October 8, 1981, p. 1.
86.
87. *The New Prague Times*, October 12, 1981, pp. 1, 2.
88. *The New Prague Times*, October 22, 1981, p. 1.
89. *The New Prague Times*, October 29, 1981, p. 1.
90. *Lester Prairie Journal*, September 10, 1981, p. 1.
91. *Lester Prairie Journal*, September 17, 1981, p. 1.
92. *Lester Prairie Journal*, September 24, 1981, p. 1.
93. *Lester Prairie Journal*, October 1, 1981, pp. 1, 8.
94. *Lester Prairie Journal*, October 1, 1981, p. 1.
95. *Glencoe Enterprise*, October 8, 1981, p. 3A.
96. *Lester Prairie Journal*, October 15, 1981, p. 1.
97. *Lester Prairie Journal*, October 22, 1981, pp. 1, 9.
98. *Lester Prairie Journal*, October 29, 1981, p. 1.
99. *Lester Prairie Journal*, November 5, 1981, p. 1.
100. *Lester Prairie Journal*, November 12, 1981, pp. 1, 4.
101. *Lester Prairie Journal*, November 26, 1981, p. 1.

Chapter Nineteen
After MEA

Grand Meadow

Grand Meadow set midnight on the Monday after MEA as their strike deadline.[1] The strike began on schedule the 20th involving twenty-eight teachers and 350 students. The two sides were $2,500 apart on money issues and disagreed on language concerning prep time and job security.[2]

A mediation session on the fourth day of the strike resulted in an impasse. Teachers reduced their request from $5,900 down to $5,546 but the board held firm on its previous offer of $3,012. Teachers said they were waiting on the board to make a move, and no talks were scheduled.[3]

Eleven days into the strike, the teachers' request was down to $5,400 and the district had come up to $4,075. Make up days had become an issue, with teachers asking for all days to be made up, while the board was adamant that none would be. The use of substitutes was under discussion.[4]

An agreement was reached November 15th providing seven make up days out of nineteen and $4,800.[5]

Eveleth

By early October, teachers in Eveleth were preparing to strike. The board was offering 27.7 percent while teachers were requesting 34.7 percent. The board placed more money than teachers suggested in the bottom of the salary range, and less at the top. Teachers said their wages had been falling behind other districts for years, and wanted wages that would bring them into line with the neighboring Virginia school district. Eveleth board members countered that Virginia had some of the highest salaries in the area and talked of layoffs, larger class sizes and eliminating extracurricular activities.[6]

A letter from the school board was published stating that they intended to hold firmly to the position of not making up strike days.[7] A mediation session was unsuccessful on October 20th and teachers voted to strike the next day. The board had increased its offer to 31.5 percent while teachers came down to 34.7 percent.[8]

A parents group formed the second day of the strike seeking a settlement.[9] The superintendent said the board didn't plan to meet until the teachers prepared a counter offer.[10] Don Hill was in town for a union sponsored rally the fourth day of the strike, telling teachers he was very impressed with the local community support.

A number of Democratic Farmer Labor (DFL) state representatives and senators also attended, supporting teachers. Dominic Elioff, a representative from Virginia, said, "I think the MSBA (Minnesota School Boards Association) targeted certain districts to strike to weaken the power of the PELRA bill."[11]

The school board responded to this statement with a letter sent to the state DFL committee saying Representative Elioff had abused the power of his office and had a conflict of interest because his wife taught in the Eveleth schools. They stated, "During an appearance at a strike rally in Eveleth he made the ridiculous and untrue statement that Eveleth had been targeted by the Minnesota School Board Association for a strike."

Teachers attempted during the next board meeting to get a date set for a session ahead of the November 5th mediation date. State finances intruded into the negotiations after the school board met with MSBA to hear about the state's revenue shortfall and possible cuts. The superintendent said projected state cuts were frightening and that he wasn't sure the board could continue with the same offer it had already made.[12]

The first negotiation session was held on day eight of the strike. Teachers lowered their salary request and then had to withdraw their offer when they discovered an error in their figures. The board said what they had been offering would already result in increased class sizes and layoffs. They urged teachers to accept it, saying that because of the state funding shortfall, they might not see an offer that high again.[13]

After nine days, vocational students presented a letter to the superintendent demanding a settlement.[14] LPN students were in danger of missing being eligible for state boards, which would not be offered for another six months.[15] Two days later, prior to a mediation session, the board said that it might have to reduce its offer in light of possible state budget cuts.[16]

A tentative agreement was reached November 12th and school began the 16th. Eight of eighteen days were made up and the salary schedule provided 32.9 percent raises for senior teachers, with newer teachers gaining 20.5 percent.

Forest Lake

The Forest Lake strike took place in a very hostile editorial environment. The vituperation heaped on the union by the local paper appeared to have little effect on the outcome.

The district faced difficult financial conditions, and had cut $200,000 from the previous year's budget. A referendum was planned for September 17 to avoid more cuts.[17] In early September, the board offered 18.87 percent while teachers asked forty-one percent. The upcoming levy vote slowed negotiations, the board stating that its offer was contingent on the levy passing.[18]

The levy passed with fifty-five percent of the vote, providing an additional one million dollars. Some cuts continued to be discussed.[19] The fourteenth negotiation session was held October 13. When it was unsuccessful, teachers voted to authorize a strike. The district offered $5,000 while teachers remained at $6,349, saying they wanted to get closer to the average of other metro districts. The board said its offer was final and already so high it would result in ten to twenty teachers being laid off the second year. An editorial called a possible strike a war and unfair to students.[20]

The board didn't move during another mediation session the following week. An editorial called school's budgeting processes 'lies' and suggested negotiating before setting budgets, and the use of binding arbitration before strikes. The local paper published the district's proposed salary schedules.[21]

The board continued to hold firm during mediation sessions on Friday and Monday before the strike began on Tuesday October 27. Teachers dropped their request to $5,800. Beginning teachers said that the increases in health insurance coverage would eat up most of the district's proposed raise. An editorial stated, "Strikes are another one of the devices of the devil put on this earth to accomplish more harm than good."[22]

The first week of the strike produced a number of incidents. Responding to anonymous telephone threats, the district hired off-duty police officers to provide protection to board members and administrators. A letter carrier had trouble crossing the picket line, saying one member was carrying a knife on his belt. The mailman later crossed with a sheriff's deputy and postmaster. Pellets were fired at the windshield of a school bus. The union denied that teachers were involved in any of the incidents. Teachers filed seven complaints against motorists for failing to stop for picket lines.

Teachers gained favorable public relations by hosting a Halloween party at a church to replace the celebrations usually held at elementary schools. A mediation session the first weekend of the strike didn't produce any formal offers, but both sides expressed some willingness to compromise.[23]

A settlement was reached during a mediation session on day fourteen. Teachers got $5,450 with seven of fourteen days made up. The agreement was approved four to three by the board and by sixty-eight percent of the teachers. The board authorized the administration to begin planning budget reductions for the second year of the contract. Make up days included twelve days extended fifteen minutes earlier and later.[24] Budget plans for next year called for laying off fourteen teachers, most at the secondary level.[25]

An editorial criticized the board for compromising at fifty dollars over half the difference between pre-strike positions and questioned why the strike was necessary.[26] It does appear that the board would have been better off settling before the strike.

Mahtomedi

Mahtomedi teachers were slow to file an intent to strike, waiting until the beginning of October. Teachers said that the district was earning $200,000 annually from its one-million-dollar reserve and that talks were being slowed down because the district's negotiator wasn't available. The union requested twenty-four percent plus full hospital medical and dental coverage. Starting salaries were among the highest in the state, but lagged behind for teachers with more experience and master's degrees. Despite the filing, negotiations were scheduled and teachers didn't anticipate striking.[27]

An indication of past labor-management relationships was evident in the case of a veteran teacher fired in 1979. She claimed it occurred because she criticized a decision to lower the number of credits high school students were required to take. The administration charged her with poor job performance, including resistance to legitimate direction and criticism. She took her firing to the Minnesota Supreme Court, which ruled in her favor.[28]

The strike began at the end of the day on Friday, October 30th. Teachers hoped that weekend negotiations would produce an agreement before they had to miss any school days. The district had offered 24.71 percent while teachers asked 30.54 percent. Teachers said their relationship with the superintendent was excellent, and hoped it would stay that way. Teachers also wanted to retain contract language which dealt with equal rights for women and minorities.[29]

A church organized a day program by day two. A union negotiator said the two sides were close on salary, but far apart on fringe benefits.[30] Informal talks continued during the second week of the strike. The complications a strike produces can be seen in the union spokesman's assertion that a recent district offer might have been accepted before the strike started, but make-up days were now an issue.[31]

A mediation session resulted in the two sides coming within a total of $50,000. The union rejected the district's offer of binding arbitration. Parents circulated a petition calling for a marathon negotiation session until an agreement was reached, but the mediator cut off the next session when he saw no movement on either side.[32]

Four church leaders were concerned enough after the strike was a month old to produce a ten point call to action that they shared with parishioners during Sunday services. The call for action encouraged phone calls to the district office and school board members. It suggested that if the board couldn't offer competitive salaries and quality teachers, it should consider consolidating with another district. A follow up march and prayer service that night was attended by eighty adults and fifty children.

The effort was criticized as being pro-teacher because it didn't include a suggestion to call union leaders. A group of parents counter-picketed at the elementary school, urging teachers to submit the dispute to binding arbitration.[33]

During a twelve-hour negotiation session in early December the board offered $5,863 if teachers would agree to submit the longevity issue to arbitration. Teachers refused and the district decided to begin hiring substitutes. The senior high would open first, followed by elementary grades.[34]

Classes reopened December 10th with forty-nine substitutes earning $100 a day. The union called some of them professional strikebreakers because they had subbed in other striking districts. Parents described feelings in town as bitter. Teachers claimed that the district's negotiator was using Mahtomedi as a painful example of what can happen if teachers strike. Others blamed the MEA for using the strike to strengthen itself.

The grievance issue revolved around a board proposal to eliminate a provision allowing teachers to grieve violations of state or federal laws. Teachers wanted to retain the right to grieve instances such as classroom overcrowding that violated state fire marshal's rules.[35]

The union filed an unfair labor practice suit in court the following week, seeking a restraining order against the use of subs. They claimed that the district was employing strikebreakers who had crossed picket lines in as many as four other strikes and was paying subs more than the district's average teacher. The board denied that, saying they were paid less than the average under the current contract.

The lawsuit came at the same time that negotiations had resulted in an agreement about average salary increases, but not how to distribute them. The union asked for twenty-two make-up days, while the district offered only five. Disagreement remained on grievance language.[36]

An agreement was reached December 19th, hours after a judge had denied the teacher's request for a restraining order against the use of subs.

He ruled that the state law limiting strikebreakers applied only to private businesses, not public employers.[37]

Teachers received 26.5 percent, longevity pay, and dental insurance.[38] The strike lasted thirty-three days, with none made up. Although teachers would take a financial hit, getting longevity pay made it worth striking.[39]

Print media coverage of this strike was limited, making it difficult to understand the nuances of the issues involved. If—as union spokesman said—teachers got along well with the superintendent, then this wasn't a bad blood strike. There were no quotes from board members or the union blaming the other side, as often happened in other strikes.

Losing thirty-three days was a financially painful way to develop longevity pay and some increased health insurance, requiring decades to recoup. Pure economics would seem to have led to settling sooner. The grievance issue was unusual. Other strikes included conflicts about basic grievance language, but no other teachers sought to grieve over violations of state and federal laws. It's not clear why teachers would want to do that, when other legal and regulatory remedies were available.

Altogether, this was quite a nasty prolonged strike in what had been a quiet small community.

Sauk Centre

Reflecting confusion that existed about the new PELRA law, teachers believed that they had to file an intent to strike notice by September 14th in order to preserve their right to strike. They described their decision to file as a matter of working within regulations governing the bargaining process. They accused the district's paid negotiator of prolonging the bargaining process in order to increase his fees and claimed he was pushing for a strike because it was in his financial interest.[40]

A levy vote was held September 17. The district said it was necessary to offset declining enrollment and a lack of state funding. Cuts planned if the levy failed would result in larger class sizes and reductions in many programs.[41] The levy was defeated by a two to one margin, forcing the district to begin planning on cutting $120,000.

The filing of an intent to strike on September 14 led to bargaining sessions on the 14 and 15. The board came up to $4,391, a twenty-two-percent raise. Teachers asked thirty-five percent. The district made strike plans, including offering subs seventy-five dollars per day—the amount of salary and fringe benefits being offered new teachers. The union talked with fifteen substitute teachers asking them to honor picket lines.[42]

There were no sessions between September 16 and October 9. The board said it had been waiting for the teachers' counter proposal. During the session on the 9th, teachers proposed a 23.5 percent for the first year and 9.73 percent the second. The board stayed at twenty-two percent, saying that offer would create a deficit of $300,000 the second year. Teachers voted to strike at the end of the school day on October 30.[43]

A mediation session was set for the day before the strike. Concerns were expressed for the volleyball and football teams, whose winning seasons had the potential to be topped off with championships.[44] Teachers went out after school on Friday, October 30, having turned down a last minute offer of $4,678. The board rejected the teachers' proposal of $4,990 because it didn't include the cost of benefit increases.

Teachers voted to allow coaches to cross the picket lines. District negotiators said they wanted to maintain a balanced education program and would not reprioritize spending to meet teachers' demands. The board held public sessions to get feedback on proposed cuts for next year.[45]

The mediator presented a compromise position during a session held the seventh day of the strike. The board accepted it but teachers turned it down. The understanding was that if either side rejected it, both would return to their respective positions.[46] The mediator had proposed $4,962 with half the days made up. The following week, teachers proposed $5,195 with six of eleven days made up. The board said the actual cost would be $500 more than that, and rejected it.[47]

The mediator suggested binding arbitration during a session held on day seventeen. The board agreed, teachers did not. The board approved advertising for subs at $100 a day—increased because teachers had turned down a similar average daily pay rate. The board chair expressed reluctance in hiring subs but said, "The teachers just don't seem to take us seriously that we will not give them back lost work days."[48]

An agreement was reached December 3rd. Teachers received $4,973 and made up eighteen of twenty-two days. Teachers had planned to open an alternative school and the district had lined up twenty-six substitutes with intentions of opening school on a partial basis.[49]

Art, Physical Education, some science, and business courses were cut for the next school year to make up a $400,000 deficit. It was proposed that as many as twenty teachers of ninety could be laid off.[50]

Jordan

After little progress had been made during three mediation sessions, the union in Jordan filed its intent to strike on September 14th. Agreement had been reached only on how much had been spent on the previous year's salaries.

Teachers' had presented nineteen language issues including personal leave, length of the work day, prep time and notification when something was placed in their personnel files. Teachers claimed that an atmosphere of unrest and overwork existed in the district that had led to a lot of teachers leaving. The district offered a total package of 21.5 percent. The union said the district was far behind and asked for 44.31 percent.[51]

Enrollment had dropped by three percent to just over 1700 students, causing the district to dip into reserve funds.[52] The board developed strike plans in late September and the superintendent began advertising for subs.

The board chair rejected the request by the union to discuss the nineteen language items directly with the board, saying that he preferred not to negotiate in public. The district was utilizing a professional negotiator who they felt should meet with teachers. The board chair was willing to talk with teachers only if they reduced the number of language issues from nineteen to five.[53]

Superficial progress was made during an October 8 meditation session. The district increased its offer to 23.33 percent. The union reduced the number of language issues from nineteen to ten. The board complained that the union had merely consolidated issues without really removing any. The union continued to reject the district's attempts to rescind previous contract language by limiting leaves, requiring staff to choose between grieving issues or taking them to court, having the right to assign additional duties and more easily suspend teachers. They voted overwhelmingly to strike.[54]

Teachers announced that they wouldn't go out on the first day possible because of a scheduled mediation session. A letter they sent to all board members blamed the district's negotiator for introducing regressive language into the last mediation session.[55] Progress was made during the next session, with the board agreeing to language about hours of service and personnel files. Three language items remained unsettled. The board increased its salary offer to 25.97 percent, which it said was in line with average settlements.[56]

A mediation session held on Sunday, the day before the strike, produced little movement. The board said it would drop all its language proposals if the teachers would accept a package settlement of $5,025, saying their language requests weren't that big an issue. Teachers reduced their demand to $5,572 and rejected the district's offer. The strike began the following day, November 2.[57]

Teachers set up a public session for November 4th, but only one board member showed up. They set up a public meeting the following night, but the same board member was the only one who attended. She said that other board members hadn't been in contact with her to say they weren't coming. The board chair said they wouldn't meet in public because they were waiting for the mediator to set up a session, justifying this by saying the teachers were the ones who had requested mediation.

An editorial criticized the board for its lack of communication. A mediation session was held on day seven of the strike, during which teachers lowered their demand by fifty dollars. No other progress was made. The superintendent announced that he would begin interviewing subs with the intent of opening schools on the following Tuesday—day twelve of the strike.[58]

Another mediation session was held after the strike had gone on for two weeks. An agreement was reached providing 31.23 percent or $5,446.75 with two of ten days made up. Language agreements included prep time, the length of the work day, extra duty assignments, an additional personal leave day and a greater contribution by the district toward health insurance. The board expressed relief that subs weren't needed to reopen schools.[59]

At first glance, this looks like a case of successful hard-ball negotiations by the district. Led by a professional negotiator, they introduced regressive language late in the process to counter teacher's requests for better language. They later offered to drop their language if teachers would accept a lower salary proposal. The district also interjected the possible use of subs as soon as teachers filed a strike vote. The superintendent's announcement of reopening schools came three days before teachers settled.

On the other hand, teachers received quite a nice settlement. Splitting the salary differences the day before the strike would have resulted in $5,299. Instead, teachers received $5,446.75. They also received most of their language requests without losing any of the regressive language measures proposed by the district.

Did the district need to employ these tactics, when in the end it conceded most of the language issues, and more than half the money difference? It appears that this was a case where the machinations of a professional negotiator played a significant part in determining the strategy of a school board.

Hibbing

Teachers in Hibbing filed an intent to strike on September 14. In addition to salary, class size and unused sick leave were issues.[60] Teachers voted Tuesday October 27th to strike the following Monday. The board offered $3,800 while teachers asked $5,100. The district had been over $500,000 in debt before a seven-mil levy passed in the summer to preserve programs. The board decided to only use two of the seven mils. Teachers wanted more of it used to increase salaries.[61]

In the week before the strike, the board moved up to $4,200 while teachers held firm at $5,100. Teachers objected to some health insurance provisions. The district said the total package was comparable to other districts and that the ball was in the teachers' court. All programs would be closed during a strike.[62]

The strike began November 2. Board members said they promised not to raise the tax levy above two mils and wouldn't go above that.[63] The status of future negotiations was confused on the second day of the strike, with each side saying they were waiting for the other to make a proposal.[64] The mediator refused to call another meeting until one side had a proposal.[65]

Don Hill was in town for a rally the fifth night of the strike, saying the state should increase taxes rather than cut aid to schools.[66] At the same time, a negotiating session was being held that resulted in an agreement.

Teachers received $4,821 and made up all five strike days. The mil levy would not increase. Additional monies to pay for the raise would come from layoffs and savings realized through retirements. Despite the quick settlement, one clergyman described the feelings of his congregation toward the strike as 'absolute hostility'.[67] The board voted to give vocational students a five-day tuition refund credited to their next tuition payment.[68]

Bemidji

The Bemidji strike had a typical beginning and strange ending. A tax levy was planned to avoid cuts.[69] The union filed an intent to strike along with other locals on September 14th.[70] The board adopted a strike plan that included no make-up days and recruiting former teachers and volunteers.[71] The levy passed by a two to one margin.[72]

The fifth mediation session was held September 18th and yielded agreement on leaves, the first progress seen during negotiations. Salaries were not discussed.[73] Additional language was agreed to a week later but the union's salary proposal was rejected. Teachers dropped a request for a cost of living clause, asking instead for a forty percent raise over two years.[74]

Teachers voted October 8 to authorize a strike if necessary.[75] Both sides moved during a mediation session, the board going to twenty-two percent while the teachers came down to 38.4 percent. A strike date was set on October 9 for November 3.[76]

Eighty one community members signed up to help during a strike. Thirty-two had teaching experience, although not all had current licenses.

The others agreed to serve as aides or do other volunteer work. Substitutes would be paid the regular sub's wage of forty-one dollars per day. Subs on the district's list were not contacted.[77]

The latest request from the teachers was down to $6,958, while the board stayed at $4,000.[78] The board produced a new salary schedule, with most of the increases given to newer teachers. Average raises were increased to $4,100.[79]

A last-minute mediation session failed, and the strike began November 4. The board offered $4,300 while teachers requested $5,500. Once the strike was announced, teachers stated that their salary request had increased to $6,558. An editorial said that the majority of citizens made less than half of a teacher's salary.[80] The union's rationale for raising their demand wasn't clear. No negotiations were scheduled.

Five classes at the vocational school reopened with supervisory staff the second day of the strike. An editorial laid the responsibility for the last minute break down in negotiations on the teachers' refusal to move from their high demand.

The district had planned to open Riverside School, a building that served emotionally disturbed children from a residential treatment center. Teachers picketed the building heavily the second day of the strike. Eight of the building's eleven teachers crossed the line, but the administration decided not to send children across. Later in the day, five teachers left the building to join picketers.

The girls' swim coach was a college student who planned to student teach in the spring and decided that he would not coach during the strike. The union president claimed that the strike was an "eye opener" for some board members, who hadn't believed teachers would really stay out on strike.[81]

Only twenty five students attended the vocational school on the second day it reopened, and the district decided to close it. Plans were made to reopen Riverside School on Monday, the fourth day of the strike.[82] During the weekend, an informal meeting occurred between the school board chair and union president to prepare for a future session.[83]

Riverside School opened Monday with seven teachers, two whom had transferred from other buildings. An informal closed door negotiating session was held with two administrators, the board chair and four members of the union negotiating team. A non-striking teacher's letter in the paper said union members had harassed her, including saying she would be ostracized; they would ruin her husband's medical career and threatened her pets.[84]

The informal session produced no new proposals, but teachers did return to their $5,500 position. A group of parents, students and taxpayers planned to counter-picket because, "They're (the teachers) are wrecking the education for the students."[85] The group cancelled their plans because they, "felt they would be pressured by the teachers."[86]

The mediator asked that only board members and union negotiators attend a session held the second weekend of the strike.[87] During the Saturday session, the board offered $4,400 with no make-up days, and informally offered $4,650. Teachers held at $5,500.[88]

Talks continued until early Sunday morning. After a twenty-three-hour session, a settlement was reached. Perhaps it was the long hours that contributed to the confusion that was evident during the announcement of the settlement. Both sides agreed that four of the eight days missed would be made up. The board said teachers would receive $4,723 while teachers calculated they were getting, "in excess of $5300."

The board pointed out that teachers had used making up all eight days in their figure, and that insurance benefits wouldn't be effective until January 1, 1982. These differences led to the disparity in calculated raises.[89] Teachers ratified the contract later on Sunday and classes reopened Monday.[90]

The board met to ratify the contract the following Thursday. The union's chief negotiator disagreed with the board's negotiator about the meaning of language changes concerning insurance. Teachers had been told prior to voting on ratification that increases in the district's contribution to health insurance would be retroactive to July 1, the beginning of the contract period. They approved it on that basis.

The board held that the language in the new agreement meant that changes would go into effect with the open enrollment period beginning January 1, 1982. Classes were held the following day, while teachers considered whether to go back out on strike.[91]

A mediation session was held two weeks later to resolve the differences in interpreting the language clause. The mediator said he didn't want to interpret the language for the two sides. The board rejected arbitrating the issue, saying it was in a "no win" situation, and believed the language was clear. The union held a meeting to discuss options.[92]

A compromise was found in early December. Teachers agreed with the district's interpretation that insurance improvements would begin January 1. Language was added that increased coverage for married couples who both taught in the district. The board voted to ratify and teachers voted to re-ratify the contract. Teachers commented that the insurance dispute lowered morale.[93] A week later, twenty-six teachers resigned from a curriculum study project they had been volunteering for.[94]

The insurance mix-up is difficult to understand. When the settlement was announced, the difference in calculating outcomes should have been a red flag for both sides that a significant misunderstanding had taken place. One source was cited by the district, which pointed to a difference in interpreting when insurance increases would begin. If it was seen that day, why wasn't it cleared up during negotiations?

The dispute also illustrates the value of taking the time to clearly write contract language. In the rush to finalize what has been a long and perhaps exhausting conflict, it can be tempting to not worry about getting the wording exactly right. If either side refuses to ratify the agreement however, the conflict can grow.

Houston

THREE MEDIATION SESSIONS failed to bring an agreement by the end of October. Teachers voted the first week of November to strike the following week if the fourth session was unsuccessful.[95] Teachers were asking $5,200 while the board offered $3,800. Referencing declining enrollment, the superintendent said that giving the teachers what they wanted would deplete the reserve fund by the end of the second year. Teachers lowered their request during the mediation session while the board held firm.[96]

The board offered $4,650 the day before the strike. Teachers voted it down, and went out November 10th, disagreeing with the way the raises were distributed. They wanted more to go to experienced teachers, while the board proposed across the board raises. An accompanying headline said residents had little sympathy with the strike. No sessions were scheduled.[97]

On the third day of the strike, the board began planning to reopen schools with subs paid eighty dollars a day. Ads were planned for the upcoming weekend. Teachers said they were paid only $83.63 a day, and wished the board was putting time into settling, rather than hiring subs. The district opened a day care center for kindergarten through sixth-grade students. One of thirty-nine teachers crossed the lines.[98]

A mediation session held on Sunday produced an agreement. Teachers settled for the same amount offered before the strike. Raises would be based on longevity the first year, and across the board the second. The district dropped several language issues including lengthening the work day and increasing the number of years required before being eligible for severance pay. A teacher negotiator said the length of the strike had been determined by the availability of the mediator.[99]

Pine River

Negotiations reached an impasse during the second mediation session, held November 3. The board made its final offer of $4,600, including a thirty minute longer work day, and three extra school days. Teachers wanted $5,700 with no change to the schedule. Teachers said their pay ranked nineteenth of twenty-one area districts and that the board had a reserve of $956,000. They voted to strike in ten days.[100]

During sessions held the two days before the strike, neither side offered formal proposals. Negotiators from both sides said they are getting along well together. Teachers said there are no bad feelings. No sessions were scheduled.[101]

Agreement was reached at midnight on the third day of the strike.[102] Teachers ratified it the next morning, receiving $5,290 and two of the three days out. The school day stayed the same length, and the year was lengthened by three days to 180.[103]

Randolph

In an unusual move, the Randolph school board voted on October 22nd to approve a strike plan before the union filed an intent to strike.[104] Teachers soon did so, and went on strike November 18 after rejecting an offer the previous day.[105] The two sides couldn't agree whether they were $900 or $1,100 apart.[106]

Teachers suggested binding arbitration after day three of the strike. The board agreed only to submitting salary, not language issues. The district said that going over its pre-strike offer of $5,019 would put the district in financial difficulty.[107]

The first mediation session held during the strike occurred on day nine. The board held to its position. Teachers said they came down $400 to $5,515. The board said they'd seen that offer before and had rejected it.[108]

An agreement was reached on December 3, providing $5,400 with none of the nine days made up. Students had staged a sit in demonstration the previous week and a group of parents had asked to meet with the superintendent.[109] With teachers losing about $100 a day, they lost a net $500 from the board's pre-strike offer.

Cass Lake

A mediation session late in November brought movement from both sides. The board came up to $3,278 and teachers down to $5,800. Teachers set a December 8 strike date and opened a strike headquarters.[110]

A twelve hour mediation session the day before the strike produced agreement on all language issues except sick leave. The board came up to $3,427 and teachers came down to $5,225. The strike began December 3. The board announced the second day of the strike that it would meet the following Monday to discuss hiring subs.[111]

The board approved hiring subs to reopen schools, beginning with seniors. Extracurricular activities could continue if certified coaches could be found. A negotiation session was held after the meeting and the board proposed some language changes.[112]

During a negotiating session on day six, teachers agreed that $5,225 would include fringe benefits and extracurricular pay. The district held firm on its total package offer of $3,427.[113] The board came up further to $3,800 during a mediation session held day nine.

Disagreement remained about adding a lane and reducing steps on the salary schedule. Teachers said the district could pay what they are asking from what was budgeted. The board countered that with anticipated reductions in state aid, almost all of the reserve would be depleted.[114]

A mediation session held December 23rd resulted in the district coming up to $4,000 while teachers held firm on their salary request. Teachers reduced their demand for all days to be made up, to nine of twelve. No further sessions were schedule during Christmas break.[115] The mediator suggested a compromise during a session Saturday January 2nd providing $4,600 and six of twelve days made up. The work day was extended a half hour to 8:00 A.M. to 4:00 P.M. [116]

Teachers settled for almost $1,800 more than the pre-strike offer, a net gain of $1,200.

---

1. *Austin Daily Herald*, October 19, 1981, p. 1.
2. *Winona Daily News*, October 21, 1981, p. 1.
3. *Austin Daily Herald*, October 28, 1981, p. 1.
4. *Austin Daily Herald*, November 4, 1981, p. 1.
5. *Austin Daily Herald*, November 19, 1981, p. 9.
6. *Mesabi Daily News*, October 14, 1981, p. 2.
7. *Mesabi Daily News*, October 19, 1981, p. 3.
8. *Mesabi Daily News*, October 21, 1981, p. 1.
9. *Mesabi Daily News*, October 22, 1981, p. 1.
10. *Mesabi Daily News*, October 23, 1981, p. 1.
11. *Mesabi Daily News*, October 24, 1981, pp.1, 10A.
12. *Mesabi Daily News*, October 28, 1981, p. 1, 2.
13. *Mesabi Daily News*, October 30, 1981, p. 1.
14. *Mesabi Daily News*, November 2, 1981, p. 1.
15. *Mesabi Daily News*, November 8, 1981, p. 4.
16. *Duluth News Tribune*, November 4, 1981, p. 2A.
17. *Forest Lake Times*, August 20, 1981, pp. 1, 11.

18. *Forest Lake Times*, September 8, 1981, pp. 1, 24.
19. *Forest Lake Times*, September 24, 1981, pp. 1, 13.
20. *Forest Lake Times*, October 15, 1981, pp. 1, 4, 10.
21. *Forest Lake Times*, October 22, 1981, pp. 1, 3, 4.
22. *Forest Lake Times*, October 29, 1981, pp. 1, 2, 4, 9, 10, 11.
23. *Forest Lake Times*, November 5, 1981, pp. 1, 2, 4, 14.
24. *Forest Lake Times*, December 10, 1981, p. 1.
25. *Forest Lake Times*, December 17, 1981, p. 1.
26. *Forest Lake Times*, November 19, 1981, pp. 1, 2, 4, 9, 22.
27. *White Bear Press*, October 8, 1981, p. 1.
28. *St. Paul Pioneer Press*, November 2, 1981, p. 17.
29. *White Bear Press*, November 5, 1981, p. 1, 3.
30. *St. Paul Pioneer Press*, November 5, 1981, p. 25.
31. *White Bear Press*, November 12, 1981, p. 1.
32. *White Bear Press*, November 26, 1981, p. 1.
33. *White Bear Press*, December 3, 1981, p. 1.
34. *White Bear Press*, December 10, 1981, p. 1.
35. *St. Paul Pioneer Press*, December 13, 1981 p. 1.
36. *White Bear Press*, December 17, 1981, pp. 1, 3.
37. *White Bear Press*, December 24, 1981, p. 1.
38. *White Bear Press*, December 31, 1981, p. 1.
39. *White Bear Press*, December 24, 1981, p. 1.
40. *Sauk Centre Herald*, September 3, 1981, p. 2.
41. *Sauk Centre Herald*, September 17, 1981, p. 1.
42. *Sauk Centre Herald*, September 24, 1981, pp. 1, 2, 5.
43. *Sauk Centre Herald*, October 15, 1981, pp. 1, 6
44. *Sauk Centre Herald*, October 29, 1981, pp. 1, 2, 8.
45. *Sauk Centre Herald*, November 5, 1981, pp. 1, 5.
46. *Sauk Centre Herald*, November 12, 1981, p. 1.
47. *Sauk Centre Herald*, November 19, 1981, pp. 1, 2.
48. *Sauk Centre Herald*, November 26, 1981, pp. 1, 2.
49. *Sauk Centre Herald*, December 10, 1981, pp. 1, 2.
50. *Sauk Centre Herald*, December 17, 1981, p. 1.
51. *Jordan Independent*, September 17, 1981, p. 1.
52. *Jordan Independent*, September 24, 1981, p. 1.
53. *Jordan Independent*, October 1, 1981, p. 1.
54. *Jordan Independent*, October 15, 1981 p. 1.
55. *Jordan Independent*, October 22, 1981 pp. 1, 4.

56. *Jordan Independent*, October 29, 1981, p. 1.
57. *Jordan Independent*, November 5, 1981, pp. 1, 5.
58. *Jordan Independent*, November 12, 1981, p. 1.
59. *Jordan Independent*, November 5, 1981, p. 1.
60. *Hibbing Daily Tribune*, September 23, 1981, p. 1.
61. *Hibbing Daily Tribune*, October 28, 1981, p. 1.
62. *Hibbing Daily Tribune*, October 29, 1981, p. 1.
63. *Hibbing Daily Tribune*, November 2, 1981, p. 1.
64. *Hibbing Daily Tribune*, November 3, 1981, p. 1.
65. *Hibbing Daily Tribune*, November 4, 1981, p. 1.
66. *Hibbing Daily Tribune*, November 6, 1981, p. 1.
67. *Hibbing Daily Tribune*, November 9, 1981, p. 1.
68. *Hibbing Daily Tribune*, November 19, 1981, p. 1.
69. *The Bemidji Pioneer*, September 6, 1981, pp. 1, 12.
70. *The Pioneer*, September 11, 1981, p. 1.
71. *The Pioneer*, September 16, 1981, pp. 1, 8.
72. *The Pioneer*, September 17, 1981, pp. 1, 2, 4.
73. *The Pioneer*, September 20, 1981, pp. 1, 5.
74. *The Pioneer*, September 27, 1981, pp. 1, 7.
75. *The Pioneer*, October 9, 1981, pp. 1, 2.
76. *The Pioneer*, October 11, 1981, pp. 1, 14.
77. *The Pioneer*, October 22, 1981, pp. 1, 2.
78. *The Pioneer*, October 23, 1981, p. 1.
79. *The Pioneer*, October 29, 1981, pp. 1, 2.
80. *The Pioneer*, November 4, 1981, pp. 1, 16.
81. *The Pioneer*, November 6, 1981, pp. 1, 2.
82. *The Pioneer*, November 8, 1981, p. 1.
83. *The Pioneer*, November 9, 1981, p. 1.
84. *The Pioneer*, November 10, 1981, pp. 1, 2, 4.
85. *The Pioneer*, November 11, 1981, pp. 1, 3.
86. *The Pioneer*, November 12, 1981, p. 1.
87. *The Pioneer*, November 13, 1981, pp. 1, 2.
88. *The Pioneer*, November 15, 1981, pp. 1, 2.
89. *The Pioneer*, November 16, 1981, pp. 1, 2.
90. *The Pioneer*, November 17, 1981, p. 1.
91. *The Pioneer*, November 20, 1981, p. 1.
92. *The Pioneer*, November 25, 1981, pp. 1, 8.
93. *The Pioneer*, December 8, 1981, pp. 1, 2.

94. *The Pioneer*, December 15, 1981, p. 1.
95. *Winona Daily News*, November 4, 1981, p. 3.
96. *Winona Daily News*, November 10, 1981, p. 1.
97. *Winona Daily News*, November 11, 1981, pp. 1, 3.
98. *Winona Daily News*, November 13, 1981, pp. 1, 5.
99. *Winona Daily News*, November 17, 1981, p. 1.
100. *Brainerd Daily Dispatch*, November 10, 1981, pp. 1, 2.
101. *Brainerd Daily Dispatch*, November 13, 1981, pp. 1, 2.
102. *Brainerd Daily Dispatch*, November 18, 1981, p. 1
103. *Brainerd Daily Dispatch*, November 24, 1981, p. 1.
104. *Cannon Falls Beacon*, October 29, 1981, p. 1.
105. *Brainerd Daily Dispatch*, November 18. 1981, p. 9.
106. *Cannon Falls Beacon*, November 19, 1981, p. 1.
107. *Cannon Falls Beacon*, November 26, 1981, p. 1.
108. *Cannon Falls Beacon*, December 3, 1981, p. 1.
109. *Cannon Falls Beacon*, December 10, 1981, p. 1.
110. *The Pioneer*, November 25, 1981, p. 1.
111. *The Pioneer*, December 4, 1981, p. 1.
112. *The Pioneer*, December 9, 1981, p. 1.
113. *The Pioneer*, December 13, 1981, p. 3.
114. *The Pioneer*, December 17, 1981, pp. 1, 2.
115. *The Pioneer*, December 23, 1981, pp. 1, 2.
116. *The Pioneer*, January , 1982, p. 1.

Chapter Twenty
1984 Strikes

Eight more districts turned to strikes to settle the next round of contracts. Negotiations began in the spring of 1983 and contracts expired in July. With no MEA strategy of mass filings of intent to strike notices, things proceeded slowly. Only one strike began in 1983, the rest early in 1984.

Duluth

First up was Duluth, a community with a history of strong labor unions. Teachers were represented by the Minnesota Federation of Teachers, a rival to the MEA that had led so many strikes in 1981. Despite being less militant, strong local union sentiment and recent labor problems led this Federation local to strike.

Frustration had been building in the teacher's union for years. After reaching an impasse while negotiating the 1979 to 1981 contract, both sides agreed to utilize arbitration. Neither side was happy with the results. The following contract was settled quickly in June of 1981. State aid was cut in 1982 and a referendum vote to restore funding failed. The district was forced to cut six-million dollars. 150 teachers—about fifteen percent of the workforce—were laid off and several schools closed.

Several administrators were laid off, and claimed to have seniority and rights to teaching jobs. The board first sided with the union and said administrators couldn't bump teachers out of their jobs. After consulting with the district's attorney, the board then sided with the administrators and several additional teachers were laid off.

The union fought the action in district court and lost, appealing the decision all the way to the state Supreme Court. Teachers felt the board was distant and had betrayed them.[1]

Teachers faced a difficult year in 1982-1983, with many having been reassigned to different schools and a number of programs cut. The following fall, little movement on salary positions had taken place despite utilizing a mediator since late summer. In early October teachers rejected the district's proposal of 13.4 percent, asking instead for 16.67 percent. When those differences persisted, teachers voted on November 18th to file an intent to strike notice, with no set date.[2]

The next Monday, teachers set a strike date of December 1st—the day after the next mediation session. Teachers claimed it would be an unfair labor practice for the district not to pay the hospitalization premium during a strike. The school board decided that all activities would be cancelled and stated that graduation wouldn't be affected unless the strike lasted more than two months.[3]

The day before the mediation session, teachers published a large ad that quoted the district's business manager saying there was plenty of money. The staff in Duluth was quite experienced, with about two-thirds having ten or more years of experience; and well educated with 74 percent having earned a master's degree.[4]

The two sides came within 1 percentage point of each other's salary offers during a negotiation session that lasted until 3:15 A.M. The district offered a salary increase of 8.7 percent while teachers asked 9.7 percent. The union said additional differences remained in severance pay and insurance. The salary difference amounted to less than 2 day's pay. The union rejected the offer, and the strike began at 7:00 A.M. December 1st, idling 900 teachers and over 15,000 students. The board chair didn't rule out the use of subs if the strike lasted a long time.

Two small school programs operating in conjunction with youth residential treatment programs stayed open utilizing residential staff, most of whom weren't teachers. The district's other 2,250 special education students wouldn't be served during the strike.

A basis for the conflict was a lack of agreement on how much additional state aid the district would receive during the next two years. The district said it would be getting six-million dollars more to use for salary increases for all staff, textbooks and maintenance. The union said the amount would be $6.8 million and would easily cover the increases they were demanding.[5] While many strikes involved disputes about projected costs, this one was unique in centering on projected revenue.

District negotiators said they were puzzled by the union's statement that significant differences existed over benefits. They understood that salary had been the stumbling block, and that benefits wouldn't be a problem.[6]

If there is a lack of communication among school board members, those who aren't part of negotiating teams can be surprised by events. Duluth was an unusual case because a member of the board's negotiating team displayed a wide misunderstanding of what was going on across the table.

Teachers demonstrated their resolve by picketing the administration building on Saturday in an effort to keep out members of a construction union who were working on a boiler. It was one of three boilers in the building and had been out of service all season because it was being converted to burn wood. The two remaining boilers were able to heat the building. When told that their efforts weren't inconveniencing the district, striking teachers maintained that they were making a statement.

Cooks and lunchroom staff were laid off the first day of the strike. The food service director made plans to continue serving free lunches to 4,000 children from low income families. In order to avoid having children cross picket lines, the union asked that area churches be utilized.[7] The food service director said this would limit the number of children who could be served, and delayed starting the program. He asked that teachers agree not to picket while children were being fed.[8] The union agreed, and the program began at five elementary schools on the ninth day of the strike.[9]

On Monday December 6, day three of the strike, union leaders called for a mediation session. None had been scheduled when the walkout began.[10] Published average salaries including benefits showed Duluth teachers making significantly less than some suburban Twin Cities districts, but more than the state average. Parents began forming a group titled "People Against Continuation of the Strike" saying they intended to stay neutral while pushing for a settlement.

In an unusual—and seemingly self-defeating move—union leaders stopped talking with local TV reporters, demanding an apology after a reporter disrupted a union executive committee meeting.[11]

Hopes rose that a settlement would be reached during a mediation session held on day six. An auditor hired by the union found that past district cost projections had been consistently higher than actual expenses. The district business manager said the numbers reported were nothing new, and illustrated the difficulties in projecting costs.[12] A fifteen hour session didn't bring any movement on salaries. Severance, personal leave and insurance remained unsettled but agreement was reached on other language issues.[13]

The parent group drew 150 people to its meeting on the second weekend of the strike, expressing frustration at the slow pace of negotiations.[14] Their plans included a student demonstration, attending the next school board meeting and a public rally. They talked of seeking to force administration members to supervise extracurricular activities. One member stated that while school days could be made up, hockey games couldn't.[15]

Thirty students picketed the administration building on day eight.[16] A dozen parents attended the school board session to push for more mediation sessions.[17]

An unannounced and informal mediation session was called for day ten, involving the union president, the district personnel director and a school board member. Some progress was made, and a "full scale mediation session" was called at 10:30 P.M. The mediator said that if it wasn't successful, another mediation session probably wouldn't be held until after Christmas.

A dispute from the beginning of preparations for the strike flared when both sides disagreed about paying health premiums. The district had sent a letter to teachers saying that premiums due during the strike would be deducted from future pay. The union claimed this was an unfair labor practice.[18] Talks recessed at 3:00 A.M. and resumed Thursday until 1:00 P.M.[19]

Meeting Friday evening, a tentative agreement was reached providing teachers with 14.94% and six make up days of twelve missed. They also received an additional leave day and insurance improvements. The board approved it by a five to four vote, with a dissenting member saying the board had caved to the union's 'take it or leave it' offer.[20] The cost of health insurance for the six days not made up would be deducted from teacher's pay.[21]

So, was it worth it? Teachers lost six days' pay in a dispute involving less than pay for two days. They also received insurance and severance pay improvements.

COLEREAINE-GREENWAY

COLERAINE IS LOCATED ON Minnesota's Iron Range, long a strongly union region. The district's 100 teachers voted to file an intent to strike notice in mid-December. A session held during Christmas break was unsuccessful, and January 3rd was chosen to begin the strike. The board offered $2,100 while teachers asked $3,800. Insurance payments were also an issue. No mediation sessions were scheduled.[22]

The board claimed teachers were the fourth highest paid in the state and that they couldn't afford what teachers were asking.[23] Teachers placed a full page ad stating that the district began negotiations by trying to take away a number of benefits. Unlike other districts, secondary teachers were required to teach a sixth class.[24]

Parents and citizens jammed a board meeting on January 9. Some citizens said that in the face of unemployment and wage reductions for miners, teachers were making enough money. Board members defended their decision not to go to binding arbitration.[25]

No progress was reported in a mediation session held on day seven. During a mediation session held on day fourteen of the strike teachers suggested binding arbitration, which the board refused. Instead, the board offered $2,388 plus a onetime payment of $100, an additional $1,000 for retiring staff, no make-up days and a cut in fringe benefits because of strike days. The district began advertising for subs at $100 per day.[26]

The board voted on day sixteen to open school for juniors and seniors the following Monday after teachers failed to respond to what the district described as their last offer. The also voted to resume extracurricular activities. Two board members voted against reopening school. One was a teacher in another district, and the other an employer who said he wanted to send a signal to his union employees.[27]

Classes were scheduled to open for grades one, eleven, and twelve on January 30th utilizing seventeen subs.[28] The Friday before that, a long session resulted in movement on both sides. The board offered $3,000 and five make up days. The union requested $3,100 and all days made up. The board suggested taking the make-up days issue to binding arbitration, but teachers refused.[29]

Two teachers met with two board members on Sunday and reached an agreement, averting a mass picketing by steelworker and trade union members the following day.[30] Teachers received $3,000 and eleven make up days out of nineteen.[31] A sour note was added to the post-strike arrangements when the board placed notes in personnel files of any teacher who had made a documented comment disparaging the board or superintendent. Threats were reported against subs, who had come to work the last day of the strike for an in-service day.[32]

The effect of the communities' milieu can be seen in this strike. One board member went out of his way not to alienate his union employees, and the entire board appears to have settled in the face of massive union picketing planed in response to opening school with subs.

Sauk Rapids

Sauk Rapids was a fairly small district, with 121 teachers. Not the kind of place you'd expect to see a prolonged, bitter strike. A number of contributing factors were cited at the time. One was the advice of the district's hired negotiator, said by a school board member to have encouraged a number of contract changes that were adamantly opposed by the union.[33] A majority of the board agreed with the negotiator's suggestions, demanding twenty-nine changes which included a merit pay system and five additional work days. The dissenting board member said the board avoided dealing with money issues, causing talks to drag on.

Reacting to these tactics by the board, teachers said their belief that the district was trying to break the union stalled talks. The union president said board members wanted to exert "dictatorial control" rather than the cooperative role they should be playing. He said the strike was caused by a lack of communication and understanding between teachers and board members.

The school board chair was also a factor. Serving as district spokesperson, she was the focus of criticism. The paper reported that she had been railed against by teachers and parents who called her dictatorial and authoritarian and accused her of pushing a personal agenda. She responded that taking flak was just part of being the board chair.[34]

The relative roles of the superintendent and board chair can be seen in the superintendent's statement that he wished to remain neutral so he could pull administration and teachers together when classes resumed.[35] In many strike cases, the superintendent appeared to be leading the charge to prevail in negotiations. Here, it was the board chair.

A merit pay system was proposed by the board in June, which was opposed by teachers. An intent to strike was filed October 5th and again on October 20. The board withdrew its merit pay proposal on November 2.[36]

If merit pay was simply a throw-away negotiations ploy by the board, it backfired by contributing to the strike. If it was a serious initiative on the board's part, it illustrates the principal that negotiations are not the place to introduce significant changes.

A strike date was set for January 5th. The board was offering $2,600, but teachers said $1,200 of that was tied up in the five extra work days, so the real increase was only $1,400. Teachers asked for $4,443. The two sides didn't agree on how to calculate costs, with the board saying the teachers' request would actually cost $7,409.[37]

A flag-waving parent crossed the picket line on January 5th, the first day of the strike, to deliver what he called a criminal complaint against the superintendent, board chair and union president. He said a state law requiring schools to provide an education was being violated.[38] Eighty parents met the first night of the strike to begin petitioning for a settlement.[39]

Both sides contacted the state mediator the second day of the strike to set up a meeting. He refused, saying both sides refused to budge. Teachers suggested meeting without him, but the board refused.[40]

A parent group joined by some students presented a petition to the school board the third morning demanding that negotiations resume and continue until a settlement was reached. The board voted to resume practice for those sports whose coaches weren't teachers. School aides and secretaries were also negotiating and filed grievances when they didn't receive automatic raises while talks were in progress.[41]

The union reacted to the possibility of nine non-union coaches crossing the lines by saying that they'd better watch what they did if they hoped to work for the district in the future. The district began advertising for subs at $125 a day. The union criticized the district for putting time into restarting athletics and advertising for subs instead of seeking a settlement.[42]

Interviewed on the fifth day of the strike, the board chair said the perception that school board members hate teachers wasn't true. The union contacted coaches and pressured them not to cross the line. Eight said they wouldn't. The board chair called the pressure distasteful and questioned the union's professionalism. The union also called board members who were not on the negotiating team, some of whom said they were being "totally left out in the dark" about issues. The union said it would be gathered every morning and ready to negotiate.[43]

The parent who delivered a criminal complaint against the school and union on the first day of the strike announced that he would meet with the Governor later in the month asking him to, "appoint a committee or something to look into this."[44]

By the end of the second week, both sides indicated that they were willing to be flexible and a mediation session first scheduled for the following Wednesday was moved up to Monday.[45] Prior to the session—the first since the strike began—the board agreed to drop the five extra school days it had been proposing and dropped its salary offer from $2,600 to $2,015.[46]

Teachers called the offer a "farce" and the session resulted in no progress with no additional sessions scheduled. Explaining the board's decision to reduce their salary offer, the chair said, "When I ask an employee to work more days or more hours or give them more responsibilities, I expect to pay for that. If I'm not going to ask any more of them, I'm not interested in paying much more."[47]

The district announced on day twelve that it would begin interviewing subs with the intent to open school, beginning with seniors.[48] A meeting set up by the district's professional negotiator and the union's chief negotiator brought no progress, but did result in a better understanding of the numbers each was using.[49] The two met again during the week, and set up a meeting for the following Saturday.[50]

The president of the National Education Association, Minnesota Education Association, and Don Hill—a graduate of Sauk Rapids and the former MEA president attended a union rally. Financial donations were presented from several other locals.[51]

Classes reopened January 30th for first and second grade, the eighteenth day on the strike.[52] The early grades were chosen because fifteen subs for those grades were available. Reopening for seniors remained a priority.[53] That same day, a mediation session saw some movement. The board increased to $2,400 while teaches came down to $4,145. The board rejected an offer to go to "final offer binding arbitration." The union accused the board of hiding funds, overestimating expenses and playing games with numbers. Teachers said they found an additional $570,000 that could be used to pay salaries.

The district threatened an injunction because all the teachers picketed at the two elementary schools that reopened. A parent group presented a memo saying, "Citizens who at one point may have strongly supported the positions of the school board or the teachers are quickly moving to a position of anger, mistrust and disgust."[54]

All the substitutes were followed home.[55] A board member said he thought the board should swallow its pride and admit they were not going to win, but would have to compromise eventually.[56] A poll conducted for the paper by a university sociologist found that fifty-eight percent of residents approved hiring subs. About six students marched around town, passing homes and businesses of school board members. An ecumenical prayer service was scheduled.[57]

Representatives from local businesses were among sixty people chanting for a settlement outside the building where the third mediation session took place on day twenty-five of the strike. A parent group called for replacing negotiators.[58] During the session, the board increased its offer to $3,000. Teachers objected to the continuing requirement for involuntary assignment to a sixth period. Parents held a vigil in the lobby of the Minnesota Department of Transportation building where the meeting was taking place and refused to move when the building closed at 4:30. They said they had promised the public, their children and God that they would maintain a vigil during negotiations. Not leaving illustrated the level of their frustration.[59]

Classes for third graders began on day twenty-seven of the strike. Teachers reported they came down to $4,000. The mediator said both sides had become entrenched in their positions. A citizen said he collected 1,000 signatures on a petition to the school board to 'hold their position'. Union members said he collected them only from senior citizens and families without students.[60]

Teachers picketed the motel where some substitutes were staying.[61] Seniors began class on day thirty-two. The parent group that had been staging vigils during negotiations gave up, saying they would put their energies into spring's school board elections. They said district residents were fed up and didn't support either side.[62]

Little movement occurred during a mediation session held after day thirty-two.[63] Teachers had come down to $3,800 and informally said they would consider substantially less. The board said it would increase its offer if coupled with acceptance of language proposals. All elementary classes were in session.[64] Teachers picketed board members' homes.[65]

A board member said the MEA executive director called saying the MEA would try to arrange a boycott of the copy machines his employer sold, and called another board member's supervisor. The union checked the licenses of what the union president termed "scabstitutes." Grades seven, eight, nine, ten, and eleven were not being held.[66]

More people joined the mediation effort during a session on day thirty-six. The director of the State Bureau of Mediation Services as well as two MEA staff members participated. Mediators described the talks as the most complex they had seen in their careers. Mediators supplied a proposal that was greeted with little enthusiasm by either side.[67]

Meeting again the following afternoon, a settlement was reached that closely followed the mediator's suggestion.[68] Teachers received $3,200 and made up fifteen of thirty-eight days.[69]

This was another illustration of a worst-case scenario. Egos, agendas, resentments and money contributed. Little negotiating was done during the strike—only five mediation sessions and several informal talks. Teachers ended up with much less than the board's pre-strike offer, students missed a lot of school and the atmosphere in the community and inside the district was poisoned by the length of the strike and use of subs.

APPLETON

FOUR MEDIATION SESSIONS were unsuccessful, and teachers struck January 16th. The district announced plans to advertise for subs and reopen schools as soon as possible.[70] During a mediation session held in Minneapolis the evening before the strike, the board refused to move from its $3,282 offer, which teachers had previously turned down.[71]

The two sides met without a mediator on the second day of the strike. Teachers came down to $4,500 from their previous $5,000. A tentative agreement was reached, but the board rejected it the next day, refusing to allow its negotiators to move from the pre-strike offer. Interviews were held with subs.[72]

The board did move up after five strike days, going up to $3,800. Teachers rejected the offer, and plans were finalized to open grades five and six the following Monday.[73] There were no incidents and the principal praised the strikers as very professional.[74] A session held during day six produced little movement.[75] The local editor, who had been at the meeting, praised both sides for working hard and treating each other with courtesy and respect.[76]

The strike ended three days later. Teachers received $3,858 and made up four of eight strike days.[77] Despite being a relatively civilized and brief strike, an editorial spoke of scars and the need for reconciliation.[78]

PARK RAPIDS

TALKS BEGAN UTILIZING A mediator in September. The superintendent requested that a professional negotiator be hired, saying his roles were becoming entangled. Some board members supported a budget that included no raises, despite having a one-million-dollar surplus.[79] In early October, teachers were requesting 19.3 percent and insurance increases while the board wasn't prepared to present a salary proposal and refused to discuss class size.[80]

A month later, the board offered $2,000 during the second mediation session. Prep time and sick leave issues were settled, and teachers dropped their proposal to limit class size. The salary proposal was rejected and teachers voted to strike, asking $5,052.[81] In late November, the board offered $2,471.[82]

Teachers set a strike day a long way off, voting at the end of November to strike January 5th. One mediation session was scheduled in the month between. The two sides calculated raises much differently. The board included automatic steps and lane increases, teachers didn't.[83] Teachers said the board cancelled a negotiations session. The board denied that, saying nothing had been scheduled.[84]

The only mediation session produced no movement. Some board members said afterwards they had made their final offer. Another session was scheduled for January 4, the day before the scheduled strike.[85] The district's paid negotiator played an unusual role just before Christmas. He proposed an offer of $3,100 and called a number of board members, urging them to accept his unofficial letter. Some board members objected, saying they weren't going to increase their offer.

An editorial spoke of teachers' previous raise of thirty percent and says the recession had hit the community hard, leading to no raises in private businesses. Citizens had become embittered against the teachers and some board members had lost long-standing friends.[86]

The union didn't renew its intent to strike notice, so even though a January 4th mediation session was unsuccessful, they didn't strike. During the session, teachers went down to $3,100 and two workshop days while the board stayed at $2,471. Teachers said they would then go back to their position of $4,500. In an extraordinary statement on the eve of a strike, a teacher negotiator acknowledged that the community was not supporting the teachers.[87]

The district developed a strike plan including no make-up days and cancellation of all extracurricular activities.[88] The board authorized hiring subs at $115 a day and rejected binding arbitration.[89] An informal session the night before failed, and teachers went on strike January 17. The union asked other locals within 100 miles to persuade subs not to cross the lines. No mediation sessions were scheduled.[90]

A parent drove his child to dance class after school with a handgun on the dashboard of his car. While crossing the picket line, he picked it up and laid it in his lap. He was arrested and charged with careless handling of a handgun.[91]

Several hundred people stood outside the building where a mediation session was held on day 5 of the strike, telling the board to "hold firm."[92] An agreement was reached, with teachers receiving $2,869 and three of five strike days made up.[93]

A board member who voted against ratifying the contract accused the mediator of splitting the board and brainwashing one of the members into accepting the agreement. He called for those board members who voted for the agreement to be defeated in next spring's elections.[94] The director of the Bureau of Mediation Services submitted a letter to the paper in which he said the board member's letter didn't reflect an informed perspective of the collective bargaining or mediation process.[95]

The board member replied several days later, angrily saying the mediator had no right to come into town and tell them what to do. He reported that the mediator had advised the board before the strike that, "if the teachers strike we would give in anyway and why not give in before the strike."[96]

It sounds to me like the mediator gave stunningly sound advice. The board's intransigence about salary and no make-up days didn't survive the strike. The lack of negotiations before and during the strike also contributed to the standoff.

Saint Louis County

The St. Louis County school district included 10 schools serving small towns and rural areas of the county with 185 teachers. The two sides utilized a mediator beginning in October. An intent to strike notice was filed December 30th. The district developed a strike policy calling for closing schools for the first twenty days, which would not be made up.[97]

The board offered $3,150 while teachers asked for $4,150. The district wanted to add a sixth teaching period to the work day which teachers opposed, saying it would lead to layoffs. The board indicated that it would not raise its offer unless teachers accepted the extra hour, and teachers voted on January 12 to strike, with no set date.[98]

The union president said they would not necessarily strike, citing the eleventh hour settlement that averted a strike in 1981. Teachers also asked for absolute seniority regarding transfers.[99]

A negotiating session January 13th was unsuccessful. The board said its offer would already result in spending $600,000 more than it took in. A levy vote would probably fail, and they couldn't afford to lay off more staff. Teachers accused the board of refusing a mediation session.[100]

Teachers gave one day's notice that they were striking. The superintendent said the board's policy of not making up the first twenty days was intended to let teachers know they would be enduring some financial loss if they struck. Coaches would be allowed to cross, but the union said none would. The boys' basketball team was undefeated. The superintendent hoped that missed games could be rescheduled.[101]

The strike began January 18th. It was nearly forty degrees below zero the second day of picketing.[102] A negotiating session held on day four produced no movement. Much of the time was spent discussing transfer language. A board member discussed how to ensure seniors could graduate, including paying tuition for them to attend schools in other districts.[103]

A mediation session held on day seven produced another deadlock, and the district began plans to hire subs at $125 a day.[104] The intention was to open school for seniors by February 6. Basketball practices resumed with substitute coaches.[105]

A proposal was developed after an all day and all night session held on day twelve. The board dropped the requirement for teaching an extra period and proposed a compromise position on transfers, utilizing seniority and limiting the number of times a teacher could be bumped. With schools almost 100 miles apart, transfer language had been a sticking point. The raise was set at $3,400 with five of twelve days made up. The board was prepared to approve the agreement, if teachers were.[106] They didn't, turning it down 144 to twenty-three.

The board chair expressed disgust, saying they would continue plans to reopen school for seniors February 7th. He said they'd given teachers everything they'd asked for except a few hundred dollars. Any further raises would result in major program cutbacks. The Nett Lake School District withdrew their fifty-five students when the strike wasn't settled the previous day and transferred them to another district.[107]

Members of the largest steelworkers local said they would picket en mass if the district tried to reopen with subs.[108] Student athletes who had been practicing said teachers had given them some flack, writing down their car's license numbers and telling them that if their parents worked for unions, students will get in trouble.[109]

A tentative agreement was worked out the day before school was to reopen for seniors. A meeting had been arranged by a state senator who was also one of the striking teachers. The agreement provided $3,600 and six of thirteen days made up.

This was the second strike settled in the face of a threat by the mineworkers' union to prevent "scabs" from opening schools, and unique in including a state—level elected official as a striker.

Moorehead

Teachers voted on January 12th to strike with no date set. The district immediately responded by advertising for subs at $125 a day. They received 150 inquiries within a week. The district employed 337 teachers, sixty-eight of them at the vo-tec school.[110] Advertising so early in the process before a strike date had been set was an aggressive move on the district's part.

The two sides hadn't met since December 21st. District negotiators said they wouldn't budge until they'd seen a more reasonable request from the teachers. The board had offered ten percent while teachers asked twenty-one percent.[111] A mediation session January 22nd was unsuccessful. Teachers said the board was unprepared, saying they were offering an additional $200 per teacher when simple math showed they were in fact offering $166 less.

The Board refused to meet without the mediator, who wouldn't be available again until February. Teachers voted to strike January 26th. The superintendent said they had interviewed 100 subs and would be opening schools. The union president said that not one person from the union had indicated they would cross the lines.[112]

The MEA vice president was in town for a teachers' rally the night before the strike. He claimed that the Moorehead school board had said that money wasn't the problem, and that the board was out to bust the union. Teachers say the average settlement had been $4,100 and they were asking for $4,400 to $4,500.[113]

The strike began January 26th. The State Department of Education issued a statement that it would no longer issue limited licenses at the request on districts during a strike. The district had interviewed over 200 subs. All athletic events were cancelled the first week of the strike, although the board authorized coaches to continue. Only the girls' basketball coach agreed to cross the lines, but the players voted not to participate. Teams from other districts indicated they wouldn't cross picket lines in Moorehead.[114]

A weekend mediation session after day two of the strike produced more confusion, with teachers saying they had dropped their request by $1,000 while the board accused them of having raised it $800.[115]

Classes began for kindergarten through fifth and tenth to twelfth on day three of the strike. Special education classes weren't held. Teachers stood in the way and shouted at buses carrying subs to orientation meetings and were nudged out of the way by security people hired by the district for the strike.[116]

A substitute teacher was interviewed (not by name). She said she wasn't working for the money, but would donate her wages back to the schools. Having lived in Michigan, she didn't believe in strikes and felt she had to stand up for what she believed in. She reported an incident of a parent who was escorting her child to school being told by a teacher who had been a friend that she would never speak to her again.[117]

A public forum held the fourth night of the strike was attended by 1,000 people. The board and union presented their views and took questions. A board spokesman said they were not trying to break the union. He stated that teachers had not struck against the board, but against parents and the district. He felt, "It will be a sad day if our ability to provide education is dictated solely by the demands of our employees." Teachers said that only half to one third of students are attending school, the district said sixty percent to seventy percent were.[118]

Sixth and eighth grades opened on day six of the strike. The hockey team began practice with the junior varsity coach who wasn't a teacher. Five students chose not to play with the team.[119] About 150 high school students left class and picketed in support of a settlement. Board members met with them. The senior class president said bitterness was growing between students.[120] Students hung a substitute in effigy.

A mediation session was held on day seven. Afterward, the board chair and union president met for an informal talk.[121] Teachers formally requested $4,500—an $800 decrease from the last session. The board didn't provide a counter offer. Both sides said they were waiting for the other to be reasonable.[122] Teachers requested a new mediator.

Junior high school and special education classes resumed on day 9.[123] The request for a new mediator was denied by the director of the Bureau of Mediation Services. It was reported that the district was paying sub's housing and mileage once a week to return home from as far away as Wisconsin.[124]

On the way into a mediation session, board members were presented with a petition signed by 2,600 citizens calling for a settlement.[125] The session was successful, resulting in a thirteen percent raise and two make up days out of twelve. A teary-eyed superintendent said that it was time to go back to what they were hired to do. The director of the Bureau of Mediation had attended the session, and took over at midnight when teachers expressed dissatisfaction with the original mediator.[126]

Perhaps the board's tactics in advertising to subs and opening schools quickly worked. Splitting the difference in pre-strike offers would have resulted in a 15.5 percent raise. Teachers settled for only thirteen percent.

Chaska

During a mediation session on February 1st, the board raised its offer to fourteen percent while teachers stayed with their request for 28.5 percent. Despite months of negotiations, a fundamental misunderstanding existed. Teachers didn't make counter offers because they believed the board wouldn't accept them. The board said that they thought not providing counter offers was the teachers' strategy. Teachers voted the next day to strike on the 27th if an agreement wasn't reached.

The board responded by advertising for subs at $115 per day. The board chair said, "It has been found if systems can get enough substitute teachers to keep classes running that strikes end more quickly."

Both sides had been using professional negotiators. The board utilized an attorney and teachers were assisted by an MEA negotiator.[127] District strike plans included permitting coaches to continue. The girls' basketball team led its division.[128] The board chair said they wanted to be supportive of student teams, but coaches claimed the offer was intended to be divisive. Coaches who were teachers said they wouldn't cross, and would quit if coaches who weren't teachers continued working.

Unresolved issues included leaves, prep time and class size. Teachers said their pay ranked thirty-eigthth of forty-eight metro districts.[129] In a session the night before the strike, the district made what it called its final offer of $4,200 while teachers came down to $5,313. Teachers had hired an independent auditor who, using a different method of calculating costs, concluded that the district did have enough money to pay substantial raises. The board said their offer of $4,200 was as high as they could go without cutting programs and staff.

The strike began February 27.[130] Schools closed the first week. A mediation session was held on day four. An agreement was nearly reached at $4,200 but broke down when the district introduced a non-litigation clause. Teacher negotiators reported to membership, who voted to request more money.

Schools opened on day six. During a face to face session that day, teachers reverted to their position of $5,313. The board offered $4,100 with additional prep time or $4,200 without it. They would have gone as high as $4,300 if most of the increase was the second year. Teachers counter offered $5,275.

The girls' basketball team won in sub regionals utilizing a substitute coach. The regular coach was in the stands.[131]

The board chair said she thought it would be dishonest for the district to find more money and that the board had offered its last pay increase proposal. Teachers said they needed the board to compromise. The board chair met with high school students after 500 of them walked out of class. Parent groups met with administrators and teachers. Prayer sessions were held and a businessman began a drive to raise the $90,000 that separated the two sides. He give that idea up after meeting some resistance to the idea.

Several hundred parents gathered for a rally at the site of a mediation session held on day ten, only to find it had been called off after ten minutes. The district paid mileage from home and motel costs for subs, sixty-five of whom worked during the Sauk Rapids strike.[132]

Two hundred parents traveled to Minneapolis to picket at the site of a mediation session held on day eleven, calling for the two sides to split the difference between their positions. A teacher negotiator said they were willing, but the board chair said they had offered all they could afford. The session produced no movement.

A substitute was fired after getting into a shoving match with a picketer after taking a sign that read, "scabs sleeping" from a snow man. Substitutes complained about harassing phone calls and pickets at motels.

Prayer vigils continued and four pastors signed a letter to the editor calling for supporters on both sides to stop calling opponents lairs. Speaking of the unhealthy climate of hostility and bitterness that existed, they called on everyone to keep a tight rein on their emotions. Saying the burden of responsibility was on the board and teachers union, they urged compromise.

An editorial said the board's position was set in concrete and criticized them for not compromising. Two non-teacher coaches resigned.[133]

The board met for the first public session on the evening of day nineteen. About 150 people told the board they'd had it with the strike. The following Saturday, the board agreed to prep time, one make up day and $4,500. Teacher negotiators turned it down.

Many parents who attended the session were unhappy, saying the board had done its part to compromise. Several parents met with union leaders on Sunday, who in turn asked for a mediation session on Monday. An agreement was reached on March 26th giving teachers $4,500, one day made up of twenty-two strike days and additional prep time.[134]

Parental input didn't seem to have much effect in many strikes, but may have persuaded teachers to take another look at the latest offer in this instance.

Children who hadn't attended school during the strike were called to the principal's office and given packets of homework due back in three weeks. Some parents protested at the amount of extra work.[135]

The district reported strike costs of $625,000.00, considerably more than normal operating expenses. A levy operating vote held in May failed. Incumbent members of the school board were reelected.[136]

---

1. *News Tribune & Herald*, December 25, 1983, p. 1A.
2. *News Tribune & Herald*, November 19, 1983, p. 2A.
3. *News Tribune & Herald*, November 22, 1983, pp. 1A, 12A.
4. *News Tribune & Herald*, November 29, 1983, p. 1A.
5. *News Tribune & Herald*, December 2, 1983, pp. 1A, 2A, 6A.
6. *News Tribune & Herald*, December 3, 1983, p. 1A.
7. *News Tribune & Herald*, December 4, 1983, p. 4A.
8. *News Tribune & Herald*, December 12, 1983, p. 2A.
9. *News Tribune & Herald*, December 13, 1983, p. 1A.
10. *News Tribune & Herald*, December 6, 1983, p. 1A.
11. *News Tribune & Herald*, December 7, 1983, pp. 1A, 8A.
12. *News Tribune & Herald*, December 8, 1983, pp. 1A, 7A.
13. *News Tribune & Herald*, December 9, 1983, p. 1A.
14. *News Tribune & Herald*, December 10, 1983, pp. 1A, 5A.
15. *News Tribune & Herald*, December 11, 1983, pp. 1A, 6A.
16. *News Tribune & Herald*, December 13, 1983, pp. 1, 8A.
17. *News Tribune & Herald*, December 14, 1983, p. 7A.
18. *News Tribune & Herald*, December 15, 1983, pp. 1A, 10A.
19. *News Tribune & Herald*, December 16, 1983, p. 1A.
20. *News Tribune & Herald*, December 17, 1983, pp. 1A, 7A.

21. *News Tribune & Herald*, December 19, 1983, pp. 1A, 5A.
22. *News Tribune & Herald*, January 3, 1984, p. 1A.
23. *News Tribune & Herald*, January 4, 1984, p. 1A.
24. *Scenic Range News*, January 5, 1984, p. 6.
25. *Scenic Range News*, January 5, 1984, p. 1.
26. *News Tribune & Herald*, January 22, 1984.
27. *Scenic Range News*, January 26, 1984, p. 1.
28. *News Tribune & Herald*, January 27, 1984, p. 1A.
29. *News Tribune & Herald*, January 29, 1984, p. 2A.
30. *News Tribune & Herald*, January 30, 1984, p. 1A.
31. *News Tribune & Herald*, January 31, 1984, p. 2A.
32. *Scenic Range News*, February 16, 1984, p. 1.
33. *Daily Times*, February 10, 1984, pp. 1C, 2C.
34. *Daily Times*, January 11, 1984, p. 7A.
35. *Daily Times*, January 19, 1984, p. 8A.
36. *Daily Times*, January 4, 1984, p. 6A.
37. *Daily Times*, December 19, 1983, p. 1A.
38. *Daily Times*, January 5, 1984, p. 1A, 5A.
39. *Daily Times*, January 6, 1984, p. 1A, 5A.
40. *Daily Times*, January 7, 1984, p. 1A.
41. *Daily Times*, January 9, 1984, pp. 1C, 2C.
42. *Daily Times*, January 10, 1984, pp. 1A, 5A, 1C.
43. *Daily Times*, January 11, 1984, pp. 1A, 7A, 1C, 2C.
44. *Daily Times*, January 13, 1984, pp. 1B, 2B.
45. *Daily Times*, January 14, 1984, pp. 1A, 3A.
46. *Daily Times*, January 16, 1984, p. 1A.
47. *Daily Times*, January 17, 1984, pp. 1A, 6A.
48. *Daily Times*, January 20, 1984, pp. 1C, 2C.
49. *Daily Times*, January 23, 1984, p. 1C.
50. *Daily Times*, January 26, 1984, pp. 1A, 6A.
51. *Daily Times*, January 27, 1984, p. 1C.
52. *Daily Times*, January 30, 1984, p. 1A.
53. *Daily Times*, January 26, 1984, p. 1A.
54. *Daily Times*, January 31, 1984, pp. 1A, 6A.
55. *Daily Times*, February 1, 1984, p. 1A.
56. *Daily Times*, February 3, 1984, pp. 1C, 3C.
57. *Daily Times*, February 6, 1984, pp. 1C, 2C.
58. *Daily Times*, February 8, 1984, pp. 1A, 6A.
59. *Daily Times*, February 9, 1984, pp. 1A 7A, 1C, 2C.

60. *Daily Times*, February 10, 1984, pp. 1A, 1C, 2C.
61. *Daily Times*, February 16, 1984, p. 1C.
62. *Daily Times*, February 17, 1984, pp. 1A, 6A, 1C, 2C.
63. *Daily Times*, February 18, 1984, p. 1A.
64. *Daily Times*, February 20, 1984, pp. 1c, 2C.
65. *Daily Times*, February 21, 1984, pp. 1C, 2C.
66. *Daily Times*, February 22, 1984, pp. 1C, 2C.
67. *Daily Times*, February 24, 1984, pp. 1A, 6A.
68. *Daily Times*, February 27, 1984, pp. 1A, 6A.
69. *Daily Times*, February 28, 1984, pp. 1A, 4A, 6A.
70. *West Central Tribune*, January 16, 1984, p. 1.
71. *The Appleton Press*, January 18, 1984, p. 1.
72. *West Central Tribune*, January 18, 1984, p. 1.
73. *West Central Tribune*, January 23, 1984, p. B1.
74. *West Central Tribune*, January 24, 1984, pp. A1, A8.
75. *West Central Tribune*, January 25, 1984, pp. A1, A6.
76. *The Appleton Press*, January 25, 1984 pp. 1, 2.
77. *West Central Tribune*, January 27, 1984, p. A1
78. *The Appleton Press*, February 1, 1984, p. 2.
79. *Park Rapids Enterprise*, September 24, 1983, p. 1.
80. *Park Rapids Enterprise*, October 1, 1983, p. 1.
81. *Park Rapids Enterprise*, November 5, 1983, p. 1.
82. *Park Rapids Enterprise*, November 26, 1983, p. 1.
83. *Park Rapids Enterprise*, November 30, 1983, pp. 1, 3.
84. *Park Rapids Enterprise*, December 10, 1983, p. 1.
85. *Park Rapids Enterprise*, December 17, 1983, p. 1.
86. *Park Rapids Enterprise*, December 24, 1983, p. 1.
87. *Park Rapids Enterprise*, January 7, 1984, pp. 1, 11.
88. *Park Rapids Enterprise*, January 11, 1984, p. 1.
89. *Park Rapids Enterprise*, January 14, 1984, p. 1
90. *Park Rapids Enterprise*, January 18, 1984, p. 1.
91. *Park Rapids Enterprise*, January 21, 1984, p. 1.
92. *Park Rapids Enterprise*, January 25, 1984, p. 2.
93. *Forum*, January 25, 1984.
94. *Park Rapids Enterprise*, January 28, 1984, pp. 1, 2, 8.
95. *Park Rapids Enterprise*, February 11, 1984, p. 2.
96. *Park Rapids Enterprise*, February 15, 1984, p. 2.
97. *Mesabi Daily News*, January 9, 1984, p. 1.
98. *News Tribune & Herald*, January 12, 1984, pp. 1A, 7A.

99. *Mesabi Daily News*, January 12, 1984, p. 1
100. *Mesabi Daily News*, January 15, 1984, p. 1.
101. *Mesabi Daily News*, January 17, 1984, p. 1.
102. *News Tribune & Herald*, January 19, 1984, p. 1.
103. *Mesabi Daily News*, January 24, 1984, p. 1.
104. *Mesabi Daily News*, January 27, 1984, p. 1.
105. *Mesabi Daily News*, January 31, 1984, p. 1.
106. *Mesabi Daily News*, February 2, 1984, p. 1.
107. *Mesabi Daily News*, February 3, 1984, p. 1.
108. *News Tribune & Herald*, February 4, 1984, p. 1.
109. *Mesabi Daily News*, February 5, 1984, pp. 1, 2.
110. *The Forum*, January 20, 1984, p. 1B.
111. *The Forum*, January 23, 1984, p. 1B.
112. *The Forum*, January 24, 1984, p. 1.
113. *The Forum*, January 25, 1984, pp. 1A, 2A, B1.
114. *The Forum*, January 27, 1984, pp. 1A, 2A, 4B.
115. *The Forum*, January 31, 1984, pp. 1A, 2A.
116. *The Forum*, January 28, 1984, p. 1A.
117. *The Forum*, January 31, 1984, pp. 1A, 5A.
118. *The Forum*, February 1, 1984, pp. 1A, 2A.
119. *The Forum*, February 2, 1984, pp. 1A, 2A, 1C, 2C.
120. *The Forum*, February 3, 1984, pp. 1A, 2A.
121. *The Forum*, February 4, 1984, p. 1A.
122. *The Forum*, February 5, 1984, p. 1A.
123. *The Forum*, February 7, 1984, p. 1B.
124. *The Forum*, February 9, 1984, p. 10B.
125. *The Forum*, February 10, 1984, p. 1A.
126. *The Forum*, February 11, 1984, pp. 1A, 2A.
127. *Carver County Herald*, February 8, 1984, p. 1
128. *Carver County Herald*, February 15, 1984, p. 1.
129. *Carver County Herald*, February 22, 1984, pp. 1, 11.
130. *Carver County Herald*, February 29, 1984, pp. 1, 14.
131. *Carver County Herald*, March 7, 1984, pp. 1, 14.
132. *Carver County Herald*, March 7, 1984, pp. 1, 12.
133. *Carver County Herald*, March 21, 1984, pp. 1, 4, 16.
134. *Carver County Herald*, March 28, 1984, pp. 1, 4, 5.
135. *Carver County Herald*, April 11, 1984, p. 1.
136. *Carver County Herald*, May 16, 1984, p. 1.

Chapter Twenty-One
1988-1992

There were no strikes during the 1985 to 1987 contract cycle. Two occurred during the next round of negotiations.

Proctor

Proctor made use of collaborative bargaining for the first time beginning in May of 1987. A dozen negotiation sessions focused primarily on contact language resulted in an impasse by early October and a mediator was brought in. The union had hired a professional negotiator.[1] Positions had hardened by mid-December and an intent to strike notice was filed. Issues included prep time, benefits and salary with the union claiming that the reserve was large enough to provide benefits similar to other area districts.

The state implemented an open enrollment program beginning in the 1988-1989 school year. Parents had until February of 1988 to decide where they wanted to enroll their students the following fall. By December, it appeared that Proctor would have a net loss of thirteen students, resulting in less state aid.[2]

Just before Christmas, the union voted to strike on or after January 5, saying they wanted their top wages to compare to area districts. The board rejected arbitration. The union said that while the relationship between teachers and the administration could be better, that negotiations had been friendly. An editorial called teachers the "working elite" in town because so many railroad workers had recently been laid off. The board offered six percent while teachers asked twelve percent.[3] The board disputed the union's contention that they are paid less than area schools and said that the union's proposal would result in higher taxes, layoffs, program cuts and larger class sizes.[4]

Instead of striking as planned, a mediation session was held January 5.[5] Both sides say they came close to an agreement, but talks were called off at 3:00 A.M. and the strike began. The board said it was already offering more that the state would provide, forcing it to dip into the reserve.[6] The district sent residents a three page letter outlining their position, while the union placed a full page ad in the local paper. It was thirty-two degrees below zero when teachers began walking the picket lines. The board chair said there were no plans to reopen schools.[7]

An agreement was reached during a session held the first weekend of the strike and school began on Monday before teachers voted on the contract.[8] Teachers made up two of three strike days[9] and received 10.2 percent. Elementary prep time was guaranteed. It was reported that the strike hadn't lasted long enough to become acrimonious.[10]

Elk River

The strike in Elk River wasn't as brief or pleasant. Negotiations were deadlocked by early January. Language issues included prep time and the district's proposals that two days be added to the calendar and layoffs be decided by criteria other than seniority. The board offered nine percent while teachers requested fifteen percent.[11]

Adding additional days to the calendar wasn't a radical request, providing the district was willing to pay teachers for them. Bypassing seniority was a significant departure from the typical practice of other districts. Certain to rile union members because it threatened their job security, it represented either an aggressive approach to negotiating or an anti-labor stance.

The district had successfully lobbied the state legislature for a substantial increase in state aid. The superintendent said the board wasn't interested in putting all that increase into teachers' salaries. Instead, students should benefit with smaller class sizes and new programs.

Union members voted to authorize filing an intent to strike notice if a mediation session on February 8th wasn't successful.[12] The board increased its offer to 9.9 percent. An union negotiator called the offer another slap in the face to teachers, saying the way the salary schedules are set up, most teachers would receive less than a previous board offer.[13]

The same day the union filed an intent to strike, the board offered binding arbitration and voted to hire subs to reopen schools in the event of a strike. All regular board meetings would be cancelled during a strike to prevent the board from being lobbied for a settlement during public meetings, allowing all negotiations to be handled at the table.[14]

The decision to insulate the board from public comment was an unusual tactic. While many school boards preferred to negotiate behind closed doors, most remained willing to stay in contact with their constituents. The announcement that subs would be hired before a strike date was set or a final mediation session held demonstrated a willingness to anger, intimidate and alienate the union.

A mediation session failed on February 22nd and teachers struck the next day. The superintendent announced that classes would be closed during the first week of the strike and that over 100 applications from substitutes had been received. Teachers rejected arbitration in part because they didn't trust the district's ability to provide accurate financial information to an arbitrator. They cited past instances of an almost three-million-dollar difference between projected and actual year end fund balances. Teachers were also unwilling to give up the protection provided by the law that said that layoffs should be by seniority, except in the case of arbitration.[15]

No negotiation sessions were scheduled. The second day of the strike, the district announced that classes would open for seniors on March 3, day eight of the strike. The following Monday, class would resume for first and second grade.[16] Subs would be paid on the same salary schedule rejected by teachers, up to $200 a day.[17]

While subs were paid what the average teacher received, including in a few cases a district's proposed offer, this is the only case where subs were paid according to the salary schedule, enabling some of them to receive the same pay as senior teachers.

A mediation session was held on day five. The district agreed to continue using seniority to determine layoffs. The number of make-up days was a new issue, with the board offering none.[18] Two hundred subs had applied by day five. Interviews were held at a motel where union members picketed while Pinkerton guards watched.[19]

The district's six home economics teachers served lunches to the 325 striking teachers each day in the Masonic Lodge. An agreement was reached the night of day six and ratified the next day. Teachers received 11.5 percent, more prep time and made up three of seven days.[20]

District officials felt that plans to open the high school ended the strike. Union negotiators said that when the district dropped its seniority language, it opened the door to a settlement. Teachers said they distrusted the school board, who had a history of claiming they had no money during negotiations only to find more after settling. The superintendent had been hired only the year before and was viewed by some teachers as tyrannical and dictatorial. Picketers had worn crowns to show the community what they thought of the superintendent.

Editorial comments said that those teachers who sought to get rid of the superintendent or school board members would be disappointed.[21] The board and union said they would look into non-adversarial bargaining for the future.[22]

Three of four incumbents were reelected to the school board the following May.[23] The superintendent remained through 2000, when he retired.[24]

The 1987-1989 contract years were quiet. One strike occurred the following year, largely the result of difficulties that occurred while consolidating districts.

Aurora-Hoyt Lakes-Biwabik

THE TWO SCHOOL DISTRICTS OF Aurora-Hoyt Lakes and Biwabik agreed in 1989 to consolidate. That process hadn't been completed by the fall of 1990. Both school boards were working to combine their separate teacher contracts into one, as well as negotiating for the current contract cycle.[25] The two teachers' unions—both members of Minnesota Federation of Teachers—worked closely together and claimed that the two school boards went in different directions.

A last minute negotiation session failed and the strike began January 10th, 1990. The boards offered zero percent the first year and five percent the second while teachers requested 2.5 percent and six percent. No talks were scheduled. The district announced no plans to hire subs.

A new state effort to settle teacher contracts in a timely manner levied a reduction of twenty-five dollars per pupil in state aid if contracts weren't signed by January 15th. For the two districts, it amounted to $50,000. Additional money was at risk because the state had pledged $800,000 over two years to help the consolidation effort.[26]

On January 17th, it was announced that the district would be assessed a $44,000 penalty for failing to settle their contract. All other districts in northeastern Minnesota had settled before the deadline. District officials announced that any wage increases would be decreased by the amount of the penalty, amounting to $500 per teacher.[27]

Both sides ran full-page ads explaining their positions. The boards said that giving the teachers what they wanted would produce a debt larger than the state would allow. Teachers also wanted no cap on health insurance and participation in decisions about transfers and student discipline.[28]

The second mediation session was held on day eleven of the strike. Details weren't released, but talks were described as encouraging.[29] A session was held beginning the next evening. After negotiating all night, an agreement was reached at 6:00 A.M.[30] Teachers received a 10.5 percent increase in benefits and wages.[31] Four days would be made up of thirteen missed. Eighteen athletic events were missed and would be made up.[32]

The next cycle of negotiations brought three strikes

ROCHESTER

THE RELATIONSHIP BETWEEN the union and the Rochester schools had been troubled for a decade. Teachers had come close to joining other districts in striking in 1981, but at the last minute the business manager found a significant amount of additional money and a settlement was reached. Ten years later, the union continued to distrust district figures.

The two sides engaged in numerous disputes, ending up twice before the Minnesota Supreme Court as well as engaging in numerous grievances.[33]

A new superintendent started in 1987. He'd served as an assistant superintendent in another state.[34] A dynamic change maker, he championed outcome based education and a middle school concept. He was described as a strong presence.[35]

Negotiations started out positively in 1991, with both sides attending collaborative bargaining training in June. The previous contract had been settled by collective bargaining[36] and both sides said the method enabled them to work out problems together.[37]

Breaking with tradition, financial issues were brought up early in negotiations, during the second session.[38] The union president said the collective bargaining system created a more open feeling. Sessions were scheduled for twice a week in late June.[39]

Agreement was quickly reached on compensation for covering other teacher's classes[40] and a restructuring of the salary schedule.[41] A stumbling block was reached in early August. The district said six percent was the maximum they could offer, since it would result in one million dollars in cuts. Teachers disagreed with how financial projections were developed. The two sides agreed to put salary talks on hold and to focus on fringe benefits.[42]

Responding in September to a district request, the union presented a salary package of 10.2 percent. The district felt that was too much and suggested mediation. Both sides agreed to drop the collaborative bargaining approach and scheduled a mediation session in three weeks. It was felt that the collaborative approach was producing results too slowly.

A large bond issue was scheduled for early December, and the state deadline of settling before January 15 to avoid penalties was a concern.[43]

Raises for top administrators surfaced as an issue. Most top administrators received over eight percent per year for the last three years, while the union was told the district couldn't afford to raise teachers' salaries over three percent.[44]

The first mediation session, held in mid-October, was spent exploring issues.[45] Another session was scheduled for the end of the month.[46]

The bond issue of $69.8 million scheduled for December 12th was the largest in state history, designed to build a third high school and additions to five buildings.[47] A citizen's group formed in opposition to the bond issue.[48]

The district adopted a strategy of aggressive traditional negotiations during a bargaining session on November 8th. They put all their original positions back on the table, negating the agreements that had been reached in earlier collaborative bargaining sessions. This move infuriated union negotiators.[49]

District negotiation tactics were being directed by the hired negotiator in conjunction with the superintendent and human resources director, not the school board.[50] Aware of who was driving the discussions, teacher anger was focused on the superintendent.

The district modified its proposal during a mediation session on November 19th, dropping demands for extending the teaching year by four days, the work day by fifteen minutes and increasing contact time by one hour for secondary teachers. Administrators still sought to cap insurance benefits, reduce severance payments by half and exert more control over teacher assignments.

Reacting to the anger of their leaders, teachers said they felt they weren't being treated as professionals, and voted to strike on December 2. The MEA president attended the vote rally and blamed the superintendent for turning negotiations into a grudge match over past grievances, accusing him of trying to take back gains made by the union in past contracts.[51]

The union president said it was unfortunate that the bond issue vote was scheduled for shortly after the strike date and that the timing was a coincidence. The superintendent agreed.[52]

December 2—the scheduled first day of the strike—was the first day a mediator could meet.[53] The union delayed the strike date until December 4 to allow for negotiations and informally lowered its request to 10.3 percent. The board set strike plans including closing schools and allowing sports to continue with qualified coaches. A provision of the plan allowed hiring subs, but the superintendent said that was not the intent.[54]

Both sides met with business leaders to explain their positions.[55] The district presented a proposal that teachers accept 5.9 percent and the district would drop all language proposals, or accept some language and negotiate a higher wage settlement. Differences in calculating costs were evident in the district's assertion that the teachers' latest proposal represented an increase in costs, not the decrease the union claimed.[56]

Later, the board increased its offer to 7.1 percent with all their language issues dropped. They hinted that they would be willing to settle at 8.1 percent. Teachers proposed 10.1 percent with all language proposals dropped except allowing early childhood and family educators to join the union. The district said subcontracting was a management right and talks broke down.[57]

The school board voted the day before the strike to cancel the bond issue, saying they were responding to citizen's concerns.[58] It was the first case in Minnesota history of a school board cancelling a bond issue vote.[59]

The strike began December 4th. Teachers walked the lines in two hour shifts in a wind chill approaching fifty degrees below zero. Firefighters and parents delivered coffee. The MEA president visited teachers and announced that the MEA would donate $134,000 to pay for teachers' fringe benefits during the strike.[60] The district could miss four days before meeting the state's minimum number of school days.[61]

Two teachers had scheduled their wedding for the evening of what turned out to be the third day of the strike. Both of them decided to picket during the day, although it put them behind in their wedding preparations. An administrator said the district continued to consider the option of hiring subs.

One of the high school swimming coaches wasn't a teacher, and a meet was held. The visiting team didn't bring its divers, out of respect for the striking diving coach. A woman with a small child in the car failed to stop at the line, and a picketer pounded on her window, frightening the occupants.[62] The swim coach decided the next day to honor the picket lines.[63]

The first weekend of the strike, the superintendent said the district would stand firmly behind its decision not to make up any days. The personnel director said the district was saving $182,000 a day during the strike. If the strike lasted beyond four days, the district will begin to lose $162,000 because it would be below the state's minimum number of school days.[64]

Teachers said that the board's regressive stance early in negotiations still rankled, even though the requests had been withdrawn. By day four of the strike, a petition was being circulated by some parents and students seeking a settlement.[65]

A mediation session lasting sixteen hours was held on day four, leading to a settlement.[66] Teachers received nine percent with no days made up.[67]

The two sides had traded positions on arbitration. The district first proposed bringing both subcontracting and salary to arbitration. The union refused, saying they thought that without clear contract language, their position wouldn't prevail. When subcontracting language was agreed to, teachers suggested submitting salary to arbitration but the district wasn't interested.[68] The subcontracting issue was settled by allowing the district to continue the practice with early childhood and family educators, but not with any union positions.[69]

Several school board members said they wouldn't run again. The board said it would have to make cuts because of the settlement, but the union disagreed.[70] In April, the board made plans to cut $621,000, citing low state funding.[71]

The board evaluated the superintendent several months after the strike. They gave him passing grades but said his leadership methods and communication skills were weak points. The board president said the superintendent's leadership and personal style raised concerns about restoring trust and morale in the district. The superintendent acknowledged that many people criticized him for the strike and canceled bond issue.[72]

A year later, teachers said the strike was about respect and having a say in planning. The superintendent agreed that a process was needed to provide a two-way conversation.[73]

A scaled-down bond issue for $45.4 million held eighteen months after the strike failed.[74] A survey said primary reasons for the defeat were monetary issues and a lack of trust, including a dislike of the superintendent.[75] The following January, the superintendent announced he was leaving to become superintendent in another state.[76] He said that he learned that when change comes from the top down, it isn't likely to be accepted.[77]

This would appear to be primarily a bad blood strike. The MEA president blamed the superintendent before the strike and teachers cited the district's early regressive demands as the reason they were picketing. Trust had broken down on both sides, with the district feeling assaulted by having lost court cases.

The subcontracting issue involved very few teachers, but when the union witnessed the district's attempt to strip them of rights, it feared that subcontracting could be expanded to include existing teachers' jobs. The board and the superintendent himself acknowledged a need for better communication and collaboration after the strike.

The two sides were only two percent apart in salary offers the day before the strike began. Teachers settled for splitting the difference with no days made up, losing money. The subcontracting issue was also a compromise, which may have required the pain of a strike to achieve.

The weather also played a factor. Brutal wind chills in the range of minus forty to fifty degrees below zero increased sympathy in the community for picketers.

The combination of an inexperienced superintendent with a strong leadership style combined with regressive contract demands would be seen in future strikes.

Spring Lake Park

Spring Lake Park teachers complained that starting salaries hadn't kept up with other districts. The union president said that in seven years they had gone from being $3,690 above a comparable district to being $1,666 under. The board chair countered that the district was in trouble after a second levy vote failed the month before, resulting in having to cut one million dollars.

Communication difficulties were evident in the board chair's surprise that stating salaries were an issue for teachers.[78] The mediator halted a session December 14th, saying the two sides were too far apart. The district offered 9.5 percent while teachers sought 11.8 percent. The union said the district's offer was really 8.9 percent.[79] Complicating calculations was the state requirement for lengthening the school year, adding three days to the calendar. When teachers included the extra days it lowered per day/per hour gains.

The strike began December 16th involving 260 teachers. Teachers said they had been willing in the past to put a higher priority on educational programming and student needs but now it was time to put a priority on teachers.[80]

Both sides cited the recent eleven percent settlement in a neighboring district as influencing teachers' expectations.[81] A mediation session held on day three resulted in a slightly higher offer from the district but no agreement.[82] Christmas break began, and the next session was held on January 3.

An agreement was reached providing teachers 10.66 percent with no days made up. Students would make up four of the five days missed by converting workshops to regular school days. The superintendent said the settlement was more than the district could afford, and would result in the layoff of twenty teachers.[83]

International Falls

Instead of returning from Christmas break and settling the contract because the state's January 15th deadline was looming, a mediation session on the second produced no progress. The superintendent said the district was facing a shortfall so it could offer no pay increase. Teachers requested 5.7 percent the first year and 4.6 percent the second. The district was also negotiating with its aides, custodians, bus drivers, secretaries and food service workers, proposing no pay increases for them.[84]

Another unsuccessful session was held the sixth and teachers voted to file an intent to strike on the ninth. The state's deadline was missed, costing the district $50,000 and the rest of the month was allowed to pass without meeting. Teachers mailed their notice of intent to strike at the end of the month.[85]

Both sides said they were willing to meet but were waiting for a request. Teachers set a strike date of February 14. The student counsel sent a letter urging the two sides to meet. A letter from the school's auditor was entered into the school board record and sent to staff explaining that the district faced a budget shortfall.[86]

The earliest a mediation session could be scheduled was the Sunday following the projected start of the strike on Friday. Saying they hadn't heard of any offers from the board, teachers decided not to change the strike date.[87] The district announced that home games would be cancelled and away games played with administrators for coaches.

Both sides produced comparisons supporting their positions; the superintendent saying teachers were well paid, and the union saying the district had adequate reserve funds. The superintendent defended the size of the reserve, saying interest earned helped pay bills.[88]

The board requested a session the day before the strike and a hundred high school students walked out of class to protest the pending strike.[89] The board offered zero percent the first year and two percent the second. Teachers said they would lose money the first year because of increased health insurance costs and rejected the offer.

The strike began on February 14 in relatively warm twenty-eight degree weather.[90] Some teachers on the lines blamed the superintendent, displaying signs, "Recycle Roberts." Others wore buttons displaying a chicken with a dollar bill in its beak and the phrase, "The sky has fell," explaining that in previous negotiations the superintendent played Chicken Little.[91]

A mediation session was held on the weekend, after one day on strike. No agreement was reached and no further talks were scheduled. Teachers said they felt they weren't being respected. The board chair commented, "I think our staff is treated as professionally as any other. But if your only guide as a professional is how much money you get, you're in the wrong profession."

The board chair expressed concern about the simultaneous negotiations being conducted with most other district employees. He said any pay raise given to teachers would probably have to be given to the others.[92]

The teachers escalated the conflict on the second day of the strike. Picketers, including the union president, were part of an informational picket line outside a school board member's business. He protested saying, "Being singled out like this is really a low blow. This is a school issue and that's where it should be kept."[93]

On the second day his business was picketed, some customers pulled up but left when they saw the picket lines. He said, "This is a union town and some people aren't going to walk through picket lines." The board chair called the picketing "goon squad tactics," and "terrorism." The board chair and some parents also questioned the union's tactic of taking photographs of participants and fans during away games, saying it was intimidating and used children as a weapon.[94]

On day four, the board said they were willing to meet but the union said there was no reason because the district wouldn't move from its salary offer. The union removed pickets from the board member's business, saying they had served their purpose.[95]

Other unions in the community showed their support on day five. Some county workers took vacation time to picket, while pipefitters donated to the strike fund. Teachers erected a sign by the high school to keep a running tally of when graduation would be delayed. In an unusual show of frustration by an administrator, the high school principal said, "If I had a gun, I'd get them in a room with a Porta-potty in the corner and send in pizza. I wouldn't let them out until they settled." [96]

The board met in a closed session during the second weekend of the strike. A union member brought several calves to join the picket line at the building where the meeting was taking place. The cows were a response to buttons worn by school board members saying they would resume negotiations when the cows came home. Teachers had some fun, saying they were seeking "moovement" about the issue of "moolah."

During the meeting, the board decided to ask for a mediation session as soon as possible.[97] A four hour mediation session on day six included proposals from each side, and mutual rejections.

Teachers said the board only moved money around without adding any and called the meeting a "cruel hoax." The board chair said that charge only made the board more rigid in its position. Teachers introduced a request to be paid for all days lost, and suggested using cost of living to calculate pay raises. The board said that could lead to as many as ten to twelve staff layoffs, which the union labeled a scare tactic.

The union also criticized the board chair for leaving on a week's vacation, saying he was the only experienced member of the district negotiating team.[98]

The board published an open letter explaining its position, citing declining enrollment and past budget cuts as reasons they couldn't offer teachers more money.[99] An editorial linked increasing salaries with larger class sizes and program cuts. Speaking of the superintendent's past practice of declaring financial crises during contract talks, it concluded that teachers' unhappiness with the superintendent shouldn't be an issue in contract negotiations. Referencing the poor economy, it said many people in the community received smaller wages than they wanted.[100]

Face to face meetings were held on day fifteen and the following Saturday.[101] A mediation session in St. Paul the following Monday produced a settlement.[102] Teachers received two percent the first year and 2.5 percent the second along with increases in insurance and incentives for early retirement. All days would be made up using holidays and some Saturdays.

Twenty five students transferred to private schools or other districts. A board member said it would take some time for the community's wounds to heal.[103] Two board members whose terms were ending, one of whom was the board chair, decided not to seek reelection.[104]

This strike packed a lot of nastiness into less than two weeks. Precipitated by distrust from past negotiations and an unpopular superintendent, teachers stuck it to the board by picketing a member's business on the second day of the strike. Board members got into the spirit of "us versus them" by wearing buttons that they would resume negotiating when the cows came home. Charges and counter charges and radical positions such as using cost of living complicated finding a settlement. Fortunately, all this was set aside and a compromise was found during the second weekend.

The effects of the strike on the community can be seen in an editorial from 2002, during the run-up to a subsequent strike. "Remember, area residents still harbor resentment over the last strike ten years ago."[105]

1. *The Proctor Journal*, October 8, 1987, p. 1, 3.
2. *The Proctor Journal*, December 17, 1987, pp. 1, 12.
3. *The Proctor Journal*, December 24, 1987, pp. 1, 12, 14.
4. *The Proctor Journal*, December 31, 1987, pp. 1, 16.
5. *Duluth News Tribune*, January 5, 1988, p. 3A.
6. *Duluth News Tribune*, January 7, 1988, pp. 1A, 8A.
7. *The Proctor Journal*, January 7, 1988, pp. 1, 3, 5.
8. *Duluth News Tribune*, January 12, 1988, p. 2A.
9. *The Proctor Journal*, January 14, 1988, pp. 1, 12.
10. *The Proctor Journal*, January 21, 1988, p. 1.
11. *Elk River Star News*, January 26, 1988, pp. 1, 3.
12. *Elk River Star News*, February 1, 1988, pp.1, 5.
13. *Elk River Star News*, February 9, 1988, pp. 1, 4.
14. *Elk River Star News*, February 16, 1988, pp. 1, 3.
15. *Elk River Star News*, February 23, 1988, pp. 1, 2.
16. *St. Paul Pioneer Press*, February 25, 1988, pp. 1B, 3B.
17. *Minneapolis Star*, February 25, 1988, pp. 1B, 3B.
18. *Elk River Star News*, March 1, 1988, pp. 1, 12.
19. *St. Paul Pioneer Press*, March 1, 1988, pp. 1B, 4B.
20. *St. Paul Pioneer Press*, March 3, 1988, pp. 1A, 4A.
21. *Elk River Star News*, March 8, 1988, pp. 1, 2, 3.
22. *Elk River Star News*, March 15, 1988, p. 1.
23. *Elk River Star News*, May 24, 1988, p. 1, 8.
24. *Elk River Star News*, December 27, 2000.
25. *Duluth News Tribune*, January 10, 1990, p. 5A.
26. *Duluth News Tribune*, January 10, 1990, pp. 1A, 6A.
27. *Duluth News Tribune*, January 17, 1990, p. 5A.
28. *Aurora-Hoyt Lakes Range Facts*, January 18, 1990, pp. 1, 5, 6.
29. *Duluth News Tribune*, January 25, 1990, p. 2A.
30. *Duluth News Tribune*, January 27, 1990, p. 1A.
31. *Duluth News Tribune*, January 29, 1990, p. 1.
32. *Aurora-Hoyt Lakes Range Facts*, February 1, 1990, pp. 8, 10.
33. Interview with previous Rochester union leader, Spring 2011.
34. *Post Bulletin*, December 10, 1991, p. 8A.
35. *Post Bulletin*, February 1, 1994.
36. *Post Bulletin*, June 7, 1991, p. 9A.
37. *Post Bulletin*, June 17, 1991, p. 3B.
38. *Post Bulletin*, June 20, 1991, p. 3B.

39. *Post Bulletin*, June 22, 1991, p. 5A.
40. *Post Bulletin*, June 28, 1991, p. 3B.
41. *Post Bulletin*, July 6, 1991.
42. *Post Bulletin*, August 3, 1991, p. 4A.
43. *Post Bulletin*, September 20, 1991, p. 3A.
44. *Post Bulletin*, October 1, 1991, p. 1B.
45. *Post Bulletin*, October 15, 1991, p. 1B.
46. *Post Bulletin*, October 16, 1991, p. 2B.
47. *Post Bulletin*, November 2, 1991, p. 1A.
48. *Post Bulletin*, November 20, 1991, p. 1A.
49. Interview, former Rochester union leader, Spring 2011.
50. Interview, former Rochester school board member, Spring 2011.
51. *Post Bulletin*, November 21, 1991, pp. 1A, 2C, 6B.
52. *Post Bulletin*, November 22, 1991.
53. *Post Bulletin*, November 22, 1991.
54. *Post Bulletin*, November 26, 1991, pp. 1A, 5B.
55. *Post Bulletin*, November 28, 1991, p. 1A.
56. *Post Bulletin*, December 2, 1991, p. 1B.
57. *Post Bulletin*, December 4, 1991, pp. 1A, 1C, 3C.
58. *Post Bulletin*, December 3, 1991, pp. 1A, 3B.
59. *Post Bulletin*, December 11, 1991, pp. 1A, 1B.
60. *Post Bulletin*, December 4, 1991.
61. *Post Bulletin*, December 3, 1991.
62. *Post Bulletin*, December 6, 1991, pp. 1A, 1B, 5B.
63. *Post Bulletin*, December 7, 1991, pp.1A,5A, 8A.
64. *Post Bulletin*, December 7, 1991, pp. 1A, 5A, 8A.
65. *Post Bulletin*, December 9, 1991, pp. 1A, 5B.
66. *Minneapolis Star Tribune*, December 11, 1991 p. 1B.
67. *Post Bulletin*, December 17, 1991, p. 1A
68. *Post Bulletin*, December 12, 1991, p. 4B.
69. *Post Bulletin*, December 16, 1991, pg1A.
70. *Post Bulletin*, December 17, 1991, p. 1A.
71. *Post Bulletin*, April 8, 1992, p. 3B.
72. *Post Bulletin*, March 25, 1992, p. 3A.
73. *Post Bulletin*, December 5, 1992, p. 1A.
74. *Post Bulletin*, May 19, 1993, p. 1A.
75. *Post Bulletin*, June 19, 1993, p. 1B.
76. *Post Bulletin*, January 19, 1994.

77. *Post Bulletin*, March 5, 1993.
78. *St Paul Pioneer Press*, December 16, 1991, p. 6B.
79. *Minneapolis Star*, December 15, 1991 pp. 1B, 5B.
80. *St Paul Pioneer Press*, December 17, 1991 pp. 1B, 2B.
81. *Minneapolis Star*, December 17, 1991, pp. 1A, 14A.
82. *Minneapolis Star*, December 19, 1991.
83. *St Paul Pioneer Press*, January 4, 1992, pp. 1A, 12A.
84. *The Daily Journal*, January 7, 1992, pp. 1, 12.
85. *The Daily Journal*, January 29, 1992, p. 1.
86. *The Daily Journal*, February 4, 1992, p. 1.
87. *The Daily Journal*, February 10, 1992, p. 1.
88. *The Daily Journal*, February 12, 1992, pp. 1, 6.
89. *The Daily Journal*, February 13, 1992, p. 1.
90. *Minneapolis Star*, February 14, 1992, pp. 1B, 3B.
91. *The Daily Journal*, February 14, 1992, pp. 1, 3.
92. *The Daily Journal*, February 17, 1992, pp. 1, 6.
93. *The Daily Journal*, February 18, 1992, p. 1.
94. *The Daily Journal*, February 19, 1992, pp. 1, 7.
95. *The Daily Journal*, February 20, 1992, pp. 1, 7.
96. *The Daily Journal*, February 21, 1992, pp. 1, 8.
97. *The Daily Journal*, February 24, 1992, pp. 1, 10.
98. *The Daily Journal*, February 26, 1992, pp. 1, 12.
99. *The Daily Journal*, March 2, 1992, pp. 1, 12.
100. *The Daily Journal*, March 3, 1992, p. 2.
101. *The Daily Journal*, March 9, 1992, p. 1.
102. *The Daily Journal*, March 10, 1992, pp. 1, 3.
103. *The Daily Journal*, March 11, 1992, pp. 1, 12.
104. *The Daily Journal*, March 16, 1992, p. 1.
105. *The Daily Journal*, September 27, 2002, p. 2.

Chapter Twenty-Two
Recent Strikes

International Falls

Under the same union president and a different superintendent and board chair than the 1992 strike, the district and union in International Falls weren't able to settle a contract during the entire first year of the 2001-2003 cycle. Mediation had begun in March, with the last session held in July. The board's last proposal included freezing contributions to insurance and a two-percent raise each year. Teachers said that would leave them with less money than they had two years ago. Teachers announced in mid-August that they were preparing a strike vote.[1]

The board responded by saying teachers' salaries were above the state average, they were willing to negotiate, and that their offers were not final.[2] Teachers arranged a strike vote for early September. No mediation sessions were held from mid-July through the end of August.[3]

The board formed strike plans before the union held a vote to decide whether to strike. The superintendent said the most pressing issue would be continuing to provide special education services. Whether the rest of the school would be reopened would be determined later. Reiterating that their offer was not final, the superintendent said the ball was in the union's court.[4]

Teachers voted the next day to file an intent to strike.[5] A mediation session produced an offer by the board of two percent each year and some insurance improvements. The union president rejected the board's offer, saying it only reshuffled the same amount of money. The board offered binding arbitration,[6] but teachers voted to strike, disputing the way the district was computing costs. The union said it was using the method that had always been used across the state.[7]

The strike began September 20th with the board offering zero percent and two percent while teachers sought 3.5 percent and three percent. Just before the strike began, a board member who had two sons who were starters on the football team resigned. She said the union was trying to use the additional pressure on her as a parent of two members of the winning football team to try to get a larger settlement.[8] Special education classes continued with paraprofessionals. Other classes closed. Non-union coaches were allowed to continue working but the coach of the undefeated volleyball team hadn't decided what to do.[9]

Seven students picketed for an end to the strike on the second day. Complaining that it was homecoming week, they didn't understand why teachers couldn't have put off the strike for a few days. Students were also concerned about being able to take their SAT tests for college admission. The board announced that missed days wouldn't be made up and no sessions were scheduled. Teachers said they had made it known they were ready to return to the table, while the superintendent said she was waiting for the Bureau of Mediation to call them together.[10]

The first mediation session since the strike began was set for the weekend, after six strike days. Prior to the meeting, the superintendent reiterated the board's offer of binding arbitration and spoke of plans of quickly returning students to class if the session was successful.

In response to questions about having to make up days, the Minnesota Department of Children, Families and Learning said that graduation requirements were up to local school boards. Teachers said they were willing to compromise, while the district said its position was very fair. A petition was presented to the board asking that sporting events continue, but the homecoming game was cancelled.[11]

A thirteen hour mediation failed. The board increased its offer to one percent the first year and four percent the second, with the entire insurance premium paid the first year, and ninety percent the second. Teachers continued to reject the district's method of cost computing, saying it was outdated and no longer used by other districts. The superintendent said she wasn't aware of how other districts computed costs.

Both sides were willing to accept a successor agreement that would have settled the next contract as well. Salary comparisons were tossed back and forth, with the superintendent holding the position that the district had offered all it could.[12]

Make up days and the insurance costs caused the talks to fail. The district offered a basic and more comprehensive health insurance plan. Teachers objected to how much they would have to contribute to the optional and more expensive plan.[13]

No talks were held the third week of the strike, each side claiming the other needed to move.[14] A letter to the editor said that twenty-nine percent of the district's children were on free or reduced lunch, and might not be getting breakfast or lunch during the strike because their parents hadn't included those meals in their tight budgets.[15]

There was a perception in the community that outsiders were making negotiations more difficult. The board was utilizing a lawyer from St. Paul as chief negotiator, and the union utilized a representative from the MEA. On day thirteen, the union proposed a mediation session with only the board and local union members present.[16] The superintendent said the board was willing to meet for as long as necessary, and hoped for a successor contract covering an additional two years to be signed as well. They wouldn't insist on it if that would interfere with finding a settlement.[17]

A sixteen hour session ended at 2:30 A.M. with no agreement.[18] Another session the following day resulted in an agreement. Teachers received zero percent the first year and 5.5 percent the second with none of the sixteen days made up. The district would pay 100 percent of health insurance premiums. Talks for an additional two year agreement died because the district would have difficulty proving their structural balance that far ahead. Negotiations for the next contract were scheduled to begin in three months.[19]

No cuts were anticipated as a result of the settlement but might be needed because of declining enrollment.[20] Forty two students left the district during the strike and hadn't returned.[21]

Teachers seemed to gain little during the last days of the strike. They'd been offered five percent on day six and settled ten days later for 5.5 percent. They did gain an agreement that the district's contribution for health insurance would go from ninety percent of the basic plan's premiums to 100 percent for both plans. Their demand for make-up days was not met. Previous strikes often saw some days made up if subs hadn't kept schools open. In this case, the State's ruling that days didn't have to be made up allowed the district to hold firm.

Red Wing

Teachers in Red Wing were also working for the second year without a contract, with some important local differences that helped cause and intensify the strike.

Administrators were provided a health insurance plan far better than any other employee group, justified as necessary to attract and retain quality staff.[22] Teachers had accepted increases in the previous contract of only 1.95 percent and 1.25 percent in order to help the district escape statutory operating debt. Soon after settling with teachers, administrators received large raises and improved health insurance.[23] Many teachers believed the rumor that their new superintendent had said during an administrator's conference that he was out to break their union.[24]

During the first year of the contract cycle, the district didn't provide teachers with raises earned for longevity or additional education. Typically received automatically beginning with the new paycheck of each year, most Districts provided these raises according to the terms of the old contract while a new one was being negotiated. Red Wing fell back to a hard-nosed interpretation not seen since the early days of PELRA, saying the terms of the old contract didn't apply. The union filed a lawsuit in August, charging unfair labor practices.[25]

Teachers voted September 23 to file an intent to strike. The union asked three percent each year and no changes to health insurance premiums or severance programs. The district was offering zero percent the first year and 2.2 percent the second, with no step raises and higher insurance premium payments. The union and superintendent said they hoped a settlement could be reached. Flying in the face of these conciliatory comments, the superintendent was quoted as saying there would be no days made up, and that he would look for substitutes and pay them $200 per day.[26]

An editorial pointed out that talk of a strike jeopardized the success of a proposed operating levy referendum.[27] The board approved strike plans which included the possibility of hiring subs. Students complained that they hadn't been asked how they felt about a possible strike.[28] Secretaries, cooks, paraprofessionals and custodians were also negotiating while the district's auditor's report said they remained in statutory operating debt.[29]

A fifteen hour mediation session was held October 7th. Although no agreement was reached, both sides said the fact that they were talking was a good sign. Another session was scheduled the following week.[30]

Belying that optimism, two weeks before the end of the strike window, teachers began removing personal belongings from their classrooms. The superintendent announced that 120 sub applications had been received. They would be paid $275 a day. The district planned to open early elementary grades after two strike days. The union representing the paraprofessionals voted to file an intent to strike notice.[31]

Both sides in the teachers' dispute presented four counter offers during a mediation session October 14th. Teachers complained that paying more for health insurance would nullify any pay increases. According to the district, the two sides remained $645,000 apart. No further sessions were scheduled.[32]

The next day, the school secretaries and support staff voted to file an intent to strike, raising the possibility that three unions—all affiliated with Education Minnesota—might strike the district.[33,34]

A mediation session held a week later was unsuccessful. The union said some members would take home less money because of increases in health premiums. Teachers struck the next day, October 23. The superintendent said the district was going ahead with plans to reopen, paying subs $275 a day—twenty dollars less per day than the average teacher.

On the same day, the district announced how it planned to get out of statutory operating debt. Declining enrollment and increasing health care costs would require $750,000 in reduced spending and the passage of a levy referendum by December 20.[35]

Background checks began for 150 applicants. Strikes for the two other unions could begin as early as the following week. That night, the football team lost a quarter-final playoff game under two administrators who had never coached a game. The regular coaches, one of them the parent of a senior, watched from the stands.[36]

During the second day of the strike the custodians became the fourth union to file an intent to strike notice.[37] No other district has ever seen a similar display of disaffection by so many employee groups. Members of the Minnesota Association of Professional Employees presented the union president with a check for $500 and a pledge of a similar amount each week of the strike. Education Minnesota had supported the MAPE union during its strike the previous fall.

The girls' volleyball team, under their non-union assistant coach, won their initial playoff game.[38]

The superintendent objected to letters sent out by the union to potential subs saying they would be banned from union membership for ten years. Plans to reopen elementary schools the second week of the strike were cancelled when not enough special education subs could be found.[39] This is the first instance when federal and state requirements that special education services be provided halted reopening school during a strike.

On day four, the union president said she had not heard that any teachers found the district's latest offer acceptable, and defended having sent letters to subs. She said teachers on the picket lines assumed that the $50,000 a day the district was saving would be used in the eventual settlement.[40]

The district announced that the levy vote would be held December 17. The board voted to increase the amount being requested in order to maintain current programs.[41] An eleven hour mediation session was held on day five. The district offered proposals insuring that no teacher would lose take home pay after premium adjustments, and included a uniform health insurance package. Teachers offered four proposals, but the district said only one of them represented a decrease in costs.

The union disputed how costs were being calculated. The superintendent replied that they were using the method recommended by the Minnesota School Board Association, the same method that had been used for years. No new sessions were scheduled.[42]

This dispute over cost calculations was the opposite of the one in International Falls. There, the union wanted the same method used by other districts. In Red Wing, the union objected to the common method.

The presidents of the National Education Association and Education Minnesota addressed teachers during a rally the evening of day six.[43] The superintendent confirmed that the district was saving about $50,000 a day because a change in the state funding formula no longer required a minimum number of school days. He rejected the idea that these monies could be converted to increased salaries, because that would be unaffordable during the next round of negotiations.[44]

Speakers at a school board meeting held on day ten shared that the strike was tearing the town apart, pitting neighbor against neighbor and friend against friend. Some pointed out that many in town had received little or no raises and had to pay rising health costs. One said she didn't feel it was fair that the superintendent was being made a scapegoat. An editorial called for teachers to join the rest of the community in paying increased health care costs.[45]

By day fourteen, it appeared that as many as twenty students were transferring to other districts. The district calculated it would cost them $90,000 in lost state aid.[46] The union placed an ad on day fifteen saying it was willing to compromise, saying the district would soon have saved one million dollars from the strike.[47]

A face-to-face mediation session was held on day fifteen that made progress.[48] Representatives from the two sides met in subgroups the following day and a mediation session was held on day seventeen that resulted in an agreement.

In a creative and finessed solution, raises were staggered. They received a one percent retroactive raise for the first contract year that had already passed, and a two percent raise each semester of the second year, with a final one percent in May. These would be used as the basis for 2.5 percent raises each of the next two years of what ended up as a four year agreement. Three of the seventeen days missed would be made up. Teachers would move to a less comprehensive health plan and split future cost increases with the district.

Both sides got what they needed. Costs to the district stayed at about 4.5 percent because the raises were staggered, the last one implemented only for several months. Teachers ended with a six percent raise that served as an adequate base for future increases.[49]

The superintendent announced that over forty-five students left the district during the strike, causing a loss of $230,000.[50] The paraprofessionals' and cooks' unions settled by the end of the month.[51] The district's business manager resigned at the beginning of December, and the school board chair resigned to accept a judgeship.[52]

The levy referendum failed. The superintendent announced that a committee would begin planning cuts designed to bring the district out of statutory operating debt.[53] An editorial blamed the vote loss on the bitter feelings in the community over the strike.[54]

The strike became quite personal for the superintendent when someone cut down some trees in his yard, leaving him disappointed that someone thought that would contribute to the process. He was offered a renewal of his contract, but announced in December of 2003 that he had accepted a job as superintendent of a different district. He feels that teacher's resistance to increasing insurance costs and the district's statutory operating debt were primary contributing factors leading to the strike. He describes it as the worst experience of his career.[55]

Crosby-Ironton

THE NEXT CONTRACT CYCLE would bring a strike with some similarities. Crosby-Ironton had been negotiating for over a year, utilizing mediation services for eleven months.[56] The district went into statutory operating debt at the end of the 2001-2002 school year, cutting twenty-five percent of the staff.

Teachers accepted the unusual sacrifice of foregoing automatic step increases in their next contract in order to help the district deal with its financial problems.[57] The superintendent was inexperienced, having served previously as a department director in a different district before being hired by Crosby-Ironton nearly three years previously.[58] The district sought to remove health benefits that had been in place for over thirty years and had been maintained by teachers' acceptance of smaller raises.[59]

There was a history of labor trouble in the district. Crosby-Ironton teachers had held a vote of no confidence in the previous superintendent in

2000, who then took a job elsewhere. The new superintendent attempted to change the definition of "union business" in the contract that had been used for twenty years. Substitutes had always been hired when union members were in mediation sessions during school days. Now, the superintendent billed the union for the cost of the substitutes. The union disagreed with the change and filed a grievance, which the district disallowed. The union then took the issue to an arbitrator, who ruled in favor of the union.[60]

There were some differences with Red Wing as well. The C-I District had a history of going through superintendents rapidly. A board member was critical of past decisions, saying the board had been overbearing and micro-managing.[61]

A measure of the breakdown in communication between the district administration and union can be seen in the superintendent's expression of surprise that the union had taken a strike vote. When informed by the local paper that a vote had taken place, she said, "I'm very surprised. It's never been mentioned. The district has been negotiating in good faith and we're surprised to hear from the media that the teachers have taken a strike vote."

Saying they were very disgruntled by the lack of progress in negotiations, the vote to authorize a strike held on October 12, 2004 passed by ninety-five percent of the union's eighty-seven members. Union leaders hoped a settlement could be reached through mediation. The district suggested arbitration, but the union rejected that, saying they had been badly burned by an arbitration decision several years before.[62]

Little progress was made in the next two months and a second strike authorization vote was held January 4, 2005. The district offered zero percent the first year and one percent the second. The percentages could increase if teachers would accept reducing or eliminating health insurance for current employees and retirees. The union asked for zero percent and 4.65 percent with no reduction in benefits.[63]

A seven-hour mediation session held two weeks later produced no agreement. The Education Minnesota president attended a union rally the next night where it was announced that the union would file its notice of an intent to strike the following Friday. A board member claimed the union had been posturing to strike for quite a while and added, "Because once you go on strike, there is no turning back. They're going to split this small community down the center. A small community just can't stand that."[64]

The district said it planned to get out of statutory operating debt by June. The two sides rejected each other's cost projections of health insurance for retirees and the district's use of consultants. The board, in an emergency meeting, set strike plans. They called for cancelling all activities, but if the strike continued for an extended period school could be resumed on a case-by-case basis. The union president said he wished they had put that much effort into negotiating.[65]

A twelve-hour mediation session held January 31st was unsuccessful. The union requested another meeting saying the mediator and board were ready, but that the superintendent and district attorney didn't respond to their request. They informed the district that they would strike on February 9th. They had originally planned to strike February 4th, but delayed the starting date because a high school student had been killed in a car accident.

The union said that in three of the last five contracts, they had received lower increases than the state average, resulting in one of the lowest beginning salaries. They were paying $2,600 more per year for family health insurance than they did two years before. Other districts who were in statutory operating debt were able to afford increases near the state average of 1.9 percent and 2.3 percent. They said the issue came down to priorities.[66]

The union didn't rush to strike, allowing their first vote held in late October to expire. They then waited over a month after again authorizing filing a strike notice before going out. Bargaining sessions were fairly infrequent during the three and one-half weeks between the first vote and the strike's beginning.

A last minute mediation session was held beginning at 3:30 the afternoon before the strike. No progress was made and talks broke off after three and one-half hours. The Education Minnesota field representative was quoted, "I think this set of bargaining sessions in Crosby-Ironton has been the worst I've ever seen. I see less concern by the employers and by the employer's attorney to get this settled. Their only interest is to hurt employees in the process. They don't worry about hurting the community."

An Education Minnesota attorney accused the superintendent of unfair labor practices in connection with the contract negotiations. Teachers received a letter encouraging them to retire, promising them greater retiree health benefits than they might receive under the new contract. The union said it was illegal to negotiate with anyone but union officials or attempt to coerce teachers. The district's attorney denied the superintendent had engaged in illegal conduct, saying the letter contained only public factual information.

The strike began on February 9th, idling eighty-seven teachers and 1300 students. A half-dozen of the town's residents—many of whom were retired—were interviewed in a local café. They said no one in town supported the teachers. One was quoted, "We have to pay for our insurance, why should we pay for theirs?"[67]

The district began advertising for substitutes, but the superintendent said no decision had been made about whether any would be hired.[68]

Interviewed after the first week of the strike, the board president said that the teachers' demands would put the district back in statutory operating debt. Rising health care costs made providing up to nine years of health benefits to retirees unaffordable. He denied that the board was weak and being controlled by the superintendent and district attorney and said, "Strikes always hurt our community. They certainly hurt our children because they're not in school. Friends become enemies, families become divided. And those bad feelings can last a long time."

The union president planned to retire at the end of the school year. He said, "We're out to respect the obligation the district has promised us for thirty-plus years. It's not fair to take this away from people."[69]

By Monday of the second week, surrounding communities were receiving requests from parents to enroll. The Aitkin superintendent said that while open enrollment had been closed for several months, that the seventy-plus Aitkin students who had chosen to attend Crosby-Ironton would be allowed to transfer.[70]

Union leaders said they had been asking the board every day to meet. The superintendent replied that they were going through the state mediator. If the union contacted that mediator, then they'd meet. The mediator in turn was waiting to call another session until both parties were willing to move closer to a settlement saying, "Calling a premature mediation session can sometimes do more harm than good. You have expectations and then nothing happens and it can exacerbate the situation." He pointed out that the two sides could meet on their own.[71]

These tangled expectations reflect the poor communications that were evident in October. While it is true that it can be difficult to see what's going on at the time, each sides' waiting on the other was reported in a single newspaper article. If confusion was the only obstacle to resuming negotiations, that should have removed it.

An informal meeting was held between the superintendent, Board President, and two union leaders the evening of President's Day, after seven strike days. Talks broke off after only twenty-five minutes when it became clear that the only topic the district was interested in was allowing non-certified coaches to lead the girls' basketball team in the section playoffs. The union president described that effort as an attempt to break the strike.

Teachers had hoped the meeting would start the two sides talking again. Union members had been contacting board members for days, trying to set up a face to face meeting in the public library the following morning. The board president said that was not the way to set up a meeting. The district began putting together a list of substitutes.

Members of the girls' basketball team had contacted board members and gone to strike headquarters to talk with teachers. The union president said that if the Monday meeting had resulted in any progress, they would have given the team a partial blessing to play. That didn't happen, and the girls said they felt they were being used by both sides. Their team had forfeited five games, dropping from second seed to fifth. The boys' hockey team didn't participate in sectionals, while the wrestling and dance team competed with their non-union coaches.[72]

Four board members and the superintendent met with teachers the following day at the library, breaking off after an hour. The union president said he was appreciative that four board members came, but disappointed that they weren't ready to negotiate. Principals had been calling parents asking whether they would send their children to school if it opened with substitutes. The superintendent said they were concerned about younger children falling behind, and seniors having enough credits to graduate.[73]

Board members and union negotiators met overnight on day nine in the first mediation session since the strike began and made some progress. First grade opened with substitutes the next morning. Most picketers withdrew when the children arrived to avoid frightening the children or intimidating their parents.[74]

Another mediation session was held the following day. A union spokesman said the mediator told them they could not talk publicly about what happened during the sessions. The superintendent said they hadn't been told that, and issued a statement outlining their offer of seven percent plus an increased contribution toward health insurance. The union disputed the figures, saying the district had included costs not normally calculated into increases and that additional health insurance money wasn't included.

By comparing the cost of retirees' health insurance to the savings realized when new teachers were hired to replace them, the union claimed that the district would save over six million dollars.

The superintendent announced that subs were being paid $300 a day, rather than the usual ninety-five dollars. A spokesperson for Education Minnesota said subs' membership in the union would be revoked. Subs were transported in a van from the bus garage. On the second strike day, teachers gathered at the garage at the end of the day and yelled obscenities at the subs, who appeared distraught and remained at the bus garage until police arrived. The police chief arrived after teachers had left and said that yelling at the subs was not illegal.[75]

Second graders returned February 28th, the 13th day of the strike. Teachers had invited board members to attend a negotiation session at the public library and waited an hour before leaving. The board president said the district would wait until the mediator called them back together. Until then, they would focus on bringing back more grade levels. The union president called that a sad primary goal and called for more negotiations.[76]

A group of parents organized a community meeting the evening of day fourteen, which was attended by 400 people. Board members weren't able to attend until near the end of the meeting because they were in a previously scheduled closed door session. Teachers who attended walked out when offers from the previous week's mediation sessions were presented. The union said that violated the mediator's gag order and that they would investigate whether this constituted an unfair labor practice. The majority of comments from community members were critical of teachers, who said they would not attend future sessions.[77]

The local state representative called for binding arbitration saying, "It's time to end this before the community is so divided that it will take generations to heal the wounds." The superintendent and board chair said they were willing to go to arbitration, but the union president rejected the idea, saying the union had been badly burned by a former arbitration decision.

The superintendent announced that eighty-one students had left the district as a result of the strike. A number of residents visited strike headquarters to say that they supported teachers and rejected the statements made by other community members during the previous night's community meeting. Teachers again reserved space at the public library for a possible negotiation session.[78]

Seven community members joined substitutes at the bus garage late in the fourth week. The union said they would pull teachers from the site the following Monday, because they had no beef with the community and that the situation was becoming too confrontational.[79] The board chair and another member met with the union president and chief negotiator at a restaurant on Sunday for an informal meeting that had been arranged by a citizen. Both sides described the meeting as helpful.

The board held a closed door session the following evening and didn't support more informal sessions, which disappointed the union president who said the four of them could have resolved the strike if they'd met a few more times.

Third graders returned on March 7, day eighteen. Three hundred community members gathered that evening and formed six committees to end the strike. Committee goals included encouraging both sides to accept arbitration, encourage daily talks, lobbing for legislation to support arbitration and end teachers' right to strike, working for mutual respect and common decency and ways to heal the community, supporting seniors and facilitating extracurricular activities. It was announced that the spring prom had been organized by parents and would be held April 9 at a near-by lodge.[80]

A listening post was held by members of the Minnesota House Education Policy Committee the following evening to hear how the strike was affecting parents, students and teachers. A shouting match erupted outside before the meeting began between picketing teachers and a citizen. One citizen compared the situation in town to the American Civil War.[81] Kindergartners returned on day twenty and fourth graders on day twenty-one.[82]

A mediation session held in St. Paul on Sunday after week five produced no progress.[83] Following thirty hours of meetings the following Tuesday and Wednesday, the district declared an impasse, opening the possibility of seeking court permission to alter the teachers' contract without their approval. Education Minnesota filed a lawsuit, claiming that the district hired unlicensed substitutes and paid them more than labor law allowed.[84]

The district released the names of replacement teachers Thursday. Eight of the forty-two names didn't appear on a state Department of Education list of licensed teachers. The union president reacted strongly saying, "The bottom line is, they are trying to break the union. They're trying to make this strike last as long as possible." He called for the board to break away from the administration and develop a settlement.[85] The superintendent denied that some subs were unlicensed. The board chair said that just because they weren't on a Department of Education web site didn't mean they weren't licensed.

Juniors and seniors returned to school on March 16, day twenty-fifth. Fifth grade was added two days later.[86]

The CI union president attended the Education Minnesota Representative Convention held the weekend after week six. Delegates voted to donate $10,000 to the CI teachers.[87]

The civil lawsuit was moved to a neighboring county to be heard.[88] The district agreed the first day in court to re-assign any subs not licensed by the following Monday to non-teaching duties. The district also agreed to provide public information about employees within two to five days of the request. Teachers' names would become public once they were selected for an interview. The superintendent revealed that subs were all hired without an interview, leading the union to question the well-being of students.

The union dropped its restraining order, allowing the district to proceed with hiring more subs. A further hearing was planned to take up the issue of excess sub pay.[89] The school board took comments from the public on day thirty-three for the first time since the strike began. Over 500 people gathered in an auditorium. Most comments called for an end to the strike, many urging the board to hold firm.[90]

Minnesota Attorney General Mike Hatch attended a teachers' rally and said there were four subs issued temporary licenses. In his view, the state Board of Teaching couldn't issue temporary licenses on the basis of a hardship because a district was on strike. When contacted, the CI attorney disagreed. The board chair said he was disappointed that the attorney general had sided with the union. The union president repeated his offer to meet at any time.[91]

Following a typical practice in preparing for the upcoming school year, and responding to the loss of at least 200 of its 1300 students because of the strike, the district developed plans to lay off thirty of its eighty-seven teachers and close programs. The chief union negotiator called it a reprisal and claimed the superintendent was trying to destroy the school district by waging war on employees for the last three years.

The school board chair denied that it was a reprisal.[92] The district's business manager reported that 342 students—about twenty-five percent of the total enrollment—had left the district during the strike. Over $625,000 had been spent so far on substitutes and security during the strike. Four of the seven members of the union's negotiating team were on the layoff list. Planned cuts included the only foreign language teacher, gifted and talented programs, reading programs and elementary art.[93] The union disputed the district's numbers, saying they estimated that no more than 130 students left.[94]

A mediation session was held on day thirty-eight with some different members. It was the first since March 16th. The board chair didn't attend, and was replaced by a different board member. Neither the union president nor chief union negotiator attended. Instead, the Education Minnesota attorney took part. The meeting had been called after the union proposed that the two sides split the difference, a suggestion considered by the board in a closed session.[95]

The session ended at 2:00 A.M. and talks resumed the next morning, resulting in an agreement. Teachers received zero percent the first year and 3.27 percent the second. A contract agreement for the next two years was also completed, granting 2.4 percent and four percent. Days made up included 2.5 in the current year and four days each year of the following contract, allowing 10.5 of the thirty-nine days lost.

The biggest break came when the Education Minnesota attorney suggested the creation of a Voluntary Employee Benefit Annuity for current employees. Teachers hired in the future would not be eligible.[96] The board chair said he regretted that negotiators hadn't thought of the idea sooner.[97]

Was it the possibility of large number of students leaving, threats of mass layoffs, or the timely suggestion of Education Minnesota staff that led to a settlement? Perhaps it was a combination of all three. Some residents had complained that Education Minnesota was inserting itself as outsiders into a local dispute. The board chair recognized the crucial role played by the Education Minnesota staff members' broader perspective.

The board set a budget the following month covering the upcoming year, based on a pupil count of 1382 student units, reflecting a loss of ninety-one students during the strike.[98] The following year, the district employed seventy-nine teachers, eight fewer than during the strike. It would appear that the district's threat to lay off thirty-five teachers was a tactic to bring pressure for a settlement.

In November, ninety-seven percent of the tenured teachers voted that they had 'no confidence' in the superintendent's leadership. In a letter sent to board members, the union asked that they begin a process of non-renewal of the superintendent's contract. The board chair released the contents of what the union had hoped would be an internal letter, saying the board would not be held hostage by the teachers' union and would soon begin discussing renewing the superintendent's contract.

The Board Chair said he would consider meeting with the union, but on the board's terms, not the union's.[99] The superintendent's contract was renewed, and then she applied for and was granted a mobility leave in March 2006. She announced that she would not be returning to the school district when her leave was over.[100]

The district's decision to terminate one of the striking teachers reverberated in court for years. In the fall, the district hadn't rehired a non-tenured teacher who had served on the union's negotiating team. The union took her case to arbitration, and a state arbitrator ruled that the district acted in retaliation when it terminated her. The district decided to fight the ruling in court.[101] In January of 2007, a district judge upheld the arbitrator's decision, ordering the district to reinstate her with full back pay and benefits.[102] The district brought the case forward and the Minnesota Court of Appeals upheld the lower court decision in April, 2008.[103]

An operating levy vote failed in November of 2007 by a wide margin. District officials had said that a failed vote could lead to closing the elementary school and going to a four day school week.[104]

The Crosby-Ironton strike had a number of contributing factors. Financial difficulties, an unpopular and inexperienced superintendent, a District negotiating stance that included removing benefits, a board willing to fight and infrequent negotiations.

Despite paying substitutes $300 a day, they were unable to open grades seven through ten and lost nine percent of their students due to the strike. A year later, it was reported that friendships and family relationships weren't the same, and perhaps never would be. Teachers said some people in town wouldn't talk to them and merchants avoided talking about it because it might cost them customers. Even students avoided the subject, calling it 'the break' to avoid possibly hurting other student's feelings.[105]

---

1. *The Daily Journal*, August 13, 2002, p. 1.
2. *The Daily Journal*, August 20, 2002, pp. 1, 13.
3. *The Daily Journal*, August 30, 2002, pp. 1, 14.
4. *The Daily Journal*, September 3, 2002, p. 1.

5. *The Daily Journal,* September 13, 2002, pp. 1, 12.
6. *The Daily Journal,* September 18, 2002, pp. 1, 10.
7. *The Daily Journal,* September 19, 2002, p. 1.
8. *Minneapolis Star Tribune,* September 20, 2002, p. 4B.
9. *The Daily Journal,* September 20, 2002, pp. 1, 12.
10. *The Daily Journal,* September 23, 2002, pp. 1, 7.
11. *The Daily Journal,* September 25, 2002, pp. 1, 11.
12. *The Daily Journal,* September 30, 2002, pp. 1, 10.
13. *The Daily Journal,* October 1, 2002, pp. 1, 11.
14. *The Daily Journal,* October 7, 2002, pp. 1, 14.
15. *The Daily Journal,* October 8, 2002, p. 2.
16. *The Daily Journal,* October 9, 2002, p. 1.
17. *The Daily Journal,* October 10, 2002, pp. 1, 13.
18. *The Daily Journal,* October 11, 2002, pp. 1, 12.
19. *The Daily Journal,* October 14, 2002, pp. 1, 11.
20. *The Daily Journal,* October 18, 2002, pp. 1, 11.
21. *The Daily Journal,* October 19, 2002, pp. 1, 10.
22. *Red Wing Republican Eagle,* October 11, 2002.
23. *Red Wing Republican Eagle,* October 22, 2002, p. 1.
24. Interview with former Red Wing teacher.
25. *Red Wing Republican Eagle,* September 23, 2002, p. 1.
26. *Red Wing Republican Eagle,* September 24, 2002, pp. 1, 2.
27. *Red Wing Republican Eagle,* September 25, 2002.
28. *Red Wing Republican Eagle,* September 30, 2002, pp. 1, 9.
29. *Red Wing Republican Eagle,* October 1, 2002, p. 1.
30. *Red Wing Republican Eagle,* October 8, 2002, pp. 1, 9.
31. *Red Wing Republican Eagle,* October 11, 2002, pp. 1, 5.
32. *Red Wing Republican Eagle,* October 15, 2002, p. 1.
33. *Red Wing Republican Eagle,* October 15, 2002, p. 1.
34. *Red Wing Republican Eagle,* October 19, 2002, pp. 1, 20.
35. *Red Wing Republican Eagle,* October 22, 2002, pp. 1, 2.
36. *Minneapolis Star Tribune,* October 23, 2002, p. 1A.
37. *Red Wing Republican Eagle,* October 23, 2002, p. 1.
38. *Red Wing Republican Eagle,* October 24, 2002, pp. 1, 10.
39. *Red Wing Republican Eagle,* October 25, 2002, p. 1.
40. *Red Wing Republican Eagle,* October 26, 2002, p. 1.
41. R*Red Wing Republican Eagle,* October 28, 2002, pp. 1, 2.
42. *Red Wing Republican Eagle,* October 29, 2002, pp. 1, 2.

43. *Red Wing Republican Eagle,* October 30, 2002, pp. 1, 2.
44. *Red Wing Republican Eagle,* October 31, 2002, pp. 1, 2.
45. *Red Wing Republican Eagle,* November 5, 2002, pp. 1, 2.
46. *Red Wing Republican Eagle,* November 9, 2002, pp. 1, 2.
47. *Red Wing Republican Eagle,* November 11, 2002, p. 1.
48. *Red Wing Republican Eagle,* November 12, 2002, p. 1.
49. *Red Wing Republican Eagle,* November 14, 2002, pp. 1, 2.
50. *Red Wing Republican Eagle,* November 19, 2002, pp. 1,2.
51. *Red Wing Republican Eagle,* November 26, 2002, p. 2.
52. R*Red Wing Republican Eagle,* December 3, 2002, p. 1.
53. R*Red Wing Republican Eagle,* December 18, 2002, pp. 1, 2.
54. *Red Wing Republican Eagle,* December 19, 2002, p. 2.
55. Phone interview with former superintendent September, 2010.
56. *Brainerd Dispatch,* January 6, 2005, pp. 1A, 5A.
57. *Brainerd Dispatch,* January 21, 2005, pp. 1A, 5A.
58. *Brainerd Dispatch,* March 29 2002, pp. 1A, 7A.
59. *Brainerd Dispatch,* February 8, 2005, pp. 1A, 5A.
60. *Brainerd Dispatch,* January 13, 2005, p. 1A.
61. *Brainerd Dispatch,* March 29 2002, pp. 1A, 7A.
62. *Brainerd Dispatch,* October 20, 2004.
63. *Brainerd Dispatch,* January 6, 2005 pp. 1A, 5A.
64. *Brainerd Dispatch,* January 20, 2005, pp. 1A, 5A.
65. *Brainerd Dispatch,* January 21, 2005, pp. 1A, 5A.
66. *Brainerd Dispatch,* February 8, 2005, pp. 1A, 5A.
67. *Brainerd Dispatch,* February 9, 2005, pp. 1A, 5A.
68. *Minneapolis Star Tribune,* February 19, 2005, p. 1B.
69. *Brainerd Dispatch,* February 13, 2005, pp. 1A, 8A, 9A.
70. *Brainerd Dispatch,* February 15, 2005, pp. 1A, 5A.
71. *Brainerd Dispatch,* February 17, 2005, p. 1A.
72. *Brainerd Dispatch,* February 22, 2005, pp. 1A, 5A.
73. *Brainerd Dispatch,* February 23, 2005, pp. 1A, 5A.
74. *Brainerd Dispatch,* February 24, 2005, pp. 1A, 7A.
75. *Brainerd Dispatch,* February 26, 2005, pp. 1A, 5A.
76. *Brainerd Dispatch,* March 1, 2005, pp. 1A, 5A.
77. *Brainerd Dispatch,* March 2, 2005, pp. 1A, 5A.
78. *Brainerd Dispatch,* March 3, 2005, pp. 1A, 5A.
79. *Brainerd Dispatch,* March 6, 2005, pp. 1A, 8A.
80. *Brainerd Dispatch,* March 8, 2005, p. 1A.

81. News.minnesota.publicradio.org March 9, 2005.
82. *Brainerd Dispatch*, March 10, 2005, p. 5A.
83. *Brainerd Dispatch*, March 14, 2005, p. 1A.
84. News.minnesota.publicradio.org March 17, 2005.
85. *Brainerd Dispatch*, March 18, 2005, pp. 1A, 3A.
86. *Brainerd Dispatch*, March 20, 2005, p. 6A.
87. *Brainerd Dispatch*, March 21, 2005, pp. 1A, 5A.
88. *Brainerd Dispatch*, March 22, 2005, pp. 1A, 5A.
89. *Brainerd Dispatch*, March 24, 2005, pp. 1A, 3A.
90. *Brainerd Dispatch*, March 29, 2005, pp. 1A, 7A.
91. *Brainerd Dispatch*, March 31, 2005, pp. 1A, 3A, 5A.
92. *Brainerd Dispatch*, April 2, 2005, p. 1A.
93. *Brainerd Dispatch*, April 5, 2005, pp. 1A, 5A.
94. *Minneapolis Star Tribune*, April 7, 2005, p. 1B.
95. *Brainerd Dispatch*, April 6, 2005, pp. 1A, 3A.
96. http://emcil325.educaitonminnesota.org/index, April 13, 2005.
97. *Brainerd Dispatch*, April 7, 2005, pp. 1A, 7A.
98. *Brainerd Dispatch*, June 28, 2005, p. 3A.
99. *Brainerd Dispatch*, November 23, 2005, p. 6A.
100. *Brainerd Dispatch*, March 14, 2006, pp. 1A, 5A.
101. *Brainerd Dispatch*, September 19, 2006, pp. 1A, 5A.
102. *Twin Cities Daily Planet*, Workday Minnesota, January 23, 2007.
103. *Brainerd Dispatch*, April 29, 2008, pp. 1A, 3A.
104. *Brainerd Dispatch*, November 7, 2007, pp. 1A, 6A.
105. *Minneapolis Star Tribune*, January 17, 2006, p. 1B.

Conclusion

This has been a book about conflict, for strikes are the ultimate expression of struggles between labor and management. More than that, this is a compendium of broken relationships. Seventy-one times in Minnesota, school districts and teachers found some issue that was more compelling than continuing to educate children.

Most of the people involved in these strikes were surprised by the forces they had loosed. Only a few settled quickly with only a tiny blip—scarcely noticeable—in the fabric of their district. Others tore apart their communities, creating rifts that continued for decades.

The ultimate responsibility lies with the electorate. Schools function in a manner that reflects the values and priorities of the community. Parents want their children to receive an excellent education. Others in the community want lower taxes; a particular view point taught (or not taught); unions eviscerated (or supported); or a focus on certain students. When groups coalesce for or against any of these issues—or simply can't agree on what an excellent educational program is—disagreements will probably be reflected in who gets elected to the school board.

If citizens won't recognize the appropriateness of a process of compromise, it's not surprising that a school board representing them can lurch into radical strategies. Individual members, pushing personal agendas or seeking to launch political careers, can also lead boards in unusual directions and push to keep them there.

School boards can be too passive, taking direction from a superintendent who may have ideas at odds with local priorities. The advice of professional negotiators—usually lawyers with backgrounds in labor relations—can alter the direction of negotiations. In every strike, school boards said they were strong and in charge. Whether they were or not, it's incumbent on local citizens to make sure that community priorities guide their district in the desired direction.

In a nasty divorce, children can be used as tools for parents to gain some kind of advantage. Communities can use schools in similar ways. It would be easy to blame the teachers, superintendent or school board for the disastrous strike in Crosby Ironton. Each did play a role. What happened was a reflection of long-standing disagreements within the community.

Compared to others in the area, teachers were well paid. Enrollment and revenues were declining. Teachers had been doing what teachers do—serving children as well as they could. How much should hard-working, loyal employees be asked to sacrifice because the employer's revenue is constrained? How important are the schools to the community?

With a community evenly divided and each side vehement in their beliefs, the Crosby-Ironton strike was allowed to drag on while each side waited for the other to capitulate. None of this needed happen if the district had been operating in a collaborative, problem solving manner.

The big question for communities is how they want classrooms to function, for that's where education takes place. Do they want teachers who are entirely focused on educating their students, or teachers who are dissatisfied and worse yet, preoccupied with worrying? None of us would perform well at work if we believed that a venomous snake was hiding somewhere nearby. Teachers can't concentrate on the children if they might be arbitrarily fired or laid off.

It makes no sense to want teachers who are intelligent and energetic, and then expect them to blithely accept being mistreated. These are American citizens, who resist injustice. I have worked in buildings where the faculty was a seething, roiling mass of dissatisfaction. The vast majority of conversations between teachers centered around how angry they were about the latest outrage imposed by the administration. Time that otherwise would have been spent collaborating, exchanging information and planning was squandered on complaining.

This is the natural consequence of mistreating staff. Citizens, the school board or superintendent may feel that they stuck it to the teachers who got what they deserved, but are they in turn getting from teachers what they want?

DOES THE COMMUNITY WANT THE SCHOOL BOARD, SUPERINTENDENT, AND TEACHERS TO BE PARTNERS, OR OPPONENTS?

If the answer is opponents, the fruits will include reflexive resistance to change (no matter who suggests it) and conflict. You can't have it both ways either, kicking teachers around during negotiations and expecting them to willingly cooperate later.

If you want an excellent school district power must be shared, the focus must be on children, trust is the foundation and everyone must accept responsibility for outcomes. There is no 'us and them', for by definition there is only us. We may have different roles, but share goals.

The negotiation table is a very difficult place to begin forming these kinds of relationships. Far better that the school board, superintendent and union leaders sit down together year round, exchanging concerns and problem solving. Respect for each other's needs can lead to trust, the key ingredient lacking in situations that led to strikes.

If this optimistic scenario doesn't work out and despite everyone's best efforts to develop a solution none is found, compromise is called for. As has always been the case, and as this history illustrates, the choice is:

COMPROMISE NOW, OR GO THROUGH A STRIKE AND COMPROMISE AFTER TEARING APART THE COMMUNITY AND DAMAGING THE SCHOOL DISTRICT.

Index

Albany, xv, 21, 58, 129, 131.
American Federation of Teachers, 11, 45, 77, 81, 83.
Andersen, Elmer, 79.
Anderson, Wendell, 91.
Anoka, xvi, 21, 30, 40, 59, 153, 155, 156.
Appleton, xvi, 23, 221.
Audubon, xv, 14, 131.
Bemidji, xvi, 21, 49, 201.
Biwabik, 17, 237.
Buhl, xv, 21, 125.
Burnsville, xv, 21, 127, 128.
Cambridge-Isanti, xvi.
Cass Lake, xvi, 21, 206.
Chaska, xvi, 23, 24, 26, 59, 229.
Crookston, xvi, 21, 172.
Crosby-Ironton, xiv, xvi, 17, 18, 23, 24, 26, 27, 30, 31, 47, 55, 56, 59, 61, 63, 258, 260, 261, 269, 273.
Deer River, xvi, 21, 149, 150.
District 916, xv, 15, 125, 129.
Duluth, xii, xvi, 11, 22, 31, 49, 54, 211-213.
Eden Prairie, xvi, 21, 162.
Elk River, xvi, 23, 49, 235.
Eveleth, xvi, 16, 17, 21, 190, 191.
Faribault, xv, 15-17, 20, 21, 46, 64, 111, 117, 118.
Forest Lake, xvi, 22, 142.
Glenwood, xvi, 22, 173.
Grand Meadow, xvi, 22, 190.
Granite Falls, xvi, 14, 22, 181.
Greenway-Coleraine, 16.
Hatch, Mike, 266.
Hermantown, xv, 21, 54, 96, 97, 99.
Hibbing, xvi, 22, 200.
Hill City, xvi, 18, 22, 176.
Houston, xvi, 22, 38, 54, 204.
Howard Lake-Waverly, xvi, 16, 23-25, 31, 32, 45, 63, 99, 100, 155, 158.
Interest Based Bargaining, 63.
International Falls, xvi, xvii, 15, 17, 23, 30, 31, 47, 56, 244, 251, 256.
Isle, xvi, 23, 176.
Jordan, xvi, 22, 40, 198.
Lake Benton, xv, 21, 23, 24, 59, 122, 124, 125.
Lake City, xvi, 22, 61, 159, 160.
Lakefield, xv, 21, 124, 125.
Lester Prairie, xvi, 22.
LeVander, 6, 89.
Luverne, xv, 21, 107, 109, 112.
Mahtomedi, xvi, 16, 22, 193, 195.
Messabi East, xvi, 23.
Minneapolis, xiv, xv, 4-6, 11, 12, 16, 21, 30, 32, 35, 40, 46, 53, 69, 80, 82, 83, 86, 87, 89, 90, 108, 113, 130, 158, 221, 229.
Minnesota Education Association, vii, 32, 99, 131, 137, 139, 219.
Minnesota Federation of Teachers, 90, 99, 137, 162, 211, 237.
Minnetonka, xv, 21, 118.
Moorehead, xvi, 16, 23-25, 225, 226.
National Education Association, 11, 137, 219, 257.
New Prague, xvi, 22, 40, 184.
Park Rapids, xvi, 23, 221.
Paynesville, xvi, 22, 140, 141.

PELRA, 13, 52, 70, 96, 99, 102, 131, 135, 138, 146, 147, 155, 163, 167, 169, 177, 191, 196, 254.
Pine River, xvi, 22, 205.
Popovich, 62.
Prior Lake, xvi, 18, 22, 24, 63, 147-149.
Proctor, xvi, 22, 23, 31, 49, 59, 169, 234.
Randolph, xvi, 22, 206.
Red Wing, xvi, 18, 23, 26, 30, 46, 47, 55, 56, 255, 256, 259.
Rochester, vii, xvi, 18, 23, 25, 30, 41, 55, 56, 59, 65, 145, 238.
Rockford, xvi, 22, 160.
Roseau, xvi, 21, 105.
Rural St. Louis County, xvi, 16, 23.
Sauk Centre, xv, xvi, 21, 23, 48, 117, 119, 135, 196.
Sauk Rapids, xvi, 22, 53, 54, 216, 219, 229.
School Board Association, xii, 13, 16, 20, 33, 43, 59, 62, 67, 122, 191, 256.
Spring Lake Park, xvi, 18, 23, 61, 243.
St. Cloud, 11, 54, 143-145, 171.
St. Paul, xii-xv, 3, 11, 16, 21, 77-80, 101, 138, 171, 172, 247, 253, 265.
Thief River Falls, xvi, 14, 22, 180.
Tracy, xvi, 22, 52, 142, 143.
Wabasha-Kellogg, xvi.
Walnut Grove, xvi, 16, 18, 22-24, 31, 71, 165.
Winona, xv, 21, 59, 60, 99, 101, 102, 104.